Brigance's
# SPEECH COMMUNICATION

# Brigance's

# SPEECH

# COMMUNICATION

### Third Edition

### J. JEFFERY AUER
*Indiana University*

New York

APPLETON-CENTURY-CROFTS

Educational Division

MEREDITH CORPORATION

# Preface

The first edition of this brief textbook, published in 1947, was described by its author, William Norwood Brigance, as one that "included only the minimum essentials, treated fully and vividly, and left out others, however useful or helpful they might be. It was a risk, but a calculated risk, as all life is a calculated risk." It turned out to be a risk well taken, and a second edition, in 1955, was shaped in part by counsel from the many teachers who had used the first one. Similarly, this third edition bears the imprint of suggestions gratefully received from nearly half of the teachers who used the second. Additional changes in emphasis and coverage, though not in basic purpose, undoubtedly reflect the hand of a new author. I hope that I have not confused mere change with progress, and that this edition continues to refine the minimum essentials of speech communication.

J. J. A.

# Contents

# CONTENTS

# 1

# The Rights and Obligations
# of Listeners

Why begin a book for speakers with a chapter on listeners? Because speaking is for listening. A *speaker* tries to communicate *ideas* by making them clear and by making them persuasive to *listeners*. The complete act of communication requires all three elements: speaker, ideas, listeners. In the 1960's it has become fashionable to express this notion by referring to the necessity of communication through public "dialogues" on public questions. *Time* reports on "the national dialogue over foreign aid that breaks out in the U. S. each spring." Walter Lippmann listens for the "informed public debate" on the Vietnam conflict. Religious editors describe the first step in the ecumenical movement as "opening up a dialogue." Educators blame student outbreaks on "a breakdown of student-administration-faculty dialogues." And on network television many public affairs programs are dialogues between public officials and interrogators: "Meet the Press," "Face the Nation," and "Issues and Answers." The ideal "dialogue" requires speakers capable of creating or adapting ideas and then communicating them intelligently, effectively, and responsibly. It also requires listeners capable of understanding ideas and then evaluating them critically, discriminatingly, and purposefully. This chapter is about that joint enterprise.

Citizens of the twentieth century have grown up with *eight physical media of communication*: books, magazines, newspapers, the stage, the public platform, moving pictures, radio, and television. But in all history man has had only *three basic forms of communication* via these eight media: prose, poetry, and public address. You have long studied prose and poetry, both producers and consumers. But most of you have not studied public address at all, so let us begin by examining how it differs from prose and poetry.

Prose and poetry are composed by absentee authors, set down on paper, and perused at a time and place that suits the reader's convenience.

1

Not so with public address. Of course the speaker composes his material *in absentia*, but this is only a first step in speechmaking. The second step is to *create* the speech by appearing in person and talking to a specific audience of listeners. These listeners sit before the speaker and are visible to him—except on radio and television, where they are not physically present although they listen at the moment of utterance and are clearly in the "mind's eye" of the speaker. As he truly creates his previously composed speech the speaker talks *to* and *with* these listeners. And he looks *at* them, because their visible reactions are a form of "talking back" to him. He sees understanding nods or misunderstanding scowls. He senses their attentive behavior that says "I am interested," or their restlessness that says "I am bored." In short, public address—unlike the editorial page in the school newspaper or the essay in *The Saturday Review* —is not set down on paper for somebody to read tomorrow or next week. It is spoken to people at the moment it is heard. It is not merely composed in the isolation of a library or study, but is *created on the instant and in the presence of the listeners.*

For a speaker to do this well he must understand and practice many skills: reasoning, or the analysis of evidence and synthesis of arguments; clarification and persuasion, or the management of ideas by organization and phrasing; and the ultimate act of physically creating the speech before an audience. These tasks are so complex that many books on speechmaking are concerned almost entirely with the speaker. Lest we fall into the same error of emphasis we shall look first at the listener, his legitimate expectations and his proper obligations.

## THE LISTENER'S RIGHTS

It cannot be said that critical listening is more *difficult* than effective speaking, but in a democratic society it is clearly as *important*. Speakers have already made up their minds, but listeners commonly have not, and "in a republican nation," as Thomas Jefferson put it, "whose citizens are to be led by reason and persuasion, and not by force, the art of reasoning becomes of first importance." If the listener is to reason his way through to intelligent conclusions the speaker must provide him with the means. The listener has a right to hear intelligent, effective, and responsible talk. Unfortunately, in the word waves that nearly engulf the modern listener, there is far too little such talk. Read this pessimistic comment by a contemporary philosopher, Harry A. Overstreet: "In no area of our maturing . . . is arrested development more common than in the area of communication. It is so common that it is . . . taken for granted as natural. The person who is mature in his communicative powers is noted as an exception to the rule. The person who is immature—halting, clumsy, obscure, rambling, dull, platitudinous, insensitive—is the rule."[1]

Some of this inadequate communication may be deliberate: Raymond G. Smith identifies "the speech to confuse," expressly designed by a speaker to obscure his true opinion or hide his real motivation. (One presidential hopeful in 1966, for example, described himself ". . . as conservative as the Constitution, as progressive as Teddy Roosevelt, and as liberal as Mr. Lincoln.") More of it is unintentional, perpetrated by self-made speakers who have never learned how to create a speech on the instant and in the presence of listeners. Some of them have never learned how to manage their ideas in private; others have never learned to manage themselves in public. Some have never learned either. Undoubtedly you have been unfortunate enough to encounter the speaker who believes that "anybody can talk," and demonstrates that fallacy with a vengeance. Or the one who has "nothing to say," and insists on proving it at length. Or the one who speaks "off the cuff," and shows that impromptu speaking usually reflects impromptu thinking.

A busy world has no time for such speakers. One of them, talking for only ten minutes before an audience of twenty-five listeners, actually commands a total of more than four hours of precious time. There is no justification for this collective expenditure unless a speaker is worth listening to. *A speaker is worth listening to only when he delivers useful ideas to the listener.* In sum, every listener has a right to expect two things from a speaker who asks for his ear: 1. Useful ideas. 2. Ability to deliver those ideas. Let us consider these rights of listeners in some detail.

### Listeners Have the Right to Expect Interesting and Useful Ideas from a Speaker

The typical educated person hears approximately one hundred speeches a year. Why listen to so many? Why listen to *any?* Not because we are forced to, for we are free to listen or not. Rather we are driven to listen by forces within us. We are human beings, living in a very real world. In that world we face problems that in a free society must be understood and resolved by responsible people. We are beset by choices and temptations. We are haunted by real and imagined threats to our security. Thus we listen to speakers because we hope they will throw light on our problems, sharpen our alternatives, or allay our fears. We listen because we hope they will give us new information, new ideas, or will simply adapt and vitalize old ideas. We listen because we want to be given encouragement, to renew our faith, to strengthen our determination. Or perhaps we listen because we want to escape from reality for a time, even to laugh and forget our troubles.

A century and more ago, when newspapers, books, and other vehicles

[1] *The Mature Mind* (New York, 1949), pp. 54-55.

of popular culture were scarce, the orator played many roles: persuader, educator, and entertainer. As a political advertisement promised for an 1844 campaign speech by Tom Corwin, the famous Ohio Whig, "You may not only learn but laugh." This was a day when the orator was often a "spellbinder," by popular request. It is understandable that in his exuberant efforts to please his audiences he was sometimes more reckless than responsible. Fancies often submerged facts. "What orator," asked Kentuckian Mann Butler in 1834, "can deign to restrain his imagination within a vulgar and sterile statement of facts?"

Today's audiences are more sophisticated; they are better informed on a wider range of issues. And they expect public speakers to treat them accordingly. They prefer logical, not lyrical, speeches. They want an emphasis upon facts, not jests. One notable survey of audiences by William K. Clark revealed that "sincerity" ranked first among fourteen qualities expected of speakers,[2] and other studies reveal the preference of listeners for straightforwardness, fairness, and trustworthiness. In selecting and presenting evidence, in analyzing and developing arguments, it is not enough that speakers be effective; we also want them to be ethical.

These are the services expected of speakers, and listeners have the inalienable right to demand that every speaker who consumes public time shall deliver them. In the catalogue of any experienced listener there are many types of speakers who do not give value received and should be put out of business by a commission on fair trade in ideas. Consider these three examples:

1. *The Outer Spaceman*—who never gets down to earth where ordinary mortals live and breathe, but who speaks from the stratosphere of abstract and hazy words. He seldom cites facts; he rarely troubles to illuminate thought by illustrations; he never relieves a tired audience with humor. He soars on the currents of his own windy generalizations, and is always in full flight. If we are not sure just what he means, perhaps he is not either. But we can be sure that he misses the real purpose of public speaking; it is not a free flight into outer space but an earthy watering and cultivating of ideas on important subjects, using plain words, simple facts, and specific ideas.

2. *The Witless Wit*—who believes in the salvation of man by funny stories. He seems determined to confuse laughter with learning, and comes armed with twenty anecdotes—but no thoughts. He amuses himself by emptying his grab-bag of jests that illustrate no theme, and measures his success by the amount of laughter. Serious listeners, who may already have heard some or all of his jokes, will wish they had remained at home. Like Gilbert and Sullivan in *His Excellency*, they will conclude, "Humor is a drug which it's the fashion to abuse."

[2]"A Survey of Certain Attitudes Toward Commonly Taught Standards of Public Speaking," *Speech Monographs*, 18 (March, 1951), pp. 62-69.

3. *The Echo Chamber*—who reads a magazine article and echoes it, under the illusion that it will sound like a speech. Among students this is a common type. One puts off preparation until the last minute, then in sheer desperation gulps a published article, unchewed and undigested, and pretends that he has an original speech. Even if he avoids plagiarizing the language, he adheres to the original content and outline, adding nothing of his own. He becomes a mere echo chamber for another's ideas, and the speech is a failure, because not even the reciting of a good article can transform it into a good speech. It was written perhaps a year before, for people of heterogeneous backgrounds; it is probably dated, already "Reader's Digested," and mass circulated. But the student's speech is to be given today, to a particular group of listeners who may already have heard two speeches on the same general topic during the month, and who will sense from the student's voice and manner that he knows nothing about the topic except what he is reciting from his single source. In other words, a speech needs to be focused on a particular audience gathered on a particular occasion and for a particular purpose. An echo always sounds the same.

### Listeners Have the Right to Expect Interesting and Lively Presentation

Woodrow Wilson once said that "eloquence lies in the thought, not the throat." This was putting first things first, but Wilson did not mean that the manner of a speaker's physical behavior was unimportant. Many unthinking persons believe that "it doesn't matter how he says it," if a speaker will only "say what he thinks." This is a comfortable and convenient belief. It relieves the speaker from any responsibility beyond writing a paper. But it is naïve and unrealistic. It assumes that the "delivery" of a speech is like the delivery of a grocery order. It assumes that when delivered, the speech, like the groceries, will arrive intact no matter how long the delivery man took, how devious may have been his route, and whether he arrived drunk or sober. Like many assumptions, this one is false. In the sense of simple conveyance there is no such thing as delivering a speech. "Delivery" in speech communication is a *figurative* term, not an exact one. Let us examine this notion that no speaker can really "deliver" a speech.

If you deliver a can of beans, or a book, or a telegram, you pick it up, carry it to its destination, and turn it over to someone else. You cannot so deliver a speech. What we often call delivering a speech is actually *translating a set of ideas through five stages from the speaker's mind to the mind of the listener*. These are the five stages:

1. Every communication begins with an idea, concept, or proposition in the speaker's mind.

2. This idea is then encoded into a message consisting of a set of audible symbols (actually phonetic ones, produced by muscular movements of the tongue, lips, face, diaphragm, etc.) and visible symbols (muscular movements of posture, body, hands, face, and head).

3. These audible and visible symbols are then transmitted through space by sound and light waves (often referred to as the communication channel) that ultimately reach the ears and eyes of the listener.

4. When the sound and light waves are perceived by the listener they are decoded into meaningful and new audible and visible symbols.

5. Finally, these new audible and visible symbols are interpreted by the mind of the listener into the original communication, or some facsimile of it.

From this description of the mechanics of communication (and we have purposely simplified it by omitting many physiological and neurological details), it should be clear that a speech is not "delivered" to a listener in a literal sense. A speech is not a package to be handed over. Instead you *use sound and light waves to create ideas in your listener's mind.* If these ideas resemble those originally in your mind it is because you have encoded them into meaningful symbols, transmitted them distinctly and completely, and the listener has decoded them efficiently and accurately.

Perhaps we should emphasize the significance of both audible *and* visible symbols created by the speaker. The audible symbols carried by sound waves are the most refined and precise; they also require the greatest sophistication for understanding. The visible symbols carried by light waves are more general in import; their meanings are older in human history, more basic. Thus a speaker's words may reflect *what he thinks,* but his actions reveal *how he feels* about what he is saying. While actions never literally "speak louder than words," they do either reinforce or undercut words.

We have said that listeners have the right to expect not only interesting and useful ideas, but the right to expect those ideas to be presented in an interesting and lively manner. Why are we so sure that "how you say it" as well as "what you say" is an important factor in listening? For these two reasons:

1. *A listener's time is valuable and his attention-span is limited.* In an exciting, provocative, and challenging world he can find an endless array of attractions: books, movies, television programs, social activities, and so on. Given free choice he will attend only to interesting and lively matters. He is unlikely to invest his time listening to speakers who are dull, monotonous, and unattractive, either in content or presentation.

2. *Listening is not easy, even under the best of conditions.* It requires a sharp and continuing concentration in order (a) to perceive the audible and visible symbols created by the speaker, and (b) to translate

those symbols into meaningful terms. Whatever interferes with this concentration makes listening a less congenial occupation. A speaker, like a television set, can produce so much "static" that he is turned off.

Experienced listeners will identify these speakers whose manner of presentation interferes with their communication:

1. *The Fidgeter*—whose actions interrupt the listeners' concentration upon his words. The eye responds before the ear; what the listener sees takes precedence over what he hears. Hence the fidgeter's actions override his ideas. Behold his behavior: If his hands are in his pockets, he takes them out; if they are out, he puts them in. If his coat is unbuttoned, he buttons it; if it is buttoned, he unbuttons it. If he is at the center of the platform, he paces to one side; when he gets there, he turns back again. He clutches the lectern while he rocks from heels to toes. His hands and feet are always in the way, and he can't get used to them.

2. *The "And-Er" Vocalist*—whose pauses mutilate instead of punctuate. His particular brand of static links his thought phrases like this: "My—Er—subject tonight is—Er—the significance of—And-Er—the current status of—Er—the tax structure." To *Er* is human; but to listeners it is exasperating. Only the punishment of being forced to hear a continuous tape recording of his own speech will fit this speaker's crime.

3. *The Listless Mumbler*—who can hear himself and seems not to care if others cannot. He looks at the ceiling, out the window, or at his notes; anywhere but at his audience. His jaw is rigid and his lips are lazy. His voice is flat and his tones are weak. Even if he can be heard in the front rows, his speech is listless, lacking color, warmth, friendliness, or even life. He is prone to drone, alone.

These speakers, and others of their ilk, may pride themselves that what they have on their minds is so important that how they say it does not matter. But they are wrong. Audience surveys reveal a high regard for speaker "animation" and "coordinated bodily movement." Experimental studies show that such factors as pitch, loudness, resonance, rate, pronunciation, articulation, and vocal variety *influence listener attitudes toward what the speaker has to say*. The evidence is clear that listeners will remember more of what is said, remember it longer, and remember it more favorably, if it is said in an interesting and lively fashion. In short, the know-how as well as the know-what is important in speaking; and listeners have the right to demand that speakers face this fact squarely, assessing their competence and working to eliminate the static of fidgeting, "and-ering," and mumbling.

Democracy, said Macaulay, is "government by speaking." Unlike the totalitarian state built upon coercion, a democratic state is built upon persuasion. Its public issues are publicly discussed in a continuous dialogue, "talked out of existence or talked into solution." Would it be unreasonable, therefore, to hold public talkers accountable for their talk?

No citizen, in our society, may practice law or medicine without first passing an examination to establish his fitness. Engineers, architects, public accountants, and taxi drivers must also prove themselves by examination. Is it too whimsical to imagine a truly Ideal Republic where a test of competence would also be required before persons are permitted to practice the art of public speaking? Consider: first, they could be required to show themselves capable of producing interesting and useful ideas; second, to demonstrate their ability to refine those ideas into a form fit for public distribution; and third, they could be obliged to prove their mastery of that complicated process of communicating ideas from speaker to listener.

Of those who passed these tests of professional competence, an Ideal Republic could finally require an affirmation of moral responsibility, a Hippocratic oath of ethical practice, before they receive certification to speak in public:

> *I swear upon my own conscience that I will never speak in public unless I have prepared myself with substance worth saying, and unless I have put it in a form that can be understood. I further swear that when I speak before an audience I shall consider its welfare and not my own pride, that I shall not dissemble or distort, mumble or fidget, or otherwise evade or shirk my responsibility, but shall present my ideas with such honesty, earnestness, and consideration for my listeners that none can fail to hear or comprehend.*

Such would indeed by an Ideal Republic, honoring the rightful expectations of listeners. But there are two sides to every coin. If the listener has legitimate expectations, so does the speaker.

## THE LISTENER'S OBLIGATIONS

Speechmaking is not easy, and the speaker who works hard at preparing a thoughtful and responsible exposition of his ideas may properly assume two minimal commitments from his audience: 1. A fair hearing. 2. Real listening. Let us consider these obligations briefly, and how the listener can meet them.

### Speakers Have the Right to Expect a Fair and Full Hearing for Their Ideas

At least since the age of Pericles we have held to the democratic notion that "we decide or debate carefully, in person, all matters of policy, holding that acts are foredoomed to failure when undertaken undiscussed." In our own age Harold Laski has reminded us that "the art of public discussion . . . is central to the achievement of the democratic purpose." We commonly accept this belief, but in implementing it we usually emphasize the citizen's right to speak. Walter Lippmann, however, has argued that freedom of speech "achieves its central purpose only when different opinions are expounded in the same hall to the same audience. . . . For, while the right to talk may be the beginning of freedom, the necessity of listening is what makes that right important...."³

In effect Lippmann is urging the virtues of the law court, where prosecutor and defender have an equal right to be heard, or of the legislature, where "men who are free to speak are also compelled to answer." Here is not merely an expression of opinion, but a confrontation of differing opinion. In endorsing this concept we do not insist that every speaker must be replied to, formally, on the spot. But in actuality there should be a constant discussion going on between speaker and listener. Listening is an active process, not a passive one, and listeners who pay attention are silently "talking back," formulating responses that would be spoken if they had an opportunity. As President Lyndon B. Johnson once put it, "I believe every American has something to say and, under our system, a right to an audience."⁴

To listen intelligently and fairly, however, we must hear the speaker out. We must try to "grasp what other persons are saying *as they themselves understand what they are saying*," is the way Harry A. Overstreet puts it. This means that we must attempt to check our prejudices at the door and enter with an open mind, conceding a speaker even "the right to be wrong." Certainly listeners have the right to expect a speaker to deliver useful ideas, and in a lively manner, but they cannot properly insist upon hearing only congenial ideas. "Every thinker," wrote John Dewey, "puts some portion of an apparently stable world in peril." But there is an even greater peril when we deny thoughtful speakers a fair and full hearing for their ideas. Those who already know all of the answers risk an atrophy of the mind that results from disuse. And that is fatal.

### Speakers Have the Right to Expect Their Hearers to Be True Listeners

Warren Guthrie, a distinguished television network newscaster, was reflecting upon his daily broadcasts. "I know they *hear* me," he said, "but are they really *listening?*" What he asked was whether those who

---

³"The Indispensable Opposition," *Atlantic Monthly*, 164 (August, 1939), pp. 186-190.
⁴*A Time for Action: A Selection from the Speeches and Writings of Lyndon B. Johnson, 1953-64* (New York, 1964), p. 19.

automatically tuned him in for fifteen minutes each evening were alert, thoughtful, and responsive. Were they just "taking it in," or did they really think about what he was saying? For the broadcaster, unable to see his audience and judge reactions, this is a perplexing question. He may never get the answer. It is unfortunate that many public speakers—standing before their audiences—are equally perplexed. Are their hearers really listeners?

Figuratively at least this question was never asked between the invention of the printing press and the beginning of broadcasting. In the intervening four centuries educational programs emphasized reading and writing; literacy was measured in terms of reading, not listening. But the age of broadcasting—first radio, then television—reversed the trend. As people listened more than they read, research studies demonstrated that greater impact upon behavior came from the broadcast word than from the printed page, and that face-to-face speaking was more potent than either.

Even these discoveries made no immediate impress upon educational programs. We knew that efficient reading required specific training in the techniques of comprehension, not just good eyesight and normal intelligence. But we assumed that hearing acuity and normal intelligence were enough to produce efficient listening. Then other research studies revealed that without specific training in the techniques of listening, even highly intelligent persons may be very poor listeners. In terms of what average college students comprehend and retain from a speaker's words, listening efficiency may range from 10 to 70 percent. Even being warned in advance that they are to be tested on what they hear often fails to help them hold on to more than 50 percent of an informative lecture for as long as a week, and less than 25 percent after several weeks. Ralph G. Nichols, at the University of Minnesota, was probably the first to experiment with specific training in listening techniques.[5] In his studies, and in those conducted elsewhere, it was found that after training every group of students improved at least 25 percent in ability to understand the spoken word, and some improved as much as 40 percent. The evidence is clear that hearers can become true listeners.

A few pages ago we imagined an Ideal Republic, where citizens authorized to speak in public were required first to take a Hippocratic oath. In such a society the listener should not be spared a similar obligation:

> *I swear upon my own conscience that I will extend to the holder of every contrary view a fair and full hearing for the expression of it. I further swear that I will not pass judgment upon his beliefs without carefully and critically analyzing his arguments and the evidence supporting them. And even though I conclude that he is in error, I*

[5]Ralph G. Nichols and Leonard Stevens, *Are You Listening?* (New York, 1957).

*will defend his right of self-expression in an open confrontation of conflicting opinions. For a democratic society cannot exist except in a milieu of free speech, critical listening, and majority rule.*

In an Ideal Republic listeners would have not only rights, but obligations.

## THE LISTENER'S LABORATORY

The next few pages may seem more prescriptive than would be expected in the opening chapter of a textbook. But there is good reason for treating the subject of listening in some detail at this point. If you are reading this book you are in a speech class. During the term you will make a number of speeches, perhaps six or even ten. But you will hear *each* of your classmates make that many, probably over a hundred all together. For every minute that you stand on the platform as a speaker, you will sit in your seat for twenty minutes as a listener. In effect, this class provides you not only with a *speaking*, but also with a *listening* laboratory. How can you best take advantage of this opportunity? How can you progress from mere *hearing* to critical *listening*? To begin with, condition yourself for two kinds of listening:

*The first is listening to get meanings.* This is the listening that focuses on the task of perceiving a speaker's central idea, the lines of argument used in developing it, and the specific evidence employed to support it. Most of our listening experiences are in conversational situations where central ideas are seldom formally and fully developed. Listening in such circumstances is fairly simple. We catch one idea at a time. If we don't catch it, we interrupt the speaker. "Would you mind saying that again?" "I'm afraid I don't get your point. Why don't you give me an example?" But listening to a formal speech is another problem. Literally hundreds of single-idea units must be caught in sequence, without interruption, and placed together at once into a complex pattern of thought. This is the listening skill that everyone needs to develop, and the speech classroom is an ideal place to perfect it. As each classmate speaks try to find the answer to "*What* did the speaker say?" by raising such questions as these:

What is the speaker talking about? What is his central idea? What response does he want from me?

What lines of argument support his central idea? What evidence supports his arguments? How logical is the total structure of central idea, argument, and evidence? Are there any inconsistencies in what he says?

Does he appear to be a trustworthy person? Does his judgment seem to be reliable?

*The second is listening to evaluate speech communication techniques.* In acquiring most personal skills we first study guiding principles, then practice them. Thus you may learn from your instructor and from this textbook the elements of effective speech communication; then you may practice by making speeches to the class and learn from the criticism of your instructor and your classmates. A similar study-practice sequence is followed in learning many other skills, such as written composition, mathematical calculation, and laboratory experimentation. But in developing your own abilities in speech communication, you may also learn much from observing the practice of others. If you consider carefully the situation confronting each of your classmates when he speaks, and evaluate critically the way he deals with it, you may multiply many times the opportunities for learning. It will pay to be an active listener, not a passive one, lapsing into a temporary coma and rousing to attention only when the speaker pauses, changes pace, or gives special emphasis to a key word or phrase. Your own stockpile of effective techniques can grow from alert and critical observation of others; and the speechmaking of your classmates offers you also an opportunity to profit from the mistakes of others. Try making mental notes on "*How* did the speaker say it?" in terms such as these:

> How did he gain my initial attention? Did he use a device that I might employ in my next speech? Would I have tried to come to the main point sooner? Did he make his central idea seem important?
>
> Did he make that argument clear? Would an illustration or a comparison have helped? Does he use types of supporting material that I often ignore? Can I learn something from him about the use of summaries and transitions?
>
> How enthusiastic does he seem to be? Is the way he uses his voice an attribute? What can I learn about posture and bodily action from him? Am I straining to hear him? Is he checking his listeners' visible reactions?

Of course your profitable listening for speech communication techniques need not be limited to the speech classroom. You will naturally be listening to get meanings whenever you hear classroom or public lectures, sermons or newscasts, televised presidential press conferences or United Nations debates. Make them also into opportunities to evaluate speech communication techniques.

In a later chapter we will describe some of the more refined techniques for evaluating speechmaking, often called rhetorical criticism.

What follows here is a brief and nontechnical summary of helpful guides to self-training in listening.

## The Nature and Process of Listening

Because we are more accustomed to reading than to listening critically, it may be useful to note two significant differences.

1. *Listening is instantaneous.* When reading we can set our own pace, pause to ponder, and reread. In listening there is no backtracking. Skilled speakers will aid you with repetitions and summaries, but they are not like tape recorders; you cannot get a verbatim playback. Therefore, you get it straight the first time, or you probably won't get it straight at all. An alert and intelligent mind that gets meanings instantly in reading will probably do as well in listening. Even a sluggish or fatigued reader can compensate by rereading. But there is no help for the laggard listener; he is simply left behind.

2. *Listening for meanings is aided by voice and action.* No reader can obtain from the printed page the aids to understanding meanings that are provided by the voice and action of a competent speaker. Because talk is older than print, man has evolved a subtle code of meaning by vocal inflection, emphasis, and rhythm. (For a simple illustration read with the indicated stress: "*He* is a man. He *is* a man. He is a *man.*") He has also evolved a meaningful code of action, a kind of sign language by posture, facial expression, and gesture that can point, describe, divide, and discriminate. (Consider the meaning of pointed index finger, clenched fist, or a smile.) Black print on white paper can never convey the full meanings of effective talk. Not all speakers have learned effective techniques of voice and action, of course: flat droning voices anesthetize audiences; uncoordinated actions distract them. In some reasonable measure highly motivated listeners can compensate for such faults of delivery. But it demands persistence and energy that the average listener may not have or be willing to give.

Not all listening makes the same demands. In order of increasing difficulty for the listener there are at least these five types:

1. *Listening for entertainment.* The stage farce, the television variety show, the comedy movie, or the humorous after-dinner speaker tax listeners least of all.

2. *Listening for escape or sublimation.* There is a little Walter Mitty in the best of us, and we effortlessly escape our own humdrum lives or sublimate our imaginative aspirations as we listen to sportscasts, travelogues, and soap operas.

3. *Listening for inspiration.* Sermons and speeches on patriotic themes, religious music and inspiring drama are all responses to the human need for inspiration. We listen to renew our faith and uplift our spirits.

4. *Listening for information and ideas.* College students spend much of their time at this level of listening: classroom lectures, laboratory demonstrations, convocations, and the like. Newscasts and other public service broadcasts commonly provide information about the world around us, and we listen for the facts and for an understanding of what they mean.

5. *Listening for opinions and conclusions.* Most listening on controversial subjects is done with a closed mind. We usually listen not to form new beliefs, but to confirm old ones. But some people can listen critically, accepting new information, modifying attitudes, and changing opinions. This is the most difficult level of listening; some try it, get tired after a few minutes, and give up. Without directed practice they will go through life listening only for entertainment, escape, or comforting confirmation of what they already believe.

Each of these levels of listening has its place and its own utility, but for now consider primarily the last two. We assume an interest in efficient listening to acquire new information and ideas and to develop opinions and conclusions. Such listening depends upon four factors: 1. intention, 2. attention, 3. retention, and 4. evaluation.

The listener's *intention* is of first importance. Research studies show that strongly opinionated listeners learn less than others, that those who tend strongly to agree or disagree are least likely to grasp a speaker's central idea and to form valid inferences. Their attitudes are negative except to compatible information and opinions and they apparently work harder at rationalizing their own views than at understanding those they hear. Without critical intentions we tend to become mere resisters to uncongenial opinions, applauders of congenial ones.

A good intention becomes operative only through close *attention.* Audience members who figuratively fold their arms, jut out their jaws, and sit back waiting for the speaker to give them something, rarely get anything. Listening is an active, not a passive process. Like hunters, listeners must track down the game. If they lose focus even for a moment the target may escape them, and a near-miss, like a half-caught thought, has little value.

Attention to what is heard at the moment must be coupled with *retention* of what was heard earlier. Otherwise the main lines of thought, the relationship of arguments, and the significance of evidence are apt to be lost. Listening research literature often refers to the ability to "structuralize a speech," to see it as a whole, not just a collection of parts. This is another way of stating the importance of continuous retention in efficient listening.

The last step is *evaluation.* It depends upon your intelligence, what you know about the speaker's subject, your previous attitude toward it, *and* your listening ability. Evaluation begins with saying "*I understand.*" Without understanding only immature minds make judgments. When you do understand you start a "silent feedback" of analysis. "I understand, and agree." "I understand, and agree, but with these reservations. . . ." "I understand, but cannot judge without time for reflection." Or "I understand, and disagree, because I cannot accept your premise . . . reasoning . . . evidence." What you hear is fused with what you already know as you analyze a speaker's facts and opinions—sifting, measuring, and judging them.

The highest skill in listening is evaluation. Some listeners fail at the outset; if they lack understanding their evaluating is of little value. Others are efficient in pure reception of facts, but fail in combining them into thought patterns and judging their relevance. Still others have a passion for their own prejudices, and their rigid minds cannot fairly judge the thought and feelings of others. They can dispute, but they cannot evaluate.

### How to Listen Efficiently

Our description of its nature and process provides clues for the development of efficient listening habits. Now consider them in a sequence of seven steps.

1. *Get set to listen.* Research has demonstrated a close correlation between listening comprehension and "anticipatory set." This is a psychological term that means having a positive and receptive attitude. It is rarely displayed by those who seek seats at the back of a room, or near an exit where outside noises mask the speaker's voice. Nor is it reflected in those who slouch into their seats, or focus their attention on their neighbors instead of upon the speaker. Such people seldom listen efficiently. In fact, they probably did not come to listen. In preparing yourself to listen, sit where you can see and hear, assume an alert but comfortable posture, focus your eyes on the speaker and give your attention to what he has to say.

2. *Switch off "emotional filters."* Ralph G. Nichols has used this term to describe attitudes that screen out what we hear, so that only what we want to hear can get through. The fact is that people with strong emotional attitudes don't listen well. Not only do they fail to get the speaker's central idea, but they fail to make relevant judgments about it. They are so busy saying to themselves: "Any fool can see right through that argument," or "He believes exactly as I do," or "I never liked this subject, anyway," that at best they can only *hear*. They cannot *listen*. The way to listen critically is to switch off the filters and let the ideas flow in.

3. *Start listening with the first sentence.* Unlike the reader, the listener must comprehend the message at once. If he "tunes in" after it has started he may never catch up. Effective speakers may sometimes provide important background information in their opening sentences, or they may

even state their central ideas in the first minute or so. This is especially true in short classroom speeches. Start listening, therefore, with the speaker's first sentence. If he is merely warming up, check it off, but stay alert for the statement of his central idea, key definitions or basic assumptions. The first part of a speech can be critical, though it may make for the hardest listening.

4. *Find the central idea.* In any speech worth listening to there is one central idea, and it will be supported by facts, examples, testimony, and other types of evidence. Be on the lookout for the unifying concept, and beware of bogging down in specific details. Chances are that if you miss the central theme you haven't listened efficiently, for even if the speaker fails to put it into exact words, you should be able to do so for yourself. Any almanac will provide a potpourri of facts. A speech is different in that it should organize facts into orderly patterns of support for a central idea. It is up to you to find it.

5. *Link up the chief supporting ideas.* Just as "no man is an island unto himself" so no central idea exists without supporting ideas. Normally these sub-ideas have some relationship to each other; occasionally they appear to exist independently. In either case the efficient listener must identify and judge them in their function as supports. Are the supporting ideas valid in themselves? Is their place in the total organizational plan clear and logical? Do they actually shore up the central idea?

Skilled speakers will aid listeners in finding the relations among supporting ideas and their relation to the whole. Forecasts, transitions, and summaries provide handles by which separate parts of a speech may be grasped by the listener. Watch for cue phrases forecasting what is to come: "Let's look at three background facts," "We will see that our subject divides into four aspects," or "My purpose is to show that. . . ." Then listen for transitional cues that reflect movement from one part to another: "A further consideration," "Let us now turn to," or "Secondly." Finally, learn to note cue phrases indicating the completion of one part of the speech: "What I have been saying adds up to this," "Let me sum up this idea," or "Before submitting my next point." Especially watch for the summary that usually comes at the end of a speech. Here you may have a chance to get a bird's-eye view of all that has been said, and to pick up points that you missed earlier.

6. *Review and project while you listen.* From childhood you have probably been advised "never try to do two things at once." This is good advice only in reference to incompatible activities. But listening to what a speaker is saying at the moment, and reviewing what he has previously said and projecting what he probably will say, are compatible. The secret is that listeners can think four or five times as fast as speakers can talk. The average speaker talks about 150 words per minute, but laboratory studies show that the average individual can think at a rate of over 500

words per minute, and some can more than double that figure. Borrowing his phraseology from Aesop's fable, Ralph Nichols describes this as the case of the tortoise talker and the hare listener. If you can monitor a speaker's words in only one-fourth or one-fifth of your time the challenge lies in how you use the surplus. If you let your mind wander aimlessly between spells of listening you may find when it returns that you've missed the speaker's essential point. There are two things you can do, each compatible with listening.

First, you can construct your own condensed version of a speaker's speech as he is speaking, recalling the total sequence of key points and fitting the newest one into the pattern. In effect you are constantly summarizing the speech and fixing it in your memory. Second, you can project what you think the speaker will say while you are waiting for him to say it. If he has already reviewed a problem, speculate about the solution he may propose. If he is discussing an effect, try to anticipate what he will identify as the cause. With practice in critical listening you will guess right more often than not. If you are right, the confirmation will fix the speaker's point in your mind. Even if you are wrong you will have gained from the experience of comparing what he said with what he might have said.

7. *Weigh and consider.* All that we have been saying about finding the central idea, linking up the chief supporting ideas, and reviewing and projecting the movement of a speech, is aimed at getting a clear understanding of the speaker's meanings. It is more than a legal nicety to record all the facts before rendering a judgment. It is a rule of life: "With all thy getting get understanding." Then evaluate. The one must precede the other, and without both the act of efficient listening is incomplete. Evaluation is often the most difficult task, and the temptation is great to avoid it, or to equivocate by damning with faint praise. But if you have or want to develop the ability to judge critically you must cast a mature and thoughtful vote. To be critical does not necessarily mean disagreeing. Nor being disagreeable. It is evaluating as Francis Bacon said readers should: "Read not to contradict or confute; not to believe and take for granted; not to find talk and discourse; but to weigh and consider."

The reader who has followed us through this chapter may have concluded that in a speech course he is to be trained only as a listener, not a speaker. If so, let him be reassured. We *are* concerned with speech-making. But we have proceeded on the assumption that speaking is for listening. We believe that those who would be speakers must first appreciate the legitimate expectations—and proper obligations—of listeners. If we have created a sensitivity for the listener and have said something useful about how to listen efficiently, we are ready to go on. The speaker comes next.

## SUPPLEMENTARY READINGS

Arnold, Carroll C., Ehninger, Douglas, and Gerber, John C., eds., *The Speaker's Resource Book: An Anthology, Handbook, and Glossary*, 2nd ed. Chicago: Scott, Foresman, 1966. See especially William G. Carleton, "Effective Speech in a Democracy," pp. 5-12, and Robert T. Oliver, "Culture and Communication," pp. 19-26.

Haiman, Franklyn S., "Democratic Ethics and the Hidden Persuaders." *Quarterly Journal of Speech*, 44 (December, 1958), pp. 385-392. A thoughtful consideration of the societal aspects of persuasion.

Lippmann, Walter, "The Indispensable Opposition." *Atlantic Monthly*, 164 (August, 1939), pp. 186-190. A classical statement on the majority's need, as well as the minority's, for direct confrontation on public issues.

Nichols, Ralph G., and Stevens, Leonard A., *Are You Listening?* New York: McGraw-Hill, 1957. A good summary of significant research, as well as a handbook for listener training.

Stevens, Leonard A., *The Ill-Spoken Word: The Decline of Speech in America*. New York: McGraw-Hill, 1966. An analysis of oral discourse in historical context, and a proposal for its improvement in response to contemporary needs.

## EXERCISES

1. Test first your ability to listen for information. Your instructor will read a three-minute article from *Time, U.S. News & World Report*, etc. Take no notes during the reading, but immediately afterward write a brief summary stressing only important items, including its central idea and the most impressive materials that support it.

2. Listen to a public speech (on radio or television if you prefer) and write a report on (a) the speaker's central idea, (b) the chief supporting ideas, (c) your evaluation of them.

3. In listening to the next round of class speeches, evaluate the speaking techniques of each speaker. Which were well used? Which poorly used? Which were ignored?

4. Draw up a list of the factors that make it difficult for you to listen efficiently. Prepare your next speech with these factors in mind, taking special care to prepare and deliver the speech so these missing cues are given your listeners.

Attach your list of factors to the outline. On the left margin of the outline explain the methods you plan to use for giving special cues to the listeners.

5. Prepare a list of three topics you would like to hear speeches about and turn it in to your instructor. He will arrange to have a master list made available, and you can refer to it for ideas about topics that "at least some one is interested in."

6. Listen to a public speech, a lecture, or a television talk, and record your own reactions to the speaker's behavior. How do you respond to his general manner and his style of speaking? List items in his behavior that annoy you. How do you respond to his ideas? List questions that remain in your mind after he has finished.

7. Read one of the supplementary readings and prepare a three-minute oral report (about 400–500 words) on it.

# 2

# The Attitudes and Resources of Speakers

No other person who appears in public has as great an opportunity to make an impact upon the behavior of his audience as does the public speaker—or so great an opportunity to make a fool of himself. It is no wonder that so many adults protest, "Oh, I could never stand up in public and make a speech." But neither is it any wonder that year after year public speaking is one of the most heavily elected courses in adult education programs.

It might be assumed that the major problem for these persons is to acquire a linguistic sense, a feeling for organization, or something to talk about. This assumption would be wrong. These adults who come late to education, like those in college, need as much to develop proper *attitudes* toward speechmaking as they need to develop techniques of communication. They also need to develop a sense of substance about speechmaking: where to find ideas and how to nourish them. These are the topics of this chapter. First, the speaker's attitudes; second, his resources.

## THE SPEAKER'S ATTITUDES

A nontechnical but accurate definition of an attitude is that it is a point of view toward or a feeling about a concept, person, or behavior. We are concerned with a positive attitude toward speech communication. We find it easiest to describe this attitude in terms of five senses. Not the usual ones of sight, smell, and so on, but specialized ones of responsibility, humanity, leadership, communication, and security.

### The Sense of Responsibility

Throughout all of history speech has been viewed as a social force by means of which man interprets, controls, modifies, or adapts to his environment. "None of the things which are done with intelligence," wrote Isocrates, about 400 B.C., "are done without the aid of speech." In our own day Bishop Gerald Kennedy, of the Los Angeles Area of the Methodist Church, declares that "the spoken word is still the most powerful instrument for shaping society and affecting lives." And on the international scene André Maurois, Nobel prize winner and member of the French Academy, dramatizes this notion by affirming that as "contemporary leaders still have the power to voice the fears and hopes and stir the hearts of men . . . one speech may be worth three divisions."

Paralleling this agreement about the power of oral discourse is a controversy about its ethical use. It was Plato who asked whether speakers were not more concerned with winning, even if it meant making the worse appear the better reason, than with searching for truth. It fell to Aristotle, in his seminal volume on *Rhetoric,* to reply that speech is a skill that can be used for worthy or unworthy purposes. "What makes a man a sophist," he said, "is not his skill, but his moral purpose." The good man, he held, should master the art of persuasion, both to enable him to defeat the efforts of unscrupulous opponents and to make him an effective advocate of what he regards as the truth.

The dilemma of a democratic society is that it cannot bar the demogogues and the charlatans from using speech as a powerful tool in affecting social change, and at the same time keep the forum open for Quintilian's "good man, skilled in speaking." The use of automobiles, guns, and other lethal weapons, may be regulated by the state, for the welfare of society. But the weapon of speech, which can be as deadly in its effect, must in a democracy be uninhibited.

In writing a book about speech, then, or in teaching a course in speech communication, it is imperative to stress the importance of the moral integrity of the speaker. If students are to be handed a weapon they must be alerted to its proper use. Simply calling attention to the ethics of speechmaking, we realize, will not of itself make all speakers responsible. But at least we can, as George Washington observed in another circumstance, "raise a standard to which the wise and honest can repair. . . ." The standard is the simple one of credibility. As listeners would express it:

We trust the speaker who shows intellectual integrity and sound judgment.

We trust the speaker who seems to know what he is talking about.

We trust the speaker who shows restraint and good will.

We trust the speaker who seems to care about us.[1]

It is difficult to put the matter of integrity into a detailed creed, but we believe Walter Lippmann would approve, as a statement of the public speaker's responsibilities, a definition he once gave of the responsibilities of the newspaper reporter: "To bring to light the hidden facts, to set them into relation with each other, and make a picture of reality on which men can act."

## The Sense of Humanity

The greatest of public speakers have been the most humane, and they have let their sense of humanity show from the platform. The chief speaker at Gettysburg in 1863 was Edward Everett, whose polished and memorized oration projected an image of urbanity, not humanity. "When you hear him," one critic said, "you button your coat to keep from taking cold." The other speaker in only 266 words, beginning with "Four score and seven years ago," so stirred the sentiments and so touched the ideals of the people that his essential humanity is still part of the nation's heritage.

A speaker's humanity is projected by an attitude of earnestness, a sensitivity to man's needs and aspirations, and a sense of humor.

Foremost in the eyes and ears of an audience is a speaker's *earnestness*. It "moves our emotions, thaws our indifference, and gives us faith which a leader must create," said James A. Winans. Audiences will sooner forgive a lack of polish than a lack of sincerity. The late Senator Estes Kefauver was not always a polished speaker; he often faltered in delivery as he fumbled for the right word, but his obvious sincerity in wanting to find the right word won him a warm popular response. Speakers who deliberately try not to be "too smooth," however, frequently give themselves away. It was no real service to Alfred M. Landon in his presidential campaign when one supporter advised his manager: "Do urge Governor Landon not to try to improve his delivery."

A speaker's *sensitivity to the needs and aspirations of his listeners* is caught in many ways. They expect recognition and respect, and they want admiration and approval. If a speaker talks frankly with them, admitting when it is so that he does not have all the answers, but involving them in the further search, he is being sensitive to their needs. He does the same when he avoids jargon and abstract phrases, and talks in concrete and meaningful terms. Talking down to listeners displays gross insensitivity, and so does talking over their heads. Adlai Stevenson, in his presidential campaigns, sensitively tried to steer a middle course: "Let's talk sense to the American people . . . candidates for important offices . . . should not

[1]These concepts have not only morality to recommend them, but experimental research to validate them. Jon Eisenson, J. Jeffery Auer, and John V. Irwin, *The Psychology of Communication* ( New York, 1963), pp. 284-289.

treat us as fourteen-year-olds but as adults . . . with the assumption that we should and can and will respond to the appeal of reason and imagination."

A friend observes that he is not happy around people who lack a *sense of humor*. Extremists in particular have this lack, and perhaps that is why they become extremists. Perspective is necessary for the human sympathy, human tolerance, and human kindliness that marks the man with a sense of humor. Fanatics seldom see their causes in a human light, and it is the first sign of a "thaw" in Communist countries when satirists and wits become free to write and speak. Student speakers also frequently lack a sense of humor in their first efforts. They do not yet feel at home on the platform, and perhaps they do not feel comfortable talking about serious subjects in public. And so they become solemn, even doleful, as they concentrate on themselves. If the disease worsens they become pompous, pronouncing that if their particular brand of salvation is not adopted by tomorrow morning the world will end. When they gain perspective and maturity the malady will wear away. They will realize that every generation lives in "times that try men's souls," and that these trials have best been met—from Julius Caesar to Benjamin Franklin to Winston Churchill—by men of good will, good sense, and good humor.

### The Sense of Leadership

A public speaker cannot escape the implications of *leadership*. He must so speak as to command *respect* and *enthusiasm* from his hearers. Without them *both* he is lost. An Associated Press dispatch from London, October 12, 1963, put it bluntly: "Richard A. Butler muffed a big chance Saturday in his bid to succeed Harold Macmillan as Prime Minister. Given the opportunity to make the concluding address at the Conservative Party's annual convention, he won a *respectful but unenthusiastic* reception from 4,000 delegates."

To gain the respect of others, a leader must respect himself. To gain enthusiasm, he must first display it. But the novice speaker says "I don't know how to develop either one. I have doubts and fears about the whole business!" Of course he does. So has every speaker and leader worth his salt, but in their learning they have followed Emerson's rule: "Do the thing you fear and the death of fear is certain." Within reasonable limits self-respect and enthusiasm can be cultivated, if you cultivate the foundation on which they rest. How?

First, *prepare* thoroughly. If you have not really prepared your speech, you do not deserve self-respect, and deep in your heart you know it. You must *earn* the right to speak, and you cannot do it by waiting until the night before and then frantically wondering what to do. One great preacher testifies that "I have never stood in my pulpit without being prepared for the event to the very best of my ability. This is not to say that every sermon has seemed satisfactory to me. None of them have. But it has never been necessary to apologize to God or man because I let other things crowd into my time for preparation."[2]

Second, *get enthusiastic about your subject.* Enthusiasm is not a rare quality, but it is a vital one, without which speaking—and living—loses much of its interest and meaning. Without it speaking cannot rise above the level of routine; and routine speaking is seldom heard with pleasure, or looked forward to with expectancy. "The best sermon," observed William Feather, "is preached by the minister who has a sermon to preach and not by the man who has to preach a sermon." The same is true of the classroom speech. It is the difference between having to make a speech on some subject or other, and having a subject that compels you to speak.

Third, *act as if you had self-respect and confidence.* Emotions and mental attitudes can be induced by deliberately assuming the physical positions and by going through the actions that characterize such emotions and attitudes. Double up your fists, grit your teeth, stomp the floor, and frown—all the while thinking of something that provokes you—and you can work up a strong state of concern. Or smile, relax your muscles—and think of something cheerful—and you can begin to rid yourself of anxiety. In the same way, you will tend to acquire self-respect and confidence before an audience if you walk firmly to the platform, stand straight, chest out and eyes front, and think how vital it is that people believe you.

Fourth, *don't overdo self-confidence.* To put it plainly, beware of egotism or conceit. For a golden mean contrast these pointed characterizations of two contemporary English statesmen: "He is a very humble man, and he has much to be humble about," and "There but for the Grace of God goes God." You need self-respect, but you need it tempered with modesty.

## The Sense of Communication

"I knew a very distinguished man who memorized every word of each address," said Clarence B. Randall, "and did it with amazing skill, but I always felt that his slight preoccupation with the effort of memory drew an unfortunate veil between him and his audience." Randall's judgment deserves respect. At his retirement he was one of America's half dozen outstanding businessmen, and for two decades he had freely given himself in public service. An able speaker himself, recipient of a U. S. Speaker of the Year Award, he was also a discerning analyst of contemporary American speechmaking. Thus his scepticism about memorized speaking deserves respect. It was not always thus. Many earlier speakers—Edward Everett and Albert J. Beveridge, to name but two—worked hard to perfect the art, sometimes spending weeks rehearsing and preparing their memories for each performance. The fact that it was a *performance* was its weakness.

[2]Gerald Kennedy, *While I'm On My Feet* (Nashville, Tenn., 1963), p. 136.

Audiences often applauded for the art itself. Not so today. Audiences in the twentieth century have no time to admire a speech primarily as an art form. They listen bcause they need information. Because they need help in problem-solving. Because they need to have ideas watered and cultivated. They listen, hoping to hear strongly-held convictions, buttressed by solid supporting evidence, vigorously expressed by a speaker who creates a speech before them. He won't reach them by reciting polished memorized phrases. He won't influence their behavior until he projects himself into their minds. In real public speaking you must *communicate* with your listeners. Memorizers don't participate in the process of communication. They recite.

Speakers face the same handicap in using manuscripts or detailed notes. The speaker who searches his papers for the next idea breaks the mind-to-mind contact with his listeners. Each time it is broken it must be reestablished. When Alben W. Barkley made what must be regarded as one of the greatest of all political convention speeches, for the Democrats in 1952, he began, "What I shall say . . . shall be spoken from the heart and not from a piece of paper." It was an ingenuous remark, but the audience's response indicated its appreciation of the implied rebuke to the reciters, the manuscript readers, and the teleprompted. For some speakers extended notes provide a crutch. For others a manuscript confesses to a false "pride of syntax." They would rather be caught in their underwear than with an impromptu split infinitive. Would that they might have the same regard for communication!

Let us grant that most speakers today use notes or manuscripts. Also occasions do arise for manuscript speaking. We acknowledge the precision of a manuscript for a president's inaugural, or for other critical statements of policy by high officials. But we do insist categorically that while some speakers can use it well, and a few superbly, the vast majority use a manuscript poorly and will never learn to do it well. For most speakers these visible means of support are incompatible with a sense of communication, of conversing with an audience.

Speech students frequently raise questions about the differences between private conversing and public speaking. Actually, the differences are largely superficial and the likenesses are fundamental. The dividing line is hard to see. In his *Public Speaking* text James A. Winans put the matter vividly. He hypothesized a man who had seen a great battle, meeting a friend on the street and pausing to tell him about it. Others gathered; he raised his voice so that all might hear. Still others came; so that they might see as well as hear him, he mounted a cart and continued. It is clear that he began a private conversation and ended with a public speech. Where, asked Winans, did the change take place?

We might pick any point as the transitional one. Perhaps the conversation becomes a speech when the number of listeners reaches fifteen, or fifty, or when the speaker stands on a cart or platform. Any one of these points is an arbitrary choice. None marks the real transition. In truth, conversation *gradually* becomes public speaking; public speaking is simply *enlarged* conversation. Forget the notion that you are "making a speech" when you stand on a platform. You are not talking *at* people, or in front of them. You are not declaiming to the walls, the ceiling, or into thin air. You are talking *with* people, and they will talk back to you.

Of course they will seldom talk back with words. Some speakers may hear an occasional "Amen!" or "Give 'em hell, Harry!" But for the most part the listeners respond with visible cues. They frown their disapproval or their misunderstanding, nod or applaud their approval. These reactions are as good as words. Alert speakers "read" them and adapt accordingly. If a number of audience expressions say to a speaker "I don't quite understand that generalization," he interrupts what he had planned to say, and inserts a fresh illustration that makes the generalization come alive. Or if listener grimaces say "I'm bored; why don't you sit down?" the wise speaker probably omits a few illustrations and hurries to his conclusion!

There is a danger in viewing public speech as enlarged conversation. Not everyone is a good conversationalist. Poor ones bore only you in private; from the platform they can bore everyone. Thus it is misleading to advise such persons to "Talk naturally. Be conversational." They are "naturally" dull, uninspired, uninteresting. Even those who speak passably in private may do less well in public; as all else is enlarged, so are modest faults. Let us therefore examine some of the attributes of good enlarged conversation.

1. *Looking the listener in the mind* is a part of all earnest conversation. Instead of staring out the window, at the floor or the ceiling, good conversationalists look each other in the eye. Actually their eye-to-eye contact is part of *looking each other in the mind*. No matter how large or small the audience, part of the mental attitude of the good public speaker is a compulsion to look each listener in the mind. Though he may vary his voice, action, or general manner to fit the occasion, this compulsion is constant. Let Adam Smith, the great eighteenth-century university lecturer, exemplify the point. He was great because he spoke not only to the patient ear of the earnest student, but also because he spoke to the shallow ear of the poorest student and to the callous ear of the great outside world. He attributed his success, said his biographer, "very largely to the vigilant care with which he watched his audience; for he depended very much upon their sympathy. 'During one whole session,' he is reported to have said, 'a certain student with a plain but expressive countenance was of great use to me in judging my success. . . . If he leant forward to listen, all was right; but if he leant back in an attitude of listlessness I felt that all was wrong, and that I must change either the subject or the style of my address!'."[3]

[3]Francis W. Hirst, *Adam Smith* (London, 1904), pp. 34-35.

2. *Physical vitality* is a hallmark of the earnest conversationalist. Watch one as he leans forward on the edge of his chair, punctuates his words with gestures, and speaks with animation. To be effective on the platform before twenty people in a classroom, or a hundred in an auditorium, requires five, ten, or a hundred times as much energy, if his voice is to be as loud, earnest, and direct as in private conversation. For many beginning speakers the amount of vitality required is unbelievable. As one reporter observed of Alessandro Gavazzi, the brilliant Italian preacher who fought with Garibaldi, he "did not speak merely with his lips. He was eloquent to his finger tips, and to the soles of his sandaled shoes." The enthusiastic platform speaker must be heard and seen by his whole audience, not just those in the front rows. He opens his mouth far wider than he would ever do in private, his gestures become more expansive, and his facial expressions are exaggerated. He understands the necessities of good "enlarged" conversation and communicates uninhibitedly.

3. *The personality patterns of good talk* are easy to identify in conversation. First is the use of personal pronouns, *we, you,* and *I.* Second is the choice of simple and direct words over the more formal and abstract ones, like *think* versus "contemplate," *go* versus "proceed," or *ask* versus "inquire." Third is the rhythm of expression, primarily revealed in contractions such as *don't, won't* and *it's,* for the full forms of "do not," "will not," and "it is." Each of these language patterns of good conversation should characterize good public speaking.

That they so often do not is easy to demonstrate. Listen to speakers who avoid the pronoun simplicity of "I think," and slip into "It is my thought that." Or those who shun the plain "I want to show you" for the pompous "It is my intention to attempt to demonstrate to you." And those who pervert the natural rhythm of "He'll go" with "He will go" (although sometimes in an effort to emphasize a positive or negative word we must say "He *will* go"). What's wrong with such speakers? James Redpath knew the answer a hundred years ago when he established one of America's most successful lecture bureaus: "Literary men, as a rule, are poor lecturers. They mistake essay reading for oratory." The answer is the same today: these men stubbornly stick to "writing talk" when they should be using "speaking talk." Though they don't sound this way in conversation, it's ten to one their only preparation for speaking was to *write* an outline or even a manuscript. When they write they use "writing talk." And when they practice out loud— *if* they practice—they don't listen to themselves and sense the absurdity of many written forms when spoken.

Public speakers must remind themselves that conversational forms are basic, that written English is what Harold Whitehall calls "a rather artificial dialect," and that its formality is *compensation* for its "communicative deficiencies as compared with speech . . . the rise or fall of the voice at the ends of phrases and sentences; the application of vocal loudness to this or that word or part of a word; the use of gesture; the meaningful rasp or liquidity, shouting or muting, drawling or clipping, whining or breaking, melody or whispering imparted to the quality of the voice."[4]

## The Sense of Security

In the "Peanuts" cartoon book, *Security is a Thumb and a Blanket*, Linus observes that "security is knowing all your lines." With the characteristic discernment of all good cartoonists, Charles M. Schulz can cut through a volume of text with a single line. This one is a capsulized answer to the *in*security that lies behind the question "How can I overcome stage fright?" Because this is probably the most frequently asked question about public speaking, by novice and even experienced speakers, we must deal with it directly.

Let it be understood at the outset that there is no pat formula for overcoming stage fright. Indeed, many of our greatest public speakers (and singers, actors, and other public performers) have never overcome it. It is reported that Mrs. Lyndon B. Johnson's fear of public speaking was so great that when she was graduated from the University of Texas she turned down the valedictorian's medal rather than make the speech required of the recipient. Yet, with a course in public speaking behind her, she was able to make as many as sixteen speeches in a single day during a 1960 whistlestop campaign trip with her husband. Stan Musial, for years the "big bat" of the St. Louis Cardinals, who feared no living pitcher, was troubled by stage fright. "I'm not a speaker," he explained, "so you have nervous tension." This tension sometimes takes bizarre forms. David Low, the eminent British cartoonist, once told an audience that every time he made a speech he felt a block of ice, nine inches square, in the pit of his stomach. Afterwards Sir Winston Churchill came up to ask: "How large did you say that block of ice is?" "Nine by nine inches," Low replied. "What an amazing coincidence," commented Britain's greatest orator, "exactly the same size as mine."

For these and all other speakers who have reported their platform fears, the problem is not to overcome stage fright, but to understand what it is and to learn to live with it. Indeed, living with it, but controlling it, will make them better speakers than if they could eliminate it.

What is stage fright? Internally it is a feeling of nervousness and confusion, in its most extreme form even a forgetting of what to say next. Externally the speaker's behavior may include a quavering voice, muscle tension and random physical action. It affects men and women alike, and research studies show that it is unrelated to intelligence, reasoning ability, or personality. In short, it is a common phenomenon. In psychological

[4]"Structural Essentials of English" in Leonard F. Dean and Kenneth G. Wilson, eds., *Essays on Language and Usage* (New York, 1959), pp. 238-239.

terms we describe stage fright as a speaker's response to an approach-avoidance conflict situation. This simply means that for all human beings there are paradoxical tugs in two directions at once: on the one hand the speaker is possessed of an idea he feels compelled to communicate to an audience (approach), but on the other hand he fears to face an audience, fears that he will forget what he wants to say, fears that he may be a failure (avoidance). In short, the speaker *fears* to do what he *wants* to do.

We have so far been describing stage fright psychologically. Physiologically its effect is to pump adrenalin into the blood stream and this chemical change creates the muscle tension, quavering voice, and so on. Thus the adrenalin released in response to the speaker's fears would seem to be the culprit. But psychologists have discovered that adrenalin is also secreted by vigorous bodily action, even in the absence of stage fright or other emotions. And that the physiological changes produced can, if controlled and directed, make our behavior more efficient in meeting the speech situation. Thus it can be shown that a reasonable amount of what we call stage fright, if controlled and directed, can actually improve a speaker's performance. This is true even for experienced speakers. Interestingly enough, though he did not know the physiological facts, Cicero sensed this truth two thousand years ago: "For the better the speaker, the more profoundly is he frightened of the difficulty of speaking, and of the doubtful fate of a speech, and of the anticipations of an audience."

How is stage fright to be controlled, and even made to build an increased sense of security? Much that we have said thus far in this chapter, about developing the sense of responsibility, humanity, leadership, and communication, is a partial answer to this question. Each speaker will undoubtedly find his own special devices for controlling and directing the nervous energy induced by contemplating the speaking situation. For many speakers, however, following these three admonitions has been helpful.

1. *Know your subject.* This advice presumes that you have a subject that interests—even excites—you. Speakers sometimes forget that they are subject to the same psychological principles that govern their audiences. If listeners are most attentive to subjects that interest them, for example, then speakers are likely to be most effective with subjects that interest them. But mere interest is not enough. Effective speakers are adequately prepared speakers. No small part of an audience's confidence in a speaker is based upon his apparent self-confidence. Does he seem to be well prepared? Is he seemingly assured in his knowledge of pertinent facts and opinions on the subject? Can he expertly adapt what he knows to fit the information, attitudes, and beliefs of his listeners? A feeling of self-confidence is a feeling of adequacy in meeting the situation. Without that feeling about his subject a speaker deserves to feel subject fright, if not stage fright!

Experts on the psychology of learning offer some helpful advice that can be applied to speech preparation.

The rate of learning is accelerated when practice is spaced rather than massed. This means starting preparation as early as possible and, once the material for the speech is well organized, practicing it once or twice on a number of occasions, instead of a dozen times the night before.

Learning "by the whole" is more efficient than learning "by the parts." This means that the total speech should be practiced each time, not just units within it.

Learning is enhanced by a sense of meaningfulness about what is being learned. This means that it is helpful to think continually about the significance of what you have to say, and about your purpose in saying it to this particular audience on this specific occasion.

2. *Focus on your task, not on yourself.* In a number of different ways we have said that speech communication should be subject-and-audience-centered, not speaker-centered. At this point we relate that concept to stage fright. When a speaker focuses his attention upon himself, asks "How am I doing?" he creates rather than stills anxiety. When he becomes highly introspective he tends to forget about the *product* in his concern for the *process.* Do you remember the childhood verse about the centipede?

> A centipede was happy quite
> Until a frog in fun
> Said, "Pray, which leg comes after which?"
> This raised her mind to such a pitch,
> She lay distracted in a ditch,
> Considering how to run.

The bitter truth may be that when a speaker asks himself "How am I doing?" he gets a negative answer! Far better than being self-conscious, hypercritical, and even deprecatory about yourself is to concentrate upon your task. Though Mrs. Lyndon Johnson admits that her knees still shake sometimes when she gets up to speak, most of her old shyness is gone. "The way you overcome shyness," she found, "is to become so wrapped up in something that you forget to be afraid."[5] Let the anxious speaker be wrapped up in his subject, not in himself.

3. *Use your energy purposefully.* We have already seen that those who suffer from stage fright become physically tense, even immobilized. This creates even greater apprehensiveness; and more apprehension means more tension. There is only one way to halt this spiraling effect: *Relax.*

Relaxation is easier to prescribe than to achieve. It must be controlled relaxation, or it is no help. Those muscles used in holding the body

[5]Marjorie Hunter, "Public Servant Without Pay: The First Lady," *The New York Times Magazine* (December 15, 1963), p. 71.

poised and erect must be kept firm. Let the others go, in the arms, the hands, and above all, in the face. In short, get the body tonus back to normal, and your stage fright will be reduced.

Of course we cannot simply command our bodies to relax and expect anything to happen. We must *do* something to provide a release, to drain off the built-up excess energy. Start with your face, and smile, or at least raise your eyebrows. Then nod your head, or shake it. Use your hands in some way; a purposeful gesture is best, but even scratching your ear will help. Finally, move your feet by taking a positive step. As soon as you begin some form of physical action, you are freeing yourself for purposeful action. Unless it is purposeful by helping to communicate your thought to the audience it is likely to distract: adjusting your tie or your blouse, patting your hair or clutching your notes has nothing to do with your task, but only with you. Do these things and you once again start up the cycle of self-concern, apprehension, and tension. Instead, as Cardinal Manning once advised a young man about to make his first important public speech: "Be full of your subject and forget yourself."

But is it not possible that, despite knowing your subject, focusing on your task and not on yourself, and using your energy purposefully, you may still find yourself facing an audience and forget what you want to say next? We honestly believe that if you have followed the suggestions in this chapter and have prepared thoroughly, you just won't forget more than momentarily, if at all. *If* you have really prepared and have thoroughly rehearsed the speech out loud and while standing on your feet, you have every prospect of carrying on, even though your mind goes blank and the room blacks out.

But suppose that in spite of careful preparation and rehearsal you forget anyhow. What then? Why, you reach for a life preserver. Here are four of them.

*Don't panic, but take a deep breath and try to remember the next point*. The deep breath will help you to keep from tensing up, and the time it takes will let you think. Perhaps a step forward or a change in posture will put your mind back on the track. If nothing happens, then:

*Rephrase and repeat what you have just said*. If it was of some importance, the repetition will impress it upon the audience, and make sense. Even if the point was not a critical one, reiterating it may give you the cue for what comes next. If it doesn't:

*Summarize aloud what you have developed of the speech*. The summary may make some sense if you have already developed a major unit of the speech. In any event, it may lead you to the next idea, or at least to some idea that follows. If you get back on the track, even though not exactly where you got off, you are underway again. If you aren't:

*Tell your listeners frankly that you cannot remember the next point*. When you forget, chances are that everyone knows it anyway. Be candid,

then, and admit it. As long as you're in trouble you might as well be
gracious about it and enlist the understanding of your listeners. By the
time you have smiled at them, and they smile back, you will feel more
comfortable. Their warm sympathy will be with you and you can continue
by *saying something,* just as you would if you met a friend on the street.
Then you can *say something about your subject.* It probably won't be what
you had planned to say, but you can still follow up as you would in conversation. Maybe you will get back to your planned speech. Maybe not.
But you will have discovered that your listeners are your friends, and that
if you treat them as such they will listen earnestly, want you to succeed,
and applaud you in any event. If you can establish that kind of rapport
with your audience, you will not need to worry about forgetting.

## THE SPEAKER'S RESOURCES

Anyone planning to make a speech, on any subject, has just two resources: what he knows, and what he can find out. Each one bears a
familiar label. The first is *thinking,* the second is *investigating.* We labor
the distinction for the very good reason that students so often do not. More
than five hundred students were asked, "How do you prepare your
speeches?" Over half said the first thing they did was to look for speech
material in the library! Does this support Thomas Edison's cryptic comment that "there is nothing to which men will not resort in order to avoid
the labor of thinking"—even to reading a book? Running to the library and
to the *Readers' Guide,* or to the *Reader's Digest,* is to look first for what
other people know about your subject. But it is *your* subject. What do *you*
know?

### Taking Stock of What You Know

The Romans had a word for it, and the word was *memoria.* As developed especially by Quintilian, it referred to the speaker's "well-stocked
mind," a mental storehouse of ideas, facts, experiences, observations, and
even their arrangement into patterns of thought. Centuries later Ralph
Waldo Emerson called this his "savings bank" of ideas in which he made
daily deposits of information that could be withdrawn when he needed
them. Sometimes the storehouse yields only a single relevant item ("Don't
I remember that Emerson said something about *memoria?*"). Again, it
may furnish a whole stock of material, already organized. At the Paris
Peace Conference Woodrow Wilson listened to a speech attacking the
Monroe Doctrine, then immediately rose to his feet and effectively de-
fended it. When Colonel House and others complimented him on his ap-

parent impromptu effort he was modest: "To me at least," he said with a chuckle, "it had a very familiar ring. I was, or professed to be, a teacher of American history for twenty years, and rarely a month passed that I did not preach what the Monroe Doctrine meant to me. . . ."

Some of you who read this book have been *living* American history for as many as twenty years. It would be unreasonable to expect you to extract enough material, and well enough ordered, to make a speech like Wilson's, but there must be many topics where perhaps half the information you need for a short speech can be pulled together from your own resources. The procedure is to take stock of what you know.

Suppose that you want to make a speech about campaign debates between presidential candidates, the values of the liberal arts, federal aid to education, the state of the current novel, integration in the schools, or membership in the United Nations. These are topics of your lifetime; they have arisen, changed, or matured while you have lived history, thinking, observing, experiencing, reading, and stockpiling. How do you take stock of what you know? One way is by asking questions such as these:

> Why did I choose this subject in the first place?
> What made me think my audience might be interested in it?
> What does my audience probably know about it already?
> What do I know about it from firsthand experience?
> Do I know enough about the subject at this time—
> > to divide it into subtopics or related parts?
> > to view its development chronologically?
> > to identify its most important features?
> > to recognize its controversial aspects?
> > to understand differing viewpoints about it?
> What gaps in my knowledge remain to be filled in?

Like the linebacker in football, you must be alert to the soft spots in your defense and try to strengthen them. Investigation is your method, and you can apply it in several different ways.

### Investigating by Talking and Listening

In your previous thinking about the problem did you decide that you knew enough about the interests and knowledge of your prospective audience? It is easy to fill in the gaps here; after you leave college and classroom audiences, it won't be so easy. Now you can determine student information and opinion by the most amiable of methods: talking and listening.

We sometimes seem to think that expertness increases by the square of the distance the expert is away from home. But every college campus abounds with persons qualified to give information and authoritative opinion. What facts can you get from a physicist about nuclear accelerators? What does the basketball coach think about the new offensive penalty rule? How do the theater professors evaluate Edward Albee's newest play? What can some of the foreign students tell you, for example, about current economic conditions in their countries?

Often as important as getting new information by talking and listening is the chance to test your ideas on others. Just as the psychologist may run a pilot study on a dozen subjects before he tools up for a major experiment involving several hundred, so you can try out your ideas informally. Try them over the dinner table, during a coffee break, with your roommate, or even on a date. You may discover unanticipated questions about your proposal, that you have not explained it carefully enough, or that something about it arouses resentment. This is sensible preparation and, if done well in advance, will give you time to shore up your speech. It is well known, of course, that presidents and other men in public life constantly test their ideas before important speeches. Woodrow Wilson spoke for all of them when he said, "I not only use all the brains I have, but all I can borrow."

### Investigating by Observing

Most of us are prudent enough to reserve judgment about a blind date until we've seen her (or him). But we may be brash enough to speak against a new bill providing construction loans to colleges without actually reading the document, or to generalize about the efficiency of the city-manager form of government without watching it in action at the local city hall. Harry A. Overstreet, one of our eminent philosophers, once took a semester's leave from his teaching position and worked on a factory assembly line in order to write more perceptively about problems in industrial psychology. This is more than we can ask of college students in speech classes. But we can ask them not to speak knowingly on a new polio vaccine unless they know at firsthand what the local public health service is using now.

The cardinal rule in all of life should be to see for yourself whenever possible. The next best, of course, is to try to get accurate reports from those who have made firsthand investigations. There are those who have observed the problem of teaching English to Japanese, the operation of the Alliance for Progress, the attitudes of farmers toward wheat subsidies. And for information about the thinking of large numbers of people there are public opinion polls.

### Investigating by Reading

After having investigated by "letting down your bucket where you are," you are ready for the library. Because its resources are so vast, it will yield the most when used systematically. There are many specialized books and pamphlets on how to use libraries most efficiently, and your college library may publish one of its own. We have space here only to suggest three basic considerations in library research and a sample of basic references.

*First, read generally.* Detailed refinements are most meaningful when general concepts are understood. A succinct but comprehensive treatment of the Federal Reserve System, for example, is a background for studying its specific discount policies. A general work on modern English history should come before a more narrow concern with the specific role of the Conservative party. The general treatments will help you define and limit your topic and may also suggest further specific readings. Read first, therefore, whatever is appropriate in gaining a general background.

## GENERAL ENCYCLOPEDIAS, ALMANACS, AND YEARBOOKS

*Encyclopedia Americana*
*Encyclopaedia Britannica*
*Political Handbook of the World: Parliaments, Parties and Press* (annual, 1927 to date)
*Statesman's Year-Book: Statistical and Historical Annual of the States of the World* (annual, 1864 to date)
*Statistical Abstract of the United States* (annual, 1878 to date)
*United Nations Yearbook* (annual, 1947 to date)
*World Almanac* (annual, 1868 to date)

## SPECIALIZED ENCYCLOPEDIAS AND DICTIONARIES

*Cambridge History of English Literature*
*Dictionary of American History,* James Truslow Adams, ed.
*Dictionary of Education,* Carter V. Good, ed.
*Encyclopedia of Educational Research,* Walter S. Monroe, ed.
*Encyclopedia of the Social Sciences,* E. R. A. Seligman, ed.
*How to Locate Educational Information and Data,* Carter Alexander and Arvid J. Burke
*Literary History of the United States,* Robert E. Spiller, *et al.,* eds.
*New Dictionary of Psychology,* Philip Lawrence Harriman
*The McGraw-Hill Encyclopedia of Science and Technology*
*The McGraw-Hill Encyclopedia of World Art*
*Van Nostrand's Scientific Encyclopedia*

## BIOGRAPHICAL DICTIONARIES: PERSONS NO LONGER LIVING

*Appleton's Encyclopedia of American Biography*
*Dictionary of American Biography*
*Dictionary of National Biography* (English)
*National Cyclopaedia of American Biography*
*New Century Cyclopedia of Names*
*Webster's Biographical Dictionary*

*Who Was Who* (English)
*Who Was Who in America*

## BIOGRAPHICAL DICTIONARIES: LIVING PERSONS

*American Men of Science*
*Current Biography* (monthly, 1940 to date)
*Directory of American Scholars*
*International Who's Who*
*Who Knows—and What*
*Who's Who* (English)
*Who's Who in America*

*Second, read selectively.* Once you have established a general background of understanding for any subject you are ready to begin reading selectively. This means narrowing your focus to the specific aspect of the subject that concerns you and exploring that aspect in depth. For this purpose you will want to compile a bibliography. On many subjects specialized bibliographies have already been compiled. Here are two guides to these materials:

Theodore Besterman, *A World Bibliography of Bibliographies* (1955-56).
*The Bibliographical Index* (semiannual and annual, 1938 to date).

Your library's card catalogue, of course, includes an arrangement of materials by subjects, and thus is a third source for specialized bibliographies. It is normally limited to books, however.

Even if you locate a specialized bibliography it will doubtless have to be supplemented by looking elsewhere for listings of materials necessary to bring it up to date. If you do not find a specialized bibliography, you will have to make one. Your aim, of course, is not to create a *comprehensive* list of materials related to your subject. That process might take months and become a volume in itself. You want a *selected* bibliography, perhaps three or four times as long as you will be able to handle, since you will want to make allowance for the unavailability of some references. Don't create it simply by listing the first references you come across. Be systematic. A given item might be listed or not depending upon its date, author, source, or accessibility. The reference works listed below include a variety of indexes and guides from which bibliographies may be compiled.

*Art Index* (fine arts periodicals and museum bulletins; quarterly and annual, 1929 to date)
*Biography Index* (periodicals, journals, books; quarterly and annual, 1946 to date)
*Book Review Digest* (monthly and annual, 1905 to date)
*Directory of Newspapers and Periodicals* (annual, 1880 to date)
*Education Index* (American and British educational periodicals, books, pamphlets; monthly and annual, 1929 to date)

*Guide to Reference Books,* Constance Winchell, ed.

*International Index to Periodicals* (social sciences and humanities; quarterly and
     annual, 1907 to date)

*New York Herald Tribune Index, 1875-1906* (annual)

*New York Times Index* (semimonthly and annual, 1913 to date)

*Poole's Index to Periodical Literature* (1802-1906)

*Public Affairs Information Service Bulletin* (economic and social conditions, pub-
     lic administration, and international relations books, documents, periodicals,
     pamphlets; weekly, 1915 to date)

*Readers' Guide to Periodical Literature* (general periodicals; semimonthly and
     annual, 1900 to date)

*United States Government Publications: Monthly Catalog* (1895 to date)

*Vertical File Service Catalog* (current pamphlets, booklets; monthly, 1932 to
     date)

*Third, read critically.* "Read, mark, learn, and inwardly digest," says
the *Book of Common Prayer.* This is good counsel. It does not tell you to
believe everything or to believe nothing, but to mark (evaluate) and digest (fit into what you already know). Critical reading means judging the
author (Is he of good repute? Does he reflect a bias? Is he consistent?
etc.) as well as what he says (Are his arguments logical? Does he support
them with valid evidence? Is this consistent with what you already know?
etc.). Critical reading also means selecting carefully the material—facts,
examples, testimony, and so on—that may be important in preparing your
speech, *and recording it in some systematic and permanent fashion.*

Surely you have learned elsewhere how to record research material.
You know that completeness and accuracy are essential, that quotation
marks should be used liberally, that each item should be noted on a separate page, and so on. Just for a reminder, recall that in documenting material taken from books you will need the author's full name, title of the
book, name of the publisher, place and date of publication, and the exact
pages from which you have taken the material. For magazines you need
the author's full name, title of the article, title of the magazine, volume
number, month and year of issue, and the exact pages.

We have been referring to your investigations so far as though they
are undertaken always for a particular speech. Of necessity this will often
be true. But there are really two kinds of research: material that you must
have today, and material that you might find useful some day. In your
general reading—textbooks, non-texts, magazines, and newspapers—try to
collect the "some day" material. Record it as carefully as you do any research note, and preserve it. You will be creating your own "savings bank"
of ideas, ready to be drawn upon when you need.

We know one minister who says that the material of this sort that he
collects he simply throws into a drawer, and then when he is preparing a
sermon he digs through the drawer until he finds what he needs. He admits that it isn't very efficient, but says that it's fun. You may find some

better way of filing your research materials. One helpful suggestion is to write across the top of the page bearing the note a general classification title, such as "preparing a speech," "tax rates in England," or "fraternity values." Then use a file card box, a set of folders, or even pigeonholes in your desk, to assemble and save the material according to subject matter.

In this chapter we have been concerned with the responsibilities of speakers to their audiences, and how significant are both their attitudes and their resources. Let Elliott H. Newcomb, American Education Publications executive, have the last word on the speaker's responsibility: "He should ask himself if he really has something to say to the particular audience before he agrees to speak—and be sure the answer is affirmative—preferably emotionally affirmative as well as intellectually so—otherwise he shouldn't speak."[6]

## SUPPLEMENTARY READINGS

Aristotle, *Rhetoric*, trans. by Lane Cooper. New York: Appleton-Century-Crofts, 1932. Treatment of speaker's resources of emotional appeal and lines of argument, pp. 90-181.

Berquist, Goodwin F., Jr., ed., *Speeches for Illustration and Example*. Chicago: Scott, Foresman, 1966. See especially Karl R. Wallace, "An Ethical Basis of Communication," pp. 181-192, and Andrew T. Weaver, "Toward Understanding Through Speech," pp. 2-11.

Bosmajian, Haig A., ed., *Readings in Speech*. New York: Harper & Row, 1965. A classic treatment "On the Liberty of Thought and Discussion," from John Stuart Mill, *Essay on Liberty*, pp. 287-326.

Braden, Waldo W., and Gehring, Mary Louise, *Speech Practices: A Resource Book for the Student of Public Speaking*. New York: Harper & Row, 1958. Emphasizes resources for invention in "How Speakers Prepare Their Speeches," pp. 14-26.

Eisenson, Jon, Auer, J. Jeffery, and Irwin, John V., *The Psychology of Communication*. New York: Appleton-Century-Crofts, 1963. A research summary and prescriptive treatment of "Psychology of Stage Fright," pp. 320-327.

## EXERCISES

1. Listen to a speech and write a brief report on the speaker's directness, earnestness, rhythm of talk, and vitality. Before hearing this speaker, make a brief outline of the suggestions made on those points in this chapter.

[6]In a letter to Richard L. Weaver, II, March 22, 1966, and quoted with Mr. Newcomb's permission.

2. Listen to a public speech and observe as closely as you can all evidence of the speaker's attitudes toward what he is doing. Then select one of the five attitudes discussed in this chapter (a sense of responsibility, humanity, leadership, communication, and security), phrase a simple assertion about how this speaker reflected that attitude, and illustrate your assertion in as many ways as you can in a 2-minute, "one-point" speech.

3. Select a general topic that interests you and that might serve as a speech subject several weeks from now. "Take stock of what you know," and list those facets that require investigation, indicating whether it is likely to be by talking and listening, observing, or reading. Then decide whether you think the subject is a manageable one in the time you have.

4. Prepare to discuss the appropriate attitudes for public speakers as compared or contrasted with those for door-to-door salesmen, preachers, television commercial announcers, teachers, advertising writers, lawyers, and others who are concerned with practical persuasion.

5. Interview someone you know who does a good deal of speaking (a teacher, preacher, or lawyer), about his experiences with stage fright. If he has ever experienced it, find out what he did to overcome it. Then compare his therapies with those suggested in this chapter.

6. Test your own sense of communication, and discover for yourself the problem of reading a speech, by practicing the following selection from a well-known speech by Wendell L. Willkie, "Freedom and the Liberal Arts." As you read, try to think only of communicating the thought and mood to your listeners.

There has been a trend recently toward what is called "leadership"—but what is really nothing more than the idolization of individual men. In Italy, Mussolini took the title of Il Duce—the Leader—on grounds that he was the one man who could fulfill the destiny of the Italian people. Not long after, in Germany, Hitler began calling himself Der Führer. . . .

I do not know all the reasons for this emphasis on single individuals. But I do perceive a connection, here in America at any rate, between that emphasis and the neglect of the liberal arts. Had we more faith in liberal education, we would have, I believe, more faith in ourselves—more faith in the great leavening process of democracy, which forever pushes new men to the top.

I have had the privilege of meeting most of the great men of our time and of conversing with them intimately. . . . Yet I can say truthfully that, however impressive their abilities—and I have found them impressive—I saw nothing in them that could not conceivably be duplicated in Akron, Ohio, where I practiced law for many years, or here at Duke University. I think it was William Howard Taft who said you could find a man fit to sit on the Supreme Court bench of the United States, in any town in America of more than 5,000 population. Possibly Mr. Taft exaggerated. Yet surely the *principle* has been proved time after time in American history. The vast American educational system has set men free—free not alone to serve, but free to lead. Education is the mother of leadership.

# 3

# The First Steps in Managing Ideas

The first step in managing ideas is to get ideas to manage. But getting ideas is not easy. Great speakers are about one part talk and nine parts judgment, and they use the nine parts of judgment to tell them when and how to use the one part talk. As John F. Kennedy said after his first two years in the Presidency, "the problems are more difficult than I had imagined them to be. . . . It is much easier to make speeches than it is finally to make the judgments."[1]

Speeches grow and mature. They need *time to ripen* and they require *constant cultivation*. Some people find this incredible. "Good speakers," they argue, "can talk off the cuff." That notion, of course, is sheer fantasy. Abraham Lincoln's "House Divided" speech was one of the greatest ever given to an American political party convention. But read what Billy Herndon, Lincoln's law partner, reported about its *ripening process:*

Mr. Lincoln was a good while preparing his "house divided against itself" speech; he was at it off and on about a month. If a good idea struck him, if a forcible one, he penciled it down on a small slip of paper and put it in his hat, where he carried quite all his plunder, checkbook for the bank account, letters answered and unanswered, handkerchief, etc. After Mr. Lincoln finished his speech by putting piece to piece and note to note he came into our office one morning and said: "Billy, I want now to read my speech, and after I am done, I want your opinion of it in all directions." . . . He subsequently consulted some friends about it; some had one view of it and some another; some wanted this sentence struck out and some that, etc.[2]

There is no short cut in the *cultivating process*, either. At the age of twenty-three Sir Winston Churchill understood what was required: in *Savrola,* his novel about a man of action who made many speeches, he wrote: "This man knew that nothing good can be obtained without effort.

[1]*Time* (December 28, 1962), p. 15.
[2]Emanuel Hertz, ed., *The Hidden Lincoln, From the Letters and Papers of William H. Herndon* (New York, 1938), p. 97.

These impromptu feats of oratory existed only in the minds of the listeners; the flowers of rhetoric were hothouse plants." But only three years later the man who was to become one of the most effective speakers in history failed in his maiden speech to Parliament because he had spent too little time in the hothouse. "The truth is," Churchill later confessed, "that [I am not a good speaker and] I learned to speak, somehow or other, with exceptional difficulty and enormous practice." Even at seventy Churchill made thorough and painstaking preparation, dictating sometimes to two secretaries in relays, before he was satisfied with his elaborate speech notes. Then he rehearsed them before a mirror in order to study his gestures, and finally recorded and edited them for "clarity, voice inflection, tone quality, and general structure." This is the man, quipped Lord Birkenhead, who "devoted the best years of his life to the preparation of his impromptu speeches."

Those who naïvely accept the "off the cuff" theory should talk to the office-mates, friends, and secretaries of eminent public speakers!

The nub of this matter is that every speaker must continually earn his right to speak. "I shall never be old enough," said Abraham Lincoln, "to speak without embarrassment when I have nothing to talk about." In any college speech course a student is wasting his time until he learns this elemental truth: *a speaker must earn the right to give a speech.*

The first steps in managing ideas, then, are really the first steps in earning the right to speak. To acquire professional skill in this process requires that fundamental principles of speech communication be both understood and practiced. You can hardly wait to make your first speech until you know *all* of the principles of discourse, yet it would be artless to practice with none. So we shall devote this chapter to a series of seven elementary steps for managing your first and relatively simple speeches:
1. Choose a subject that interests you, and that can interest your audience.
2. Select only one specific part of the whole subject for your central idea.
3. Phrase the central idea into a purpose-sentence that sets your goal.
4. List two or three main points that will cover your central idea.
5. Use specific and interesting material to support each of these main points.
6. Organize the entire speech into a fairly complete outline.
7. Practice delivering the speech until you have it well in mind.

## CHOOSE A SUBJECT THAT INTERESTS YOU, AND THAT CAN INTEREST YOUR AUDIENCE

Most students, ready to get underway, ask "Where can I look for an interesting subject?" Look for a subject? First, look at your audience! It is made up of college students, mostly about your own age, and probably with similar backgrounds and aspirations. They are no longer high school students, so you cannot work off on them that speech you prepared when you were in high school. They are not yet teachers, businessmen, housewives, or professional people, and you cannot talk to them as such. But they do have a wide range of interests. Some can properly be called scholars, immersed in books and ideas. Some are interested in the sciences, and spend much of their time in laboratories. Some are interested in the humanities; for them literature and languages are life's storehouse. Some are most intrigued by business and economics. Each hopes to become an engineer, musician, lawyer, physician, or what-have-you.

Does it seem impossible to find a subject that will fit an audience with such a variety of interests? Actually such people can become interested in a variety of subjects. While many of them are already specializing in their course programs, it may be reassuring to reflect that your contemporaries are more concerned about knowledge outside of their major fields than past student generations. Thus it becomes easier to interest them in what already interests you. Try these two guide lines:

1. Choose a subject you already know something about, and about which you can find out more.
2. Choose a subject the audience may already know a little about, but wants to know more.

Are you a science major? Then explain to the class how Telstar works, or the latest developments in antibiotics. Or how the geologist "reads" history in the rocks. Or about oceanography, ornithology, or ecology. Or what Newton did. Or Darwin. Or Fermi.

Are you studying contemporary literature? Identify the newest novelists, and what they are trying to do. Explain the avant-garde theatre. Describe what is happening to the magazine publishing business. Or what Faulkner, Brecht, Pearl Buck, or Arthur Miller mean to you.

Are you an athlete? Or majoring in physical education? Try to explain to those who are spectators how a football huddle looks from the inside, how they can better understand the strategy of the game. Or report on the physical fitness of modern man, and what difference it makes.

Are you majoring in government, business, or economics? Can you report to the class on recent developments in automation, international assistance programs, current fiscal policies, unemployment, specialized agencies of the United Nations, or Far Eastern foreign policy?

"Interest speaks all sorts of tongues" among educated and intelligent people. Let this be your assurance and your opportunity.

## SELECT ONLY ONE SPECIFIC PART OF THE WHOLE SUBJECT FOR YOUR CENTRAL IDEA

The novice speaker usually hopes to wrap up the earth and all the planets in a five-minute speech. But five minutes (about 750 words) can't be stretched that far. The subject must be narrowed down to manageable proportions.

Is art your subject? Here is the interplanetary approach:

You and art
Greek and Roman sculptors
Italian painters
Dutch, Flemish, and French painters
English and American painters
Oriental arts
Modern art: Realists, Impressionists, etc.

Even the first of the seven divisions is easily worth an hour's speech, but perhaps you can chip off a fragment and treat it meaningfully for a classroom speaking assignment.

How lines and colors affect your appearance, for example, is narrow enough for a short talk. A speech on Communism, even Communism in America, is too ambitious. But "Recent Supreme Court Decisions and the American Communist Party" is an improvement, and "The Legal Status of the Communist Party" is better yet. Think of a good speech as being like a good photograph: in focus, single subject, and close-up.

Students frequently ask about speech titles. One suggestion is to remember that a topic is not a title. "New Class Attendance Rules" may make a subject for a speech, but as a title it has no more appeal than last year's license plate. The student who changed it to "How to Hold a Class Without a Rope" may have tried *too* hard, but he did get attention. A second suggestion is that any title should be attention-getting and curiosity-arousing. "Have You a Muddle in Your Middle?" (about ulcers) and "How to Get the Bird" (early morning bird walks) may qualify on both counts. A third suggestion is that titles should suggest the subject, and memorably, such as "The Hemingwayward Days" (about expatriate writers) and "He Who Laughs, Lasts" (a sense of humor and longevity).

## PHRASE THE CENTRAL IDEA INTO A
## PURPOSE-SENTENCE THAT SETS YOUR GOAL

Be certain that you understand what this principle means, for if you do not follow it you can get into trouble later on. A public speech, unlike a private conversation, needs a definite purpose. A conversation may be aimless, but a good speech moves straight toward its goal. The speaker has a target. He wants the audience to *know* something, to *understand* something, to *believe* something, to *do* something. Therefore, to keep in mind where your speech is going, and to guide you as you prepare it, put down your purpose-sentence in writing.

You are going to talk about the Peace Corps, let us assume, and you have selected this central idea: The Peace Corps as a world service enterprise. With such a central idea you might have a dozen specific purposes. Three of them are indicated by these purpose-sentences:

The function of the Peace Corps is to give mass technical and professional assistance to the people of underdeveloped countries, and on a person-to-person basis (i.e., *information*), or

The Peace Corps will be a lasting monument to John F. Kennedy (i.e., *belief*), or

The internationally-minded college graduate should welcome the opportunity to serve an internship in peace by joining the Peace Corps (i.e., *action*).

Any one of these three is a good speech purpose, but do not try to wander across all of them in a single speech. Choose *one*. Write it out in a clear-cut purpose-sentence, use it as a guide while you plan the speech, and aim at it as a goal.

A final suggestion: *For your first speeches, better avoid subjects involving argument and controversy*. At its best, argument is an explosive and you have to know how to handle it. There will be plenty of time later for controversial speeches, but start with the fundamentals. *The most fundamental thing in speaking is to be able to explain something clearly and interestingly*.

## LIST TWO OR THREE MAIN POINTS THAT
## WILL COVER YOUR CENTRAL IDEA

These main points cover the whole central idea. In Chapter 6 we shall take up some of the patterns for arranging main points, but for the present rely on your common sense and what you already know about composition. Make these main points simple and obvious. Most important, don't have too many, for listeners cannot remember them. Five main points are probably always too many. Other things being equal, three are better than four, and two are better than three. And no matter what, each one should be phrased simply and significantly for the listener.

To illustrate, let us suppose that you put together a first draft like this:

PURPOSE-SENTENCE: Your looks can be improved by skillfully using art.
*Main Points:*    I. Looking your best helps you socially and professionally.
       II. Artistic lines will help stout people.
      III. Thin people can also be filled out figuratively.
      IV. One set of colors is best for blondes with blue eyes.
       V. Other techniques will enhance dark hair and eyes.

Now look at it critically. There are too many main points; they spread the central idea too thin. The main points are clumsily phrased; they are abstract and roundabout. Try again.

PURPOSE-SENTENCE: You can improve your looks by skillful use of lines and colors.
*Main Points:*    I. If you are fat or thin, skillful use of *lines* can improve your looks.
       II. If you are blonde or brunette, skillful use of *colors* can improve your looks.

Now look at the revision. There are two main points instead of five. The two are simply phrased in parallel fashion, one dealing with *lines,* the other with *colors.* Both changes make the main points easier for listeners to remember.

## USE SPECIFIC AND INTERESTING MATERIAL TO
## SUPPORT EACH OF THESE MAIN POINTS

In the technical language of speechmaking, a statement of an idea or principle, such as each main point, is called an *assertion*. Of itself an assertion does not explain, elaborate, or prove. It just asserts the idea or principle, but actually leaves it hanging unsupported in midair. To assert that "Arthur Miller is America's leading playwright," or that "to raise the federal debt ceiling will stimulate the economy," neither increases the listener's knowledge nor changes his belief. Like an empty sack, an assertion cannot stand by itself.

In speechmaking, then, assertions serve to state the speaker's main ideas, but *they are worth little until they are elaborated or supported.* In truth, unsupported assertions are seldom even remembered by listeners, for they hear a speaker's words only once; unlike readers they cannot go back and read again, contemplate, and judge. Without elaboration or support an assertion is like a drifting cloud; it catches our attention briefly and floats out of our consciousness. What we *remember* are those things kept vividly before us, in our focus of attention. When assertions are supported by a succession of facts, examples, comparisons, and other vivid supporting material, they are hammered into our thought patterns. In point of fact we may not, a day or a week later, remember the supporting materials. But we do remember that the assertion, *at that time,* was well supported, and is thus still believable.

We move, then, to consider how a speaker can support his assertions with effective supporting materials. In Chapter 7 we will consider a variety of types. At this point and for first speeches we shall introduce only five:

1. Facts and Figures
2. Specific Instances
3. Illustrations
4. Comparisons
5. Testimony

How these supporting materials are used can be shown in this cross section of a speech outline:

I. Assertion
   A. Supporting material
   B. Supporting material

Of course a speech may be more elaborate and have two or more levels of assertions, as our next cross section will illustrate. But no matter how many levels of assertions there are, a good speech is built ultimately upon the bedrock of solid supporting materials.

I. Assertion (first level)
   A. *Assertion (second level)*
      1. Supporting material
      2. Supporting material
   B. *Assertion (second level)*
      1. Supporting material
      2. Supporting material

The above sample cross sections have shown how supporting materials appear in a speech outline. Now let us be sure that we understand the nature of the five types of supporting materials that may be most useful in managing ideas in relatively simple speeches.

1. *Facts and Figures.* Although plain facts and figures are the most elementary type of supporting material, they are notably inadequate in student speeches. Students often fail to get the pertinent facts and frequently do not use effectively what facts they do have. They tend to rely too heavily upon unsupported assertions and, worse yet, to wonder why listeners are not impressed. Make this, therefore, your basic rule: Where facts and figures are to be had, get them, verify them, and use them. Beware of alleged facts. Remember that no amount of repetition of an assertion can transform it into a fact. And even though you "saw it in print," it may be all wrong, or partly right, partly wrong, and altogether misleading. Or the truth, but not the whole truth. Educated people read suspiciously, check sources, and avoid deception.

Here is an example of the use of verified facts and figures in supporting an assertion:

| | |
|---|---|
| Main Point<br>(ASSERTION): | I. The three best-selling American novels have no common element that explains their popularity. |
| *Facts and Figures* | A. *Uncle Tom's Cabin* was a tale of slavery, written in the heat of pre-Civil War passions; it sold 3,000,000 copies. |
| *Facts and Figures* | B. *Ben Hur* was a story of the Christ, written in the Gilded Age of high living and high finance in the late 19th century; it sold 2,500,000 copies. |
| *Facts and Figures* | C. *Gone With the Wind* was a story about personal courage in the face of disaster, written in the depressed 1930's; it sold over 4,000,000 copies. |

2. *Specific Instances.* A specific instance is a briefly stated and condensed example. It gives support to an assertion by saying, in effect, "here is a case of what I mean." Because they are brief, several must usually be cited for fullest impact. If a speaker says "Early labor-management relations were marked by strife [*assertion*], such as the Haymarket Riot [*specific instance*]," we may think it a thin support for a broad generalization. Because specific instances are condensed, they must carry instant meaning to the listener. Even if we added several more specific instances in support of our generalization about labor-management strife—"the Homestead Strike and the Pullman Strike"—we would provide instant meaningfulness only for those few listeners who had studied labor history. Therefore this basic rule: When specific instances will give support, use several, and be sure they will be instantly understood by your listeners.

The following development of succinctly stated specific instances provides support for the assertion:

| | |
|---|---|
| Main Point<br>(ASSERTION): | I. Great achievements have been made by men and women under 30 years of age. By that age:<br>  A. Mozart had published over 200 of his musical compositions.<br>  B. Lord Byron had written *Childe Harold* and published 14 volumes of poems.<br>  C. William Pitt, the Younger, had been Prime Minister of England for 6 years.<br>  D. Alexander Graham Bell had invented the telephone.<br>  E. Henry Ford had produced his first automobile.<br>  F. Elizabeth Barrett Browning had published two volumes of poems.<br>  G. Margaret Mitchell had finished half of *Gone With the Wind*. |

3. *Illustrations.* An illustration is a narrative of events, usually developed chronologically. It tells the full story, but skillfully eliminates the nonessentials. With the economy of an Edgar Allen Poe short story, a good illustration has events so closely interwoven that the removal of a single one will break the entire chain. One advantage of the illustration is that its narrative form tends to hold listener attention. Another is that it symbolically represents additional cases. A single carefully chosen illustration may be strong enough to support an assertion: There is joy over "one sinner that repenteth," illustrated by the Parable of the Prodigal Son; "Who is my neighbor?" illustrated by that of the Good Samaritan.

Sometimes two, or even more, illustrations are used, as in the following:

| | |
|---|---|
| Main Point (ASSERTION): | I. It is nothing new in history to believe that the world has really attained security, or is just about to. |
| *Illustration* | A. I remember way back in that wonderful normal year of 1913. Our distinguished senator returned from Washington after serving his first term and when a group of us went to visit with him, he handed out copies of a new law, just passed by Congress that month. It was a famous law, and one you all know about even now—the Federal Reserve Bank Act. I started off the questions with an omnibus one: "Senator Sterling, what is this law for?" "Young man," he said soberly, "this is a bill to prevent depressions." I'd been born during the depression days of the 1890's and remembered the one in 1907 when I was a kid. So I asked "Will it really prevent depressions?" "I think it will," he said, and explained why. What progress we'd made! *After centuries, we were finally safe from depressions!* |
| *Illustration* | B. A few months later, in May, 1914, one of my fellow students asked our economics professor how a modern democratic government could raise the money to carry on a modern war. Here was the professor's considered answer: "You don't need to worry about a long modern war. Wars are so expensive today that they would bankrupt a little nation in six weeks or the strongest one in three months. It's just impossible to have wars today as we had in Napoleon's time." Again I was pleased with our progress. *After centuries, we were finally safe from war, as well as safe from depressions.* That was May, 1914! |

4. *Comparisons.* Likenesses and differences between things or ideas are shown vividly by comparisons. There are two circumstances when they are especially valuable as supporting materials. First, *to connect something meaningless with something meaningful.* If you say "The United States last year stood in 11th place among major nations in infant mortality rates," it conveys little sense of the seriousness of the problem. But this does: "More Americans perished just before and after birth in the single decade from 1950 to 1960 than the total number of soldiers the United States has lost in all the wars it has ever fought, from Bunker Hill to the Yalu River." And so does this: "In short, a soldier in wartime has a better chance for survival than a baby during birth."

Second, *to explain something new, about which people are suspicious, in terms of something old, which they accept.* History is an unbroken record of popular suspicion of new things and ideas: Christianity, the printing press, democracy, free public education, the automobile. Therefore, when you explain or advocate something really new, you can often do it best by showing that it is like something else, which people already know about and believe in. For example: "The undistributed profits tax is merely an extension of the individual income tax." Or, "To form a federal union of the Western nations would be following the example of the thirteen separate colonies who joined together to form the United States."

Here is a series of comparisons used as supporting material for an assertion:

| Main Point (ASSERTION): | I. New York City today is still a melting pot. |
|---|---|
| *Comparison* | A. It has more Jews (2,250,000) than Israel. |
| *Comparison* | B. It has more Negroes (1,150,000) than the whole state of Georgia. |
| *Comparison* | C. It has nearly half as many Italians (1,905,000) as Rome. |
| *Comparison* | D. It has more Irish (500,000) than Dublin. |
| *Comparison* | E. It has nearly half as many Poles (412,000) as Warsaw. |

5. *Testimony.* The authority of others is revealed through testimony. In effect the speaker is saying: "Look here, I am not alone in believing the way I do. There are two of us (or three, or more), and the others are famous people (or experts, or in a special position to know)." While the advertiser has often abused testimonial evidence (and the consumer at the same time), it is true that many of us accept authority in our churches and social groups, that all of us respect the authority of courts and judges, and that on many matters of judgment and complex ideas, we listen to qualified experts. Even in reading a book we tacitly accept its author as an authority.

The following examples show the use of testimony by competent authorities in supporting an assertion:

| | |
|---|---|
| Main Point<br>(ASSERTION): | I. For hundreds of years intelligent and respected people have been saying that education has been getting steadily worse. |
| *Testimony* | A. Former President A. Whitney Griswold of Yale is typical. He wrote of the "serious setback to education," of its "lost character," and its "dilution," and said that unless we return to older and better patterns of education we shall be neglectful "at our peril." |
| *Testimony* | B. In 1894, about the time President Griswold thought of as having an excellent curriculum, a Faculty Committee reported to the Harvard Board of Overseers on the sad state of education: Young men entering Harvard were 19 years old, yet they still had "immature thoughts . . . miserably expressed," written in "a crabbed slovenly hand," and spelled "wretchedly." Education had declined since the Good Old Days a half century before. |
| *Testimony* | C. In 1845 the Boston Grammar School Committee made an official report on the decline of education: "Boys and girls of 14 and 15 years of age, when called on to write simple sentences . . . cannot write, without such errors in grammar and spelling, and in punctuation, as we should blush to see in a letter from a son or daughter of their age." To this committee the Good Old Days, before the decline, were half a century or more earlier. |
| *Testimony* | D. In 1773, about the time to which the Bostonians had referred, Dr. Samuel Johnson testified at length that "learning had declined" since those Good Old Days when he had been a student in Oxford University, 1728-1729. |

Seldom does a speaker limit himself to one kind of supporting material. *He uses two, or three, or whatever is needed to give each assertion its best support.* Here is a development of five kinds of supporting material for a single assertion:

| | |
|---|---|
| Main Point<br>(ASSERTION): | I. The European continent is afflicted by national barriers against money and trade. |
| *Facts and Figures* | A. I don't mean the mere inconvenience of different kinds of money, for travelers get used to handling 26-cent guilders, 24-cent marks, 23-cent Swiss francs, 2-cent Belgian francs, and until recently ¼-cent French francs. |
| *Illustration* | B. One day I spent 250 Italian lire for breakfast, 9.10 Austrian shillings for lunch, and 5.05 Swiss francs for dinner; and it took only a minute to figure that in U. S. money breakfast cost 40 cents, lunch 36 cents, and dinner $1.15. That's a nuisance, but not a barrier. |
| *Specific Instances* | C. The money barriers come from countries who try to fix by law the rate of exchange on their currency, and to regulate the amount of money that comes in and goes out of that country. You could take 10 pounds into England, and 5 out; 100 guilders into Holland, and 50 out. France for twelve years fixed its rate at 350 francs to the dollar, when on the black market in France and in the open exchanges of other countries the franc sold over 400 to the dollar. |
| *Specific Instances* | D. The trade barriers came only slightly from high tariffs; more especially they came from private artificial barriers known as cartels. These cartels assigned quotas to their members, and had power to force into bankruptcy any member who violated his quota. |
| *Testimony* | E. The Common Market Treaty of 1957 undertook to erase these barriers and permit goods and workers to move as |

freely in western Europe as between New York and California. As Konrad Adenauer said: "We must part with concepts of the past."

*Comparison*  F. Of course the ideal has not yet been reached, but significant progress has been made. Skeptics should bear in mind that even with the advantages of a common language and heritage the American colonies advanced piecemeal through the Articles of Confederation to the Constitution.

## ORGANIZE THE ENTIRE SPEECH INTO A FAIRLY COMPLETE OUTLINE

Inexperienced speakers often are afraid of making their outlines too obvious. Let them be reassured that it is better to have an outline that is too evident than to have a speech that lacks plan and sense of direction. *A clear outline is the hallmark of disciplined thought.* A speech, like an essay, play, or novel, must structure a central idea and move it in the direction set by a purpose-sentence. Structure and movement can best be created, and checked, in a fairly complete outline. Anyone can learn to make an outline. Here are the basic steps:

1. Set down the purpose-sentence so you can keep in mind where you are going. (We have already discussed this; see p. 44.)
2. Make a list of the two or three main points of the central idea. (We have discussed this, too; see p. 45.)
3. Arrange these main points in the most effective order for your audience. There are special patterns best suited to particular circumstances, but for the time being rely upon your common sense.
4. Develop each of these main points with specific and interesting supporting material. (We discussed this earlier; see pp. 46-53.)
5. Plan an introduction that will (a) explain the subject, if necessary, and (b) capture the attention of your audience. Introductions usually are about 10 percent of the whole speech, though this proportion obviously varies.
6. Plan a conclusion that will in some way round out the speech. It may be a summary to help listeners remember main points, or it may be a vivid illustration, apt quotation, or something else that leaves listeners with a lasting impression. Conclusions usually are about 5 percent of the whole speech, but this also obviously varies.

To see what a good and fairly complete outline looks like, turn to pp. 102-107. We consider a fairly complete outline one that has from 30 to 60 percent of the number of words in the full speech. This is not a rule, and each speaker will develop his own best procedure. But we believe that as a rule the most *responsible* speakers—not the demagogues or loose talkers—make longer and more detailed preparation on paper. Mere glibness is not a goal for responsible speakers, but without thoroughness and accuracy it may become the only apparent end.

## PRACTICE DELIVERING THE SPEECH UNTIL YOU HAVE IT WELL IN MIND

The first six steps in managing ideas have not yet provided you with a speech. They have focused on developing ideas in your mind and then getting them down on paper. There they lie, spread out flat before you. Now comes the task of creating from them a real speech. On the second page of this book we said that a speech is "created on the instant and in the presence of the listeners." How is this done? How can you create a speech out of your thought-on-paper while standing before an audience? How can you be sure, when you rise to speak, of not forgetting these ideas, missplacing them or just rambling? How can you avoid blank pauses, or nonsensical talk? How can you keep within your allotted time? These are not idle questions. If the right words don't come when you try to speak in public, the failure is real and personal.

Some would-be speakers deserve to fail. This is not an uncharitable view, just an honest one. To create an extemporaneous speech for an audience, using the ideas placed on paper in the isolation of your study, requires a definite technique. Those who ignore it, or who look for shortcuts, run the risk of deserved failure.

Before we describe the necessary technique let us resolve any possible misunderstandings about our objective. Are we agreed that extemporaneous speaking is *not* impromptu speaking? Some people think otherwise; they think that extemporaneous speaking is speaking without preparation. No idea could be more erroneous. Unprepared speeches are *impromptu,* and we are not interested in them here simply because truly impromptu speeches are usually not good speeches. Other people think that extemporaneous speeches are those "given with hasty or meager preparation." This idea is also completely wrong. Such speeches are merely poorly prepared ones, nothing more. In point of fact, what often seems to be said on the inspiration of the moment is, by the best speakers, the most carefully prepared. Of his first parliamentary speech Winston Churchill said "I need not recount the pains I had taken to prepare, nor the efforts I had made to hide the work of preparation." Even answering questions in the setting of a "debate," where John F. Kennedy and Richard M. Nixon appeared to be "marvels at extemporization, wasting none of the precious media time in reflective pauses, never having to grasp for the elusive word," campaign reporters were not fooled. "To anyone who spent much time on tour with the two men," wrote Douglas Cater, "this was no great surprise. The dialogue was largely a paste-up job containing bits and snippets from campaign rhetoric already used many times."[3]

Let us understand, then, that *a true extemporaneous speech is one in which the ideas are firmly fixed in the speaker's mind, but the exact words are not memorized.* A speech haphazardly planned is not extemporaneous, but just haphazard.

Now, assuming that you have developed a good outline, how do you turn it into a good extemporaneous speech? Let's switch for a moment to the theater, and assume that you have been in a play or at least seen one. Actors begin to create a play from a script, complete with every word set down. But the script is not the play, for the play is a *living* thing. Similarly, an outline is not a speech. How do actors turn a script into a play? 1. They study their lines for meaning and mood. 2. They learn their lines. 3. They perfect their memory and develop action through rehearsals.

In creating an extemporaneous speech from an outline you don't follow the actor's steps, but you do use the same *process.* Obviously you need not study the outline to find its meaning, since you made it and its meaning is already yours. Neither do you "learn the lines," as in a play, by memorizing a speech word-for-word. Individual methods vary, and what suits you best will emerge as you acquire experience. Most speakers, however, follow the procedure we now describe.

First, *fix the sequence of ideas in your mind.* A photographer uses the term "fix" to describe the chemical process of making a permanent image on a film. In similar fashion, a speaker must fix in his mind a permanent image of the sequential ideas in his speech outline. Begin with the two or three main points, then fix the arrangement of supporting material for each one. Notice that we do *not* say that you memorize the outline, as you might a role in a play, or a poem. Instead, you fix the sequence, so that you can *see* the total arrangement, including each fact and figure, specific instance, and so on, and *why* it appears in your picture at a particular place. In doing this, psychologists advise us, these are the most effective steps:

1. First, read the outline *silently* from beginning to end. Read it slowly, feeling your way along, but do not backtrack even once, for backtracking breaks the process of fixing the total sequence.
2. Next, read the outline *aloud,* thinking about its meaning, but again without any backtracking.
3. Now put the outline aside and rehearse the speech *aloud,* still without

[3]"Notes from Backstage," in Sidney Kraus, ed., *The Great Debates* (Bloomington, Ind., 1963), p. 129.

backtracking. If you forget parts of the speech, go right on. Don't check the outline, and don't backtrack. You are trying to fix the total thought pattern in your mind, so don't get entangled in details.

4. Study your outline again and note any places where you may have skipped parts of the speech, or mixed up the sequence. Patch up these places mentally, and then read the outline through again *aloud*, slowly and thoughtfully, but still without backtracking.

5. Put the outline aside once again and rehearse the speech *aloud* from start to finish, without backtracking.

Now, *rehearse the speech formally from five to ten times, aloud, on your feet, and in a large room.* The rehearsals we described above were intended merely to fix the *outline* in your mind. Now you are ready for rehearsing to create a speech. From centuries of experience man has accumulated knowledge about how to create a speech from thought-in-your-mind. Here it is:

1. *Rehearse on your feet and aloud.* More than your brain is involved in remembering. You remember with your nerves and muscles also. Sometimes this is called "muscle memory," a process essential to the speaker. You will give the speech before an audience while standing up, and aloud. Therefore, rehearse while standing up, and aloud. This will make you remember not only the ideas but the muscular set for the public speech. It will also permit you to attend to your posture and action.

2. *Rehearse in a room roughly the size of the classroom.* This may not be possible, or necessary, for all of your rehearsals, but certainly for a few of them you need to stand up in a full-size room and get the feel of your voice as it comes back to you from the four walls. If you do all of your practicing in a small dormitory room the sound of your voice in the classroom may overwhelm you. It is probably best to rehearse at least once in a speech classroom, if you can, and a mutual criticism session with a classmate can be extremely helpful. Except when having a practice session with a classmate you should of course rehearse where you will be free from interruptions.

3. *Rehearse the speech formally from five to ten times.* There is no magic number of rehearsals, but few students will need less than five. Some will need more than ten. Of one thing we are certain: most students need more rehearsals than they think. During the first ones you are still fixing the speech in your mind. In the next few you can also attend to your posture, your action, and especially to your *poise*, that hallmark of mature platform behavior. In the final rehearsals you can concentrate upon projecting the fine shades of thought—the humor, suggestion, and other elements of what we call *feeling, mood,* and *attitude*—so that when you give the speech they will be apparent to every listener in the room.

Does the preparation of even a simple speech seem like a complex task? It is. But it will become easier with much practice and by following systematic procedures such as the seven steps we have outlined here. Such practice, all through his life, enabled Adlai Stevenson, in the 1952 presidential campaign, to make as many as *twelve or fourteen speeches a day* on a whistle-stop tour through Pennsylvania and New Jersey. "While they were brief," testified Wilson Wyatt, his campaign manager, each one was "on a new subject, with different expressions and different in content." He did this, Stevenson said, "out of his deep conviction that if an audience came to hear him, they were entitled to the very best he had to offer."[4]

## SUPPLEMENTARY READINGS

Aristotle, *Rhetoric*, trans. by Lane Cooper. New York: Appleton-Century-Crofts, 1932. Treatment of ethical and emotional proof, pp. 90-181.

Eisenson, Jon, Auer, J. Jeffery, and Irwin, John V., *The Psychology of Communication*. New York: Appleton-Century-Crofts, 1963. A comprehensive review of "Basic Psychological Factors," pp. 227-252, in all forms of speech communication.

McGlon, Charles A., "How I Prepare My Sermons: A Symposium." *Quarterly Journal of Speech*, 40 (February, 1954), pp. 49-62. Self-descriptions by Harry Emerson Fosdick, Joseph M. Dawson, Ralph Sockman, Vincent J. Flynn, Joseph Rauch, and Edgar DeWitt Jones.

Petrie, Charles R., Jr., "Informative Speaking: A Summary and Bibliography of Related Research." *Speech Monographs*, 30 (June, 1963), pp. 79-91. A useful review of research in terms of message, speaker, listener, and environment.

White, Eugene E., and Henderlider, Clair R., "What Harry Truman Told Us About His Speaking." *Quarterly Journal of Speech*, 40 (February, 1954), pp. 37-42. A candid question-and-answer account.

## EXERCISES

1. Go to hear a speaker and evaluate his extemporaneous ability:

a. Is his speaking punctuated by breaks in fluency?

b. As you make a key-word outline of the speech, do you find that the speaker has wandered off the line of thought?

c. Does he waste time and words simply because he has not packed his thoughts into concise form?

d. In his enthusiasm or wandering does he tend to exaggerate—for example, saying *many* when he means *a few?*, saying *absolutely* when he means *probably?*, saying *everybody knows* in place of *some people think?*

[4]*Louisville Courier-Journal* (July 15, 1965).

2. Analyze one of your instructors in the manner explained in Exercise 1.

3. Prepare a four-minute speech, following the seven steps set forth in this chapter. In order not to overlook or treat casually any step, use the following procedure: Make a time table of your speech preparation and hand it in with the outline. On it list the seven steps, and show when you started each one and when you completed it. This is a mechanical procedure, and is for beginners only. For them it is excellent, because it shows the source of trouble or failure in first speeches.

4. Study the use of supporting material by preparing a "one-point" speech outline, starting with an assertion as a main topic, and then arranging below it in subhead form a variety of supporting material: facts and figures, specific instances, illustrations, comparisons, testimony. Use the outline on pp. 52-53 as your guide.

5. Read the speech on pp. 128-136 or the one on pp. 153-161; select one main topic, and construct an outline (using the one on pp. 52-53 as a guide) showing how the speaker used a variety of supporting materials.

6. Select a possible topic for a future speech and develop an introduction of not more than one minute that will explain the subject as may be necessary, and that will capture the attention of your audience.

# 4

# Being Seen

You will remember that we saw in Chapter 1 why no one can literally "deliver a speech," that what we commonly call "delivering a speech" is actually a process of *using light waves and sound waves to make listeners think what you are thinking*. In this chapter we shall consider the use of light waves, or what the listeners see.

## WHY SPEAKERS USE ACTION

A significant thing about action is that when you ask the average listener he will say it is not important. Indeed one survey showed that only 27 percent of the people in selected audiences thought "gesture" was essential to good speaking, and only 46 percent thought "coordinated body movement" was essential.[1] So widespread is the misunderstanding of what is meant by "gesture" and "action" that we should pause for a survey of its place in thinking and in communication.

### Action Is an Inherent Part of Thinking

What do we think with? Only the brain? Hardly. The brain is like a telephone exchange, useless without the lines running into it from the outside. It is the switchboard, not the whole system. It receives incoming signals, makes proper connections, and sends messages through to their destination. For efficient service the body must function as a *whole*.

Where is your "mind"? Is it in the brain? Or perhaps in the nervous system? Actually we cannot say that the mind is in any particular *place*. It is not a thing, like a leg, or even the brain. It is an activity, a function. Aristotle, twenty-three centuries ago, observed that *the mind was to the*

[1]W. K. Clark, "A Survey of Certain Attitudes Toward Commonly Taught Standards of Public Speaking," *Speech Monographs*, 18 (March, 1951), pp. 62-69.

*body what cutting was to the ax.* When the ax is not in use, there is no cutting. So with the mind. "Mind," said Charles Henry Woolbert, "is what the body is doing." We don't think merely with the brain, or even with the nervous system. We think with brain, nerves, glands, and muscles, working together as a whole. A physically inert speaker is not thinking at his fullest.

*Total activity is necessary for thinking. Total activity is also necessary for communicating thought from one person to another.* Observe how people go about ordinary conversation. If you have never really paid attention to it, you have a surprise in store. Good conversationalists nod their heads, shake their heads, lift their eyebrows, and let change of feeling play across their faces. They bend, turn, swing, droop, and shrug their shoulders. Their hands are still hardly more than a few seconds at a time.

Now these people are not making speeches, they are simply communicating to one or two other people what is in their minds. They are not conscious of using action. They are merely human beings, talking the way human beings have talked for half a million years.

For half a million years people have talked with head, face, hands, and body. Remember that. Face frankly the fact that you cannot abolish the habits of half a million years.

## Visible Language Is an Older Code of Communication
## Than Spoken Language, and Is More Basic

When Columbus discovered America he found copper-skinned natives who had been separated from peoples of the Old World for some 18,000 years. They spoke approximately 100 different word-languages, none of them related to the languages of Europe, but these newly discovered natives shook their heads for "no," and nodded their heads for "yes," exactly as did Columbus' crew of Mediterranean sailors, and as had the Greeks, Romans, and Egyptians. These newly discovered natives raised their right arms to greet an approaching stranger, as had the knights of Medieval Europe. They turned palms down to express disapproval, palms up to express approval, and lifted their hands in supplication— exactly as other people did everywhere in the world.

Visible language, sign language, is older than spoken language. It is more uniform. It is written deeper into our organism. It carries more basic meanings. We use spoken words for refined thought, but for the deep basic meanings we use action. We are civilized, yes; but *the eye is still quicker than the ear.*

You are about to give a speech. Before you utter a word, you begin to talk to all who see. Do you stand with a timid, uncertain stance, or with poise born of confidence? Do you gaze with a frozen face and a fishy eye, or does change of thought and feeling travel across your face? *Every speaker gives two speeches simultaneously, one with words, and one with action.* If both carry the same message then you are truly communicating. But when words say one thing, and action says another, listeners usually let the words go by and give first attention to the action. Why? Action tells them the real meaning. There they see the false smile, the evasive glance, the sickly grin, the random grimaces of confusion. There is the real speech, and listeners know it. The eye *is* quicker than the ear, and sign language *is* older than spoken language.

### Action Holds Attention

Did you ever lean forward, muscles tense, while watching a game? Did you ever feel your muscles contracting as if to throw a ball, make a catch, shoot a basket, or do whatever the players are doing? Whether you know it or not, you have engaged in such mimicry. It is the spectator's basis of enjoying the game.

This phenomenon is known as *empathy*. It may be defined as *feeling ourselves into* whatever we perceive. All perception, in fact, involves this participation. We not only wind up with the pitcher, swing with the batter, and plunge with the fullback, but also feel ourselves into static situations. When we see a painting or stand before a cathedral, our like or dislike hinges largely on whether the object evokes pleasant or unpleasant tensions in our bodies. We are unconscious of this participation, to be sure, as we are of our breathing or our heartbeat. But it influences our behavior profoundly.

Now apply this to the audience. *Unconsciously they imitate the speaker.* The speaker has no option whatever on whether his action will affect the audience, for it *must* affect them in one of three ways:

1. If he uses too little action, empathy in the audience will be weak. Because it is weak, the audience will not remain physically alert, but will relax more and more into physical—and therefore mental—inaction. But the more one relaxes, the less active becomes the mind, until in complete inactivity one goes to sleep. So the speaker who uses no action puts the audience into a state too near sleep for them to follow alertly what he is saying. They will sit and half listen; but, when he is through, they will recall little of what he has said.

2. If the speaker uses distracting action, action that he never intended using and often does not know he is using, the audience will be forced into fitful and distracting responses. We have all seen the speaker who buttons his coat and then unbuttons it, or twists a handkerchief in his hands, or rocks up and down on his toes, or toys with an object on the table. "If he moves that watch again, I'll scream," whispered a woman

after a speaker had put his watch in twelve or fifteen places over the table. She did not scream vocally, nor did she listen to what he was saying. She sat tense, waiting for him to move that watch! So with all people. They are distracted by empathetic response to a speaker's uncontrolled action.

3. If the speaker uses controlled action, communicative action, listeners find it easy to follow what the speaker is saying. They participate, "feel in," and give the speaker sustained attention.

"Must I use gesture?" asks the timid, or diffident, or nervous student. The frank answer is that you cannot say "No" to life. Action is part of the process of thinking. Action is a universal sign language far older than spoken words. Action arouses attention. Action is inherent in good private conversation. Add it up yourself.

## EXERCISES

1. Prepare and give a two-minute speech on empathy. To prepare this speech, attend an athletic contest, an exciting motion picture, a circus, a television vaudeville performance, or any other event where you will witness alert bodily movements. (a) Observe carefully the stresses and tensions of your own body, and (b) observe the behavior of those around you. Do you "feel in" with the performer? Is this "feeling in" revealed chiefly by leaning forward with tension? Or does it break out into the open so that the spectator tenses or relaxes, moves to right or left, with the performer?

2. Practice in your room and demonstrate in class vigorous and appropriate action on the following:

a. "Halt! Who's there . . . Advance and be recognized!"

b. "I mean it. I propose to stand here. Not to move, but to stand *here*."

c. "Will you listen, please? What else could we have done? What else did we have a *right* to do?"

## MAKING ACTION EFFECTIVE

Effective action hardly seems like action at all. It seems natural, spontaneous, done on the impulse. Indeed, action that calls attention to itself is bad because it distracts instead of communicates. A good speaker never seems to be "gesturing" at all. He is merely a person who makes you understand him, and who happens to use light waves as well as sound waves. Hence the adage, "Great art conceals art." There are five constituent parts of this art.

## Control Your Posture

No single posture is best for everyone, although some postures are bad for everybody. From the listener's standpoint, a good posture should not call attention to itself. From the speaker's standpoint, a good posture should allow ease of bodily movement, ease of breathings, and voice projection to fill the room.

Suppose we start with a good military posture. Understand that a military posture is *not* a good speaking posture. It is too stiff and formal. But we can modify it into a good speaking posture:

1. Heels together on the same line (or, for speaking, heels fairly close together).
2. Feet turned out and forming an angle of about 45 degrees.
3. Knees straight without stiffness.
4. Hips level and drawn back slightly; body erect and resting equally on hips; chest lifted; shoulders square but not lifted.
5. Arms and hands hanging naturally at the sides.
6. Head erect, chin drawn in so that the axis of the head and neck is vertical, eyes to the front and not on the ceiling or floor.
7. Weight of the body sustained partly on the balls of the feet, heels resting on the floor.
8. The entire posture to appear natural and graceful, to be without rigidness or exaggeration, and to be one from which action is possible without first relaxing muscles that have been constrained in an effort to maintain the posture.

From this fairly rigid military posture, you can develop a speaking posture that fits your individual personality and mode of speaking. Probably the one essential of good posture is to *"stand tall."* To stand tall, reach up with the top of your head. Reach up with your spinal column. Reach up with your chest and abdomen. And with your legs reach down to the floor.

You will not learn this posture from merely reading about it. So rehearse it day after day. Practice even how to *sit tall* and *walk tall*. Make it part of your speech behavior.

## Learn How to Use a Speaker's Table

For beginners, and for those self-made speakers out in the world at large, a speaker's table or lectern is a booby trap. Beware of it. Its function is to make the platform look less bare and to serve as resting place for a water pitcher, a vase of flowers, or the speaker's manuscript or notes. But it snares the undisciplined speaker in a myriad of ways. He uses it for a crutch. He uses it for a stanchion on which to rest his weary frame. He uses it as a shelf for paper clips, watch, and other toys to be fingered and fondled.

Probably for a beginning speaker it would be a good thing if he had no table or lectern to tempt him. If it is there, however, *stand tall behind it*. Rest your hands on it if you feel more at ease that way, but don't slump down on it, or hook your elbows on the edge of it.

## Talk to the Audience, Not to Yourself

Until you have disciplined yourself to self-control you are likely to engage in random action: licking your lips, loosening your collar, smoothing your hair, shifting your feet, or letting your posture wilt. You may be startled to find that your hands have grown to enormous size; you cannot conceal their size from the audience, so you try to get them out of the way, behind your back, or in your pockets. These actions are symptoms of inner emotions. Unwittingly, but with deadly effect, you are telling the audiences that you have lost control of yourself. We have discussed this under stage fright, both causes and treatment (pp. 28-32).

There remains a milder form of disorganized action to be discussed here, namely *self-directed gestures. This is the tendency of speakers to gesture to themselves instead of to the audience*. It takes various forms:
1. You clamp the elbows tightly against your body, and gesture toward your face.
2. You guard the stomach with your forearm, often using the hand for a weak gesture but keeping that arm-block between you and the audience.
3. Or you may reach out arms and elbows toward the audience, but keep the palms—the real carrier of meanings—turned toward your face.

Now self-directed action is not really a problem of action at all. The real cause is your mental attitude. First, you are thinking about *yourself*, not the audience. You are not speaking to help the audience, for when you start helping people you are no longer afraid of them. Further, you are not enthusiastic over what you have to say. Once you get enthusiastic, you will literally "forget yourself into good speaking."

Effective action talks to the audience, not to the speaker. But get first things first. *When your action fails to talk to the audience, the trouble is not with "gesturing." It is with your mental attitude. You cannot be afire for people to hear you—all the people, even those in the back row—without reaching out to them with action as well as with voice.*

## Gesture with the Whole Body

The runner does not run with his legs and feet alone, but with his whole body. The baseball pitcher does not pitch with his arm alone, but with his whole body. The speaker does not speak with his voice alone, or with his voice plus his hands. He speaks with his whole body. This is the imperative plus of communicating by physical action.

If you want to be ludicrous, make gestures without this teamwork of muscles. Whether intending to be funny or not, you will be. The actor Charles P. Sale attained his first reputation in character parts by "speaking a piece" with detached gestures. His arms and hands moved like a puppet's pulled by strings. For an added punch he would throw in, now and then, a hand movement that came a shade too soon, or too late. He was never all in one piece, but gave the effect of one who had "studied gesturing" and was following the rule without the spirit.

Now suppose we put into practical operation this principle of all-in-one-piece action. Stand before a mirror and assume a good posture. Then speak the following without gesture but with total body vigor and strength:

Government *of* the *people,* *by* the *people,* and *for* the *people* shall not perish from the earth.

The action involves every part of your body: hand, arm, shoulder, head, torso, leg, knee, ankle, and foot. The action is *built into* the whole body action, and is not "something added on."

Now try it again, emphasizing the words *of, by* and *for* by any type of hand action—putting the whole body behind it all in one piece.

Try it still again, using 1. the right arm, 2. the left arm, 3. both arms.

## Make Your Action Definite

Effective action should point, indicate, suggest, separate, emphasize —carry some particular *definite* meaning.

Definite hand action involves three phases: the *approach,* the *stroke,* and the *return.*

The *approach* is the "get ready" movement. It is like raising a gun to take aim. You make this approach well ahead of time and you hold it until you are ready for the emphatic stroke.

The *stroke* carries the meaning. It is like pulling the trigger. If you are going to emphasize that "The time is *now,*" the approach may have been started even before the first word of the sentence is spoken. Your body is set for action, beforehand, and on the word *now* comes the stroke—backed by the whole body all in one piece.

The *return* is the "as you were." After you have held the idea before the audience long enough for them to see it fully (don't hurry it, and don't backlash your gestures), you simply let the hand fall to the side in its original position. Avoid bringing it back in a wide curve. Just let it fall naturally, without fanfare or tick-tocking.

# KINDS OF ACTION

Perhaps it will help you to consider three specific kinds of action that every speaker uses: platform movement, basic hand action, and action of the head and face.

### Platform Movement

Movement on the platform is not essentially different from movement anywhere else. But a speaker is like a fish in a glass bowl. He is before everybody's eyes, and everything he does is magnified. On the platform avoid two extremes, the extreme of standing stock-still through the whole speech, and the extreme of pacing like a caged animal. Total lack of movement tends to lose audience interest. Too much movement tends to distract attention.

In general, effective platform movement is made forward and backward, instead of from side to side. Side-to-side movement often signifies only nervousness. Forward and backward movement, on the other hand, is part of the half-million-year-old visible code. People step closer to others, or lean toward them, when they are deeply in earnest or want to be especially emphatic. Speakers do the same thing.

Backward movements, though not necessary, are useful at times to indicate divisions of thought. They are like chapter headings or paragraph indentations in print. In effect they say to listeners, "I now come to a new part of the subject."

This homely advice may seem unnecessary. It may seem like saying what everybody knows. But speakers on the platform are under nervous tension. This tension tends to find outlet in aimless wandering, until it becomes a habit. Habit is a powerful force. You had best get it on your side. What you do in practice you will likely do later in performance. Therefore, from the start, practice controlled posture and movement.

### Basic Hand Action

The following six kinds of hand action are a universal sign language, older in the human race than words, and understood by people regardless of whatever word-language they use:

1. *Locating.* You point to an idea or a thing. "A hundred years ago," you say—as you point behind you to indicate that you are speaking of the past. "Tomorrow," you say—as you point forward to indicate the future. "This idea," "that principle," "yonder map," "at the right," "on the left,"

"before us,"—all such things are pointed out for the eye of the listener. In a sense they *see* what you are talking about.

2. *Dividing*. You have a series of ideas or facts, and you want to keep them separate in the listeners' minds. Therefore, you use dividing action. "On the one hand liberals say . . . ," while with the palm held vertically you put the liberals on your left. "On the other hand, conservatives say . . . ," while with the same action you put the conservatives on your right. In the same way "this *versus* that," or "first, second, third," are divided by the hand into separate parts. In print you divide ideas with subtitles and paragraph indentations. In speech, you use dividing action.

3. *Describing*. This type of action suggests the shape, size, or movement of things. "It was this long," you say—and measure the distance with both hands. "It was round,"—and with both hands you round it out. In the same way you indicate movement. "It winds through a valley"—and you trace its winding with a finger.

4. *Approving*. More than any other, this is the gesture of friendly relation, of exchange, of giving and receiving. It is made with an open hand gesture, palm upward, held out as though to give something or to receive something. With this action you carry such ideas as, "This I do believe," or "Here is a duty we cannot escape," or "I present this for your consideration."

5. *Rejecting*. Off the platform, when people are not self-conscious, this is a common action. On the platform, most students find it difficult. This probably is because they are afflicted at least mildly by self-directed, body-guarding gestures. They cannot reject and body-guard, both at the same time; but the nervous tension that causes body-guarding is deep and fundamental, so rejecting action is blocked from their public platform behavior. What is rejecting action? It is simply the normal action any person makes in pushing away something he does not like. A baby makes it spurning food. An adult makes it in pushing away a dog with muddy paws. It is made with the palms down, or away from the speaker. With this action you say, "I don't like it," or "I distrust it," or "That's not the way."

6. *Emphasizing*. When a speaker wishes to lift a word or phrase or sentence above the level of context, he gives it emphasis. Behind the emphasis of voice he may also throw emphasis of action—an index finger, a hand thrust forward or downward, or even the clenched fist. Emphasizing action would be used to carry the following thoughts:

"You ask, 'What is our aim?' I can answer in one word: 'Victory'—victory at all costs, victory in spite of all terror."

"Don't join the book-burners!"

## The Head and Face

*The head and face are the most commonly used and among the most effective instruments of gesture.* By a nod of the head we indicate approval; by a shake, disapproval. Eyelids open in joy, surprise, amazement, or wonder; they contract in anger, envy, or concentration; they sparkle with happiness, or glitter in wrath. Lips may curve into a smile, or curl in contempt; they may be pulled down in a frown, or pursed into a determined straight line. Good conversationalists communicate that way in private speech. Good speakers do it in public speech.

## SUPPLEMENTARY READINGS

Black, John W., and Moore, Wilbur E., *Speech: Code, Meaning, and Communication*. New York: McGraw-Hill, 1955. "The Speaker's Gesture and Bearing," pp. 231-254, is a provocative treatment.

Clark, W. K., "A Survey of Certain Audience Attitudes Toward Commonly Taught Standards of Public Speaking." *Speech Monographs*, 18 (March, 1951), pp. 62-69. A basic research report.

Grimes, Wilma H., and Mattingly, Alethea Smith, *Interpretation: Writer-Reader-Audience*. Belmont, Calif.: Wadsworth, 1961. "The Interpreter's Use of His Body," pp. 245-266, has applications for manuscript readers.

Hall, Edward T., *The Silent Language*. Greenwich, Conn.: Fawcett, 1959. Excellent discussion of how total appearance and behavior "communicates," whether the speaker intends them to or not.

Oliver, Robert T., *The Psychology of Persuasive Speech*, 2nd ed. New York: David McKay, 1957. "Delivering the Persuasive Speech," pp. 366-383, emphasizes psychological factors.

## EXERCISES

1. Study the action of a poor speaker: preacher, politician, teacher, fellow student, or anyone who is invariably dull:

a. Study this speaker's muscular tone. Does his posture suggest muscular or mental alertness? Does it suggest inertness or flabbiness? Does it suggest rigidity or tension? Does he gesture with the whole body all in one piece? If not, which parts were not used? Did his action "talk to the audience," or "talk to himself"? Was it definite?

b. Study the empathy of the audience. Do most of them follow the speaker with an alert eye? Do any appear to be drowsy? Do some avoid looking at the speaker.

c. Write a paper on your assessment of the speaker's action and the audience's response.

2. Do the same thing with a notably good speaker.

3. Practice the following exercises in your room and be ready if necessary to repeat them in class. Follow these directions:

a. Use *spontaneous* action, not planned action. Pay no attention to rules, elegance, or correctness, but act on impulse.

b. Use *abundant* action; avoid restrained or half-hearted movements.

c. Use the *whole body*, all in one piece.

d. First try simply to express your thought and feeling. Later repeat the exercise in front of a mirror and observe how it would look to others.

    1) "I looked out the window. We were flying at 2,000 feet, and there was New York coming slowly toward us. The Statue of Liberty passed by on our left, looking small as a ten-cent toy. Steamships below us moved like bugs that walk on the water. Ahead were the skyscrapers. But from the air they didn't scrape the sky. They were only toys made to imitate the real skyscrapers you see from the streets. From the air, all New York was a toyland and I felt like Gulliver landing in Lilliput."

    2) "How ill this taper burns! Ha! who comes here?
        I think it is the weakness of my eyes
        That shapes this monstrous apparition.
        It comes upon me. Art thou any thing?
        Art thou some god, some angel, or some devil,
        That mak'st my blood cold, and my hair to stare?—
        Speak to me what thou art."

SHAKESPEARE, Hamlet

4. In your room practice the following kinds of action until you get the feeling behind them; then demonstrate your mastery in class:

a. Getting the *whole* body into all action.

b. Using the *approach, stroke,* and *return* in hand action.

c. Freeing the wrist so that action will not seem wooden.

d. Getting the hand *open* instead of leaving the fingers curled and awry.

e. Turning the palm toward the audience.

f. Using *both* hands, instead of one only as beginners tend to do.

5. Study the following paragraph until you have it word-perfect. Then, using the types of action you practiced in Exercise 3, communicate this paragraph by words and action:

> Nor must a young man compare himself with others or measure his success by theirs. It makes no difference how other men succeed. Their success is theirs; not yours. It matters nothing to me that Edison can invent the electric light and I can't; that Kipling can write a "Recessional" and I can't; that you can plead the law and I can't. You can do one thing; I try to do another. But success is for both of us just so far as we do well what we can do. Every man is himself, and it is in proportion as he gets out of himself the power there is within him that he succeeds—succeeds in doing the thing he is best fitted to do.

EDWARD BOK, The Americanization of Edward Bok

6. The following selection is more conversational. Try reading it and reinforcing your words with communicative action:

As Mr. John Oakhurst, gambler, stepped into the main street of Poker Flat on the morning of the 23rd of November, 1850, he was conscious of a change in its moral atmosphere since the preceding night. Two or three men, conversing earnestly together, ceased as he approached, and exchanged significant glances. There was a Sabbath lull in the air, which, in a settlement unused to Sabbath influences, looked ominous.

Mr. Oakhurst's calm, handsome face betrayed small concern in these indications. Whether he was conscious of any predisposing cause was another question. "I reckon they're after somebody," he reflected; "likely it's me." He returned to his pocket the handkerchief with which he had been whipping away the red dust of Poker Flat from his neat boots, and quietly discharged his mind of any further conjecture.

In point of fact, Poker Flat was "after somebody." It had lately suffered the loss of several thousand dollars, two valuable horses, and a prominent citizen.

BRET HARTE, The Outcasts of Poker Flat

# 5

# Being Heard

We now come to the use of *sound waves* in communicating thought. "Anybody can talk," runs a thoughtless adage; but talking is not necessarily communicating. Some people talk with voices that are weak and thin. Some have lingual inertia and immobile lips. Some do not open the mouth; they only half-open it. Some do not actually carve the sounds of speech; they only approximate them. To say that such people talk is a liberal extension of the meaning of that word. More exactly they mumble, drone, mutter, muffle, sputter, haw, and croak. We are concerned here with talk that communicates. Public address is *enlarged* conversation, and the enlarging gives trouble. It starts with the nature of hearing itself.

## THE NATURE OF HEARING

Hearing in public address is done at greater distance and under more adverse conditions than in private conversation. The nature of hearing, therefore, enters the picture. Let us look at how the ear operates.

When the sound waves arrive at the ear they must, first, be translated into thought in the listener's mind. Now what we call sound waves are really *pressure* waves. The pressure waves of the faintest audible tone at the most favorable pitch move the ear drum in and out by less than a hundred-millionth of an inch. When this movement reaches the inner ear it contacts an auditory nerve which has some 30,000 fibers. These fibers are the pathway through which the dot-dot-dot code of nerve impulses reach the brain and are translated into thought. This inner ear is the sound analyzer. Among its chief means of analysis are these:

1. *By energy of sound.* The louder the tone, the greater is the number of nerve fibers stimulated. Also the louder the tone, the more impulses pass along each fiber per second. Thus the speaker who uses greater energy in-

creases the total number of nerve impulses delivered to the listener's brain in two ways: (1) More fibers are active, and (2) more impulses are sent per fiber. Here we see why a weak voice in a large room is not enough, and why a full voice communicates more meaning.

2. *By rhythm.* Each language has a characteristic rhythm determined partly by its grammar and partly by its pronunciation. Hence a stilted or artificial speech rhythm hinders understanding.

3. *By stress and accent.* Certain melody patterns are standardized, and the ear is conditioned to translate them. So it is that by timing of syllables, and by pause between them, the ear translates additional meanings. So it is that monotonous voices, lacking stress and accent, give the ear fewer impulses to translate.

4. *By pitch.* The inner ear sorts out the various frequencies in each complex sound. Each frequency stimulates a corresponding group of the 30,000 nerve fibers. Stimulation of certain fibers causes us to hear a high-pitched tone, and stimulation of others causes us to hear a low-pitched tone. To use an analogy, "hearing a high-pitched tone corresponds to feeling a touch on the face, and a low-pitched tone to a touch on the foot."

So "hearing others talk" is far from simple. Even in a quiet living room we do not hear as much as we think. Continually we are filling in, guessing at sounds, and even words, that we don't quite hear. Listening at greater distance and in greater noise compels us to guess more and fill in more. Research on intelligibility, therefore, shows that increasingly higher levels of intelligibility are required in a friendly conversation, a small classroom, a large classroom, and on the public platform and stage.

## BEING HEARD

To be understood you must first be heard. To be heard in public address requires certain specific disciplines.

### Supply Vocal Power from Below the Larynx

A public speaker needs energy enough to be heard easily, and energy enough to carry tone color and informing inflections. Here you face two difficulties. First, some people try to get power by constricting the muscles in the throat and neck; the result is sounds that are harsh, shrill, or brittle. Second, some try to speak without adequate energy, and the result is lifeless tones without salt and spirit.

Power of voice comes from pressure behind the breath stream. This pressure, in turn, comes from muscles in the abdomen and between the ribs. In the words of the old Victorian actors, you *"pack your tones against your belt."* Lift the front wall of the chest. Harden the abdomen. Pull down the diaphragm until it draws air into the lungs like a suction pump. Now you can "pack your tones against your belt." Further steps are these:

*Maintain a steady air pressure as you talk.* In good voices there is steady muscle action in exhaling. In poor voices it tends to be jerky. Steadiness, of course, does not mean uniform pressure. You increase the pressure for emphasis and accent. You vary the graduation according to the thought. But the pressure is not wavering or jerky, not booming forth at the start of a sentence, then fading to inaudibility at the end.

*Maintain an adequate breath reserve.* You do not keep your lungs filled to the last cubic inch, or else you soon will have a chest full of air with burned out oxygen. Instead, you take a reasonably deep breath and fill the chest comfortably. In the same way, you do not keep on talking until you run out of air, but refill smoothly with short catches of breath. This ample reserve enables you to maintain vigor of voice to the end of each thought.

## EXERCISES

1. Practice breathing. Stand erect. Pull down the diaphragm and draw air into the lungs. While inhaling also: (1) Lift the upper chest. (2) Push out the ribs. (3) Harden the abdomen. (4) Try to feel the muscle-pull in the small of the back. (5) Make sure the throat is *open and relaxed.* Now exhale without a sound by letting the air flow silently through the lips.

2. Stand erect and inhale as above. Then with relaxed and open throat, speak the following with maximum energy and prolonged tones:

> *All aboard!*
> *Forward! March!*

3. Stand erect and inhale until the chest is comfortably filled. Then speak the following with maximum vocal power. Keep the throat relaxed. Supply power from below. Sustain the stressed sounds:

> Hear the mellow wedding bells—
> Golden bells!
> What a world of happiness their harmony foretells!
> > EDGAR ALLAN POE, *The Bells*

> The bell invites me
> Hear it not, Duncan; for it is a knell
> That summons thee to heaven or to hell.
> > SHAKESPEARE, *Macbeth*

### Use Ample Resonance

The vibrating vocal cords in your larynx produce only a thin and feeble tone. You must amplify and enrich this tone with the resonators. What are the human resonators? You have two types, fixed and adjustable. The *fixed resonators* are unchangeable in size: the skull bones, nose, nasal sinuses, trachea, sternum and ribs. When you use any of them you get the feeling of resonance in that part of your body. Close the lips and hum *m-m-m-m* until you get this feeling. Then put your hand on top of your head and you will know whence comes that "feeling." It is the real thing, for your skull bones are vibrating! Also feel the chest. If you are using enough energy down in your bellows, the chest bones are also vibrating.

*Adjustable resonators* are those that can be changed in size, shape, and tenseness: the mouth, pharynx, and larynx. These adjustable resonators change the pitch of your voice. They give it the rising and falling inflections. They impart the subtle variations of vocal quality. Especially they give it the vowel quality, for by changing the size and shape and tension of these adjustable resonators you can turn one sound into *e*, another into *o*, still another into *i*. You use about 15 vowel sounds. To produce each one clean and clear requires a different size, shape, and tension of the adjustable resonators.

Some people use their resonators efficiently; and we say they have "good voices." Some don't; and they have poor voices of various degrees and types.

## EXERCISES

1. Inhale (remember your breathing exercises), relax the throat, flatten the tongue and make the sounds given below. Hold the tone for 15 seconds while you feel the cranium, jaw, chest, etc., and locate which of these resonators are vibrating. Note that the mouth must be *opened wider* for each succeeding pair:

> *e* and *oo*
> *a* and *o*
> *i* and *ah*

2. Read the following with relaxed and open throat, and the power coming from bellows down below:

> I have but one lamp by which my feet are guided, and that is the lamp of experience.
>
> PATRICK HENRY, *speech in the Virginia Convention, March 23, 1775*

There are maidens in Scotland more lovely by far,
That would gladly be bride to Young Lochinvar.

Sir Walter Scott, Marmion

Ship me somewhere east of Suez, where the best is like the worst,
Where there aren't no Ten Commandments, an' a man can raise a thirst.

Rudyard Kipling, Barrack Room Ballads

## Use Your Normal Key

Your voice has a normal key. This is the general pitch level best suited to your particular resonators. Your voice will rise and fall above and below this median, but it tends always to return to it.

The normal key varies with different persons, and it varies greatly between men and women. In this respect voices are like musical instruments. Each will produce sounds within a given range, some high, some medium, some low. Outside this range it does not perform so well. Hence some women's voices are contralto, and others are soprano. Some men's voices are bass, and others are tenor.

If you do not use your normal key, you cannot attain best potential voice power or quality. If you speak below it, you tend to have a deep hollow tone without flexibility. If you speak above it, you tend to have a thin squeaky voice, with the same lack of flexibility.

The best way to find your normal key is to sing from your lowest key to your highest, including your falsetto. Your normal key is about *one-fourth* the way up from your lowest tone.

## EXERCISES

1. Using the method described above, find your normal key. By going frequently to a piano and sounding the proper key, you can keep this pitch continually in mind and help to make its use habitual.

2. Using your normal key, read the following, but do not read in a mono-pitch. Instead communicate the meaning by as much variety of pitch as you need, but use your normal key as a median:

> We hold these truths to be self-evident, that all men are created equal, that they are endowed by their Creator with certain unalienable Rights, that among these are Life, Liberty and the pursuit of Happiness.

Declaration of Independence

> Friends, Romans, countrymen, lend me your ears;
> I come to bury Caesar, not to praise him.
> The evil that men do lives after them;

The good is oft interred with their bones;
So let it be with Caesar.

SHAKESPEARE, *Julius Caesar*


# BEING UNDERSTOOD


Being heard does not mean that automatically you will be understood. We may hear words in a foreign language, or indistinct sounds in our own language, and understand them only partly or not at all. Let us look at how to be understood in enlarged conversation.

### Speak with a Flexible and Responsive Voice

The inner ear, you remember, is the sound analyzer. It takes in the sound waves, translates them into nerve impulses, and sends them to the brain along selected groups of the 30,000 fibers of the auditory nerve. But it cannot analyze what is not there. You must supply the material. The more you supply, the more analysis there is and the more meaning. The human race, in fact, has evolved a code of meaning from changes in pitch, time, and emphasis—a code that is independent of the words themselves. Its use is as involuntary as the twinkle of the eye.

## COMMUNICATING MEANINGS BY CHANGES IN PITCH

We communicate meanings by two kinds of pitch changes: *steps* and *slides* (i.e. inflections). The step is a pitch change *between* syllables, as seen in the following sentence:

```
                      he
                           do?
         What
                   did
```

The slide (inflection) is even more common, and is used constantly for communicating subtle shades of thought. It is a gliding pitch change *during* the syllable, as in saying sarcastically:

```
                        t s
                    a      o
                  a        o
                a          o    o?
                th           o o
            Is
```

For thousands of years these pitch changes have been used to communicate meanings. Each person will have his own personalized variations, but the standard meanings are far older than any words of the English language and quite as definite.

1. *A rising inflection communicates incompleteness of thought, uncertainty, or inconclusiveness.* When you ask a question, hesitate, or are in doubt, or cannot make up your mind—your voice says so with a rising inflection.

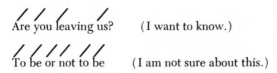

Are you leaving us?    (I want to know.)

To be or not to be    (I am not sure about this.)

2. *A falling inflection communicates completeness of thought, assurance, conviction, or determination.* This is the inflection of decision and assurance. It is used less often than rising inflections, but carries more definite and important meanings.

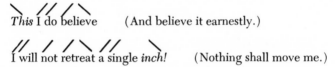

*This* I do believe    (And believe it earnestly.)

I will not retreat a single *inch!*    (Nothing shall move me.)

3. *A wave, or double inflection, communicates the rich double meanings of humor, sarcasm, and subtle thought.* Not all thought is plain and straight. Often we really say two things at once. Such meanings are communicated by a voice wave, or double inflection. In other words, when there is a double thought in the mind, there is a double inflection in the voice.

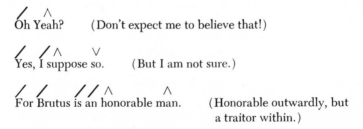

Oh Yeah?    (Don't expect me to believe that!)

Yes, I suppose so.    (But I am not sure.)

For Brutus is an honorable man.    (Honorable outwardly, but
a traitor within.)

Bare words, in short, mean little. They are given fullness of meaning by subtle shadings of voice. The word "no," said Charles H. Woolbert, can be spoken to carry at least twenty different meanings, one of them being "yes."

*In public address the special problem is to enlarge the inflection to fit the enlarged conversation.* The short inflection, suitable enough for ordinary conversation, is not enough for the enlarged conversation of public address.

## EXERCISES

1. Read the following to communicate the question-and-answer current of ideas:

> Does the road wind up-hill all the way?
>> Yes, to the very end.
> Will the day's journey take the whole day long?
>> From morn to night, my friend.
> But is there for the night a resting-place?
>> A roof for when the slow dark hours begin.
> May not the darkness hide it from my face?
>> You cannot miss that inn.
> Shall I meet other wayfarers at night?
>> Those who have gone before.
>>>> CHRISTINA ROSSETTI, *Up-Hill*

## COMMUNICATE MEANINGS BY VARIATIONS IN TIME

We don't speak at a constant rate like a steady wind blowing. We change the rate, pause, and group our words. These time variations are part of man's code of communicating.

1. *Rate.* Some people think fast and talk fast. Some think and talk at a slower tempo. Webster, for example spoke at about 80-100 words a minute, Lincoln at 100, Franklin D. Roosevelt at 117, Henry Clay at 130-160, John C. Calhoun at 180, Rufus Choate at 200, and Phillips Brooks at 215. Each talked according to his own personality and his capacity for clear articulation. If you talk too fast, the sounds become obscure. If you talk too slowly, you tend to have blank pauses, or to fill in time with *Ahs* and *Ers*. In general a rate over 150 words a minute is too fast, and if you slow to 100 words a minute, there is danger of the audience's losing interest—unless you have exceptional syllable duration and use especially effective pauses.

All this applies to the *average rate.* Actually, we do not speak long at an even rate. When dealing with narrative, suspense, or excitement, we speed up to fit the mood. When explaining or moving through a difficult thought, we slow down markedly. To sum it up: *Talk fast enough to be interesting. Take time to be distinct to those who are farthest away.*

2. *Word Grouping.* We don't talk in single words, but in groups of words. We group words together, according to the meaning. One word group, for example, may carry the central meaning of a thought and the others merely fill in details. If we change the grouping, the identical words may have exactly the opposite meaning, to wit:

The teacher said the student is a fool.
"The teacher," / said the student, / "is a fool."

The essence of grouping for clear meaning is this: *Group together those words which stand for ideas that belong together, and separate that group from others by emphasis and pauses.*

The essential of effective word grouping is the *pause.* In speech you don't have commas, semicolons, and periods. You have the pause. It is the punctuation mark of speech—the comma, semicolon, and period all rolled into one. A pause permits listeners to concentrate on what has been said and get set for what is to come. A pause is that "thunder of white silence" that causes restless listeners to look at the speaker, and to listen sharply. "I . . . made a pause," said Winston Churchill, "to allow the House to take [it] in. . . . As this soaked in, there was something like a gasp."

Beginners seldom know how to pause. They are afraid of the silence, like a child of the dark. They hurry on to fill it up with talk and rush on to that final blessed word. This is not real speaking. It is a race with time. Therefore, take stock of yourself. Do you group words firmly enough? Do you pause positively? Can you listen to the silence of your pauses, and allow listeners this moment of golden silence to digest what you have said and to get set for what is to come?

One final word. Beware of pausing at every place you find a punctuation mark in print. Pausing and punctuation often fall at the same place, but not always. Punctuation is for the eye. Pausing is for the ear. For the eye punctuation is like this:

Let us, therefore, brace ourselves to our duties, and so bear ourselves that, if the British Empire and its Commonwealth last for a thousand years, men will still say, "This was their finest hour."

But for the ear, pauses come at five places where there is punctuation, at three additional places where there is no punctuation. Furthermore, there are no pauses at two places where there is punctuation.

Let us, therefore, / brace ourselves to our duties, / and so bear ourselves / that, if the British Empire and its Commonwealth / last for a thousand years, / men will still say, / "This / was their finest hour." /


## EXERCISES

1. Which of the following would you read at a faster rate, and which slower? In succession read the two at rates that seem best for you:

> Out of the North the wild news came,
> Far flashing on its wings of flame,
> Swift as the boreal light which flies
> At midnight through the startled skies.

And there was tumult in the air,
    The fife's shrill note, the drum's loud beat,
And through the wide land everywhere
    The answering tread of hurrying feet.

T. B. READ, The Revolutionary Uprising

The Moving Finger writes; and, having writ,
Moves on; nor all your Piety nor Wit
    Shall lure it back to cancel half a Line,
Nor shall your tears wash out a Word of it.

OMAR KHAYYÁM, Rubiayat

2. Pause forcibly with packed meaning to communicate full meaning on the following:

Books are the best of things, well used; abused, among the worst.

He batted his eyes, and the lightnings flashed;
He clapped his hands, and the thunders rolled.

## COMMUNICATING MEANINGS BY DEGREES OF EMPHASIS

We don't emphasize each word equally. If we did human speech would resemble the *tap, tap, tap* of a typewriter. But speech is not like that at all. It comes in bursts and swells.

In each sentence a single idea dominates, and this idea often is conveyed in a single word—with all the other words being mere undercover support. In speaking we highlight the important idea-carrying words by emphasis, and let the others fade into the background.

I tell you *earnestly* and *authoritatively* you must get into the habit of looking *intensely* at words, and assuring yourself on their *meaning, syllable* by *syllable*—nay, *letter* by *letter*.

In public speaking emphasis is far stronger than in private conversation. This, in part, is because the audience is composed of persons of various degrees of intelligence and alertness, and it is necessary to reach all—including the dullest. Again, speaker-to-audience distance is a factor. The farther away a speaker is, the harder it becomes to read his facial expression and other minute signs of meaning, and the more the audience must depend on the speaker's distant voice and on action that cannot be seen close up. In short, *enlarged conversation demands enlarged emphasis.*

## EXERCISES

1. Read the following so as to bring out the full force of the neat insult:

    Sir, I admit your genial rule,
    That every poet is a fool,

> But you yourself may serve to show it,
> That every fool is not a poet.
>
> ALEXANDER POPE, *Epigram from the French*

2. In the following speech on "The American Scholar," Emerson attacks the traditional higher education of over a century ago. His style is condensed and it will require full emphasis to communicate the meaning. Read it as to an audience of one hundred people.

> Books are the best of things, well used; abused, among the worst. . . . The book, the college, the school or art, the institution of any kind, stop with some past utterance of genius. This is good, they say—let us hold by this. They pin me down. They look backward and not forward. But genius looks forward: the eyes of man are set in his forehead, not in his hindhead: man hopes: genius creates.
>
> RALPH WALDO EMERSON, *The American Scholar*

3. The thought in the following passage rises and falls like rolling ocean waves. Read it so as to communicate all the rising and falling, but keeping the thought rolling on to its splendid climax:

> You ask, "What is our policy?" I will say, "It is to wage war, by sea, land, and air, with all our might and wealth against a monstrous tyranny, never surpassed in the dark, lamentable catalogue of human crime. That is our policy." You ask, "What is our aim?" I can answer in one word: "Victory"—victory at all costs, victory in spite of all terror, victory, however long and hard the road may be; for without victory there is no survival. . . . But I take up my task with buoyancy and hope. I feel sure that our cause will not be suffered to fail among men. I feel entitled to claim the aid of all, and I say, "Come, then, let us go forward together with our united strength."
>
> WINSTON CHURCHILL, *On Becoming Prime Minister*

## COMMUNICATING MEANINGS BY DISTINCTNESS OF ARTICULATION

The average speaker talks at a rate of about 300 syllables a minute, or 5 per second. A listener must catch these syllables on the wing and translate them into thought. He must do it instantly, without faltering and almost without pausing. But if these 5 syllables a second are slurred, muffled, or projected weakly the listener is going to miss some of them. If, at that moment, he stops to think, "What was that he said?" then he misses also those words that come in the instant of thinking back. All in all, he has missed a whole section of what the speaker said. So it is that in public address clear articulation is vital to communication.

By articulation, of course, we mean the skillful molding of speech sounds, and the combining of separate sounds to make up intelligible speech. Loudness of speech is mainly in the vowels, but *intelligibility is mainly in the consonants*. Hence the maxim, "the vowels give beauty, the consonants give clarity." Unfortunately, consonant sounds are not loud even at close range; and, unfortunately also, they fade with distance, so that a consonant sound heard easily at 5 feet may be inaudible at 50 feet. Hence to be heard easily in public address you must sharpen the articulation of consonants. The following tested procedures will be helpful:

1. *Pack plenty of breath pressure behind the consonants.* Explode the initial *p* as is pull, *t* as in talk, and *k*-sound as in *chemist.* Use ample breath pressure to sound the medial consonants like the *zh*-sound in *measure,* the *sh*-sound in *nation,* and the *s*-sound in recent. Carry this breath pressure all the way through to the final consonants; explode the *t* in *don't,* hiss the *s* in *miss,* prolong the *l* in *control.* It takes far more breath to project consonants than to vibrate resonant vowels. Shallow breathers take note.

2. *Articulate; don't slur, mumble, or muffle.* People who really articulate open their mouths wide. They have an active jaw, lips, face, tongue, and pharynx. Ironically, not only can you hear good articulation but you can look at the speaker and also see it. There is the constant nimble movement as the visible speech organs move into position for the consonant, make the sound, and speed swiftly on to the next one. Here are two broad and convenient self-made tests.

First, look at yourself in the mirror as you talk. Do you see the swift and nimble movements that come from the strength of contact and quickness of release of the visible articulating organs?

Second, listen to your voice, both as you speak and from recording playbacks. Do you say *What's that* or *whassat? Let me* or *lemme? Don't know* or *dunno? Recognize* or *reckernize? Particular* or *partikerler? Manufacture* or *manerfacture?*

3. *Sustain the friction-like consonants:* the *s* in *sit* and *hiss,* the *z*-sound in *his,* the *sh*-sound in *motion,* the *zh*-sound in *occasion,* the *f* in *half* and *four,* the *v* in *never* and *move.* These sounds are made by partially blocking the breath stream at some place in the mouth and by forcing out the breath at this place in a *continuous* stream. Make the stream continuous.

4. *Hold the long consonants until you get them rolling:* the *l* in *hill,* the *r* in *road,* the *n* in *now,* the *m* in *home,* and the *ng* in *coming.* These are sounds that require a build-up. Therefore, build them up.

5. *Do not ignore medial consonants.* Which do you say: "twen*t*y," or "twen*ny*"? "Star*t*ed," or "star*d*ed"? Do you have the clear medial consonants in ro*s*trum, hu*n*dred, e*x*tra, di*s*prove?

6. *Sound the final consonants in a word group.* When combinations of consonants occur within a word group, we blend them, as in "the fair bree*ze bl*ew, the whi*te foam fl*ew." But when a consonant sound falls at the end of a word group, it needs to be carried through and articulated with full breath pressure:

> Night's candles are burnt ou*t,* / and jocund day
> stands tiptoe / on the misty mountain top*s*./

7. *Master the difficult consonant combinations.* The English language is infamous for its many difficult consonant combinations. There are 22 two-consonant groups that number far over 100 individual combinations. Beyond that are 58 reasonably common three-consonant and four-consonant combinations. The following list is helpful. Practice it, being careful to articulate all of the consonants without slurring or omitting any within the combinations.

## TWO-CONSONANT COMBINATION

| | | | | | |
|---|---|---|---|---|---|
| ou*ts*ide | bra*c*elet | ro*bb*ed | loo*k*ed | pa*st* | mon*th* |
| nu*mb*er | noi*s*eless | li*v*ed | pu*sh*ed | a*sk* | bri*ngs* |
| i*ns*ect | a*lm*ost | pu*lls* | wa*k*ed | my*ths* | he*lp* |
| di*sm*al | mi*lli*on | rai*s*ed | so*ngs* | bu*lb* | fee*ds* |

Remember that letters and sounds are not identical. Thus in the second column "bra*c*elet" is pronounced with the sound of *sl*, "noi*s*eless" is pronounced *zl*. Observe that in the fourth column "wa*k*ed," etc., are pronounced with a final *t*, not with *d*. Finally, do not be disturbed that words like "mon*th*" and "bri*ngs*" are spelled with three final consonant letters. They have only two-consonant sounds, since *th* and *ng* are single sounds.

## THREE-CONSONANT AND FOUR-CONSONANT COMBINATIONS

| | | | | | |
|---|---|---|---|---|---|
| e*xpl*ain | a*ptl*y | fi*x*ed | ne*xt* | hi*nged* | po*sts* |
| mi*sq*uote | exa*ctl*y | a*sk*ed | a*cts* | ·a*sks* | gue*sts* |
| di*scr*eet | dire*ctl*y | comme*nc*ed | ju*dged* | de*sks* | eigh*ths* |
| la*ngu*age | mo*stl*y | lun*ch*ed | e*dged* | te*sts* | mon*ths* |

Note that the words in column 3, although spelled *ed,* are pronounced *t.*

## EXERCISES

1. Pronounce the above word lists to a friend. Have him sit at right angles to you or with his back turned, so he cannot see you but must depend wholly on sound. Ask him to write down the words slurred or weakly articulated. Remember that these are not mere words that give you trouble; they are *sound combinations.* Note the combinations. (They are italicized in the above word lists.) Make up a list of words containing these sounds for future practice.

2. If possible make a recording of these word lists and listen to them yourself.

3. Pronounce the following pairs of words so that listeners can easily distinguish one word from the other:

| | |
|---|---|
| *p*ear | *b*ear |
| *t*oe | *d*ough |
| *f*ine | *v*ine |
| *wh*at | *w*att |
| hi*ss* | hi*s* |
| ri*ch* | ri*dge* |

4. Drill on the following words until you can pronounce them without slurring or omitting any of the sounds:

| WRONG | RIGHT | WRONG | RIGHT |
|---|---|---|---|
| ke*p* | ke*pt* | mon*ts* | mon*ths* |
| exa*ckly* | exa*ctly* | a*w*-right | a*ll* right |
| co*ss* | co*sts* | wa*d*er | wa*t*er |
| insi*ss* | insi*sts* | uni*d*ed | uni*t*ed |
| ra*err*oad | rai*lr*oad | a*ss* | a*sks* |

5. Read the following and be careful not only of articulation but also of communicating the mood and rich double meanings:

There was once a little man, and his rod and line he took,
For he said, "I'll go a-fishing in the neighboring brook."
And it chanced a little maiden was walking out that day,
    And they met—in the usual way.

ANON, The Usual Way

Maris is simple and chaste—
    She's pretty and tender and modest—
But on one or two matters of taste
    Her views are distinctly the oddest.
Her virtue is something sublime—
    No kissing—on that there's a stopper—
When I try, she says, "All in good time—
    At present it's highly improper."

GILBERT AND SULLIVAN, Haste to the Wedding

We are spinning our own fates, good or evil, never to be undone. Every smallest stroke of virtue or vice leaves its never-so-little scar. The drunken Rip Van Winkle, in Jefferson's play, excuses himself for every fresh dereliction by saying, "I won't count this time!" Well, he may not count it, and a kind Heaven may not count it; but it is being counted none the less. Down among his nerve-cells and fibers the molecules are counting it, registering and storing it up to be used against him when the next temptation comes. Nothing we ever do is, in strict scientific literalness, wiped out.

WILLIAM JAMES, Talks to Teachers

## Make Your Voice the Vehicle of Thought and Feeling

This is the final goal of all voice training. Everything else in this chapter has been on the ways and means to prepare for it. A good voice carries to listeners your finest degrees of thought and slight shade of values, every color and hue.

Foremost of all things your voice should tell is *sincerity*. To all who hear, it should say, "You may disagree with what I say, but you cannot question my sincerity." No listener, of course, really knows whether a speaker is sincere. He can know only whether a speaker *seems* sincere. "Say what you think," William Jennings Bryan used to say to his daughter, "but *feel* what you say." Now sincerity is not easily feigned. The surest way, the only safe way, to sound sincere is to *be* sincere.

Once you have established sincerity, then comes the meaning of the words themselves. Remember that when you speak or read you communicate *two* simultaneous meanings. First, you say, "This is what I am talking about." Second, you say, "Here is how I feel about it." Like the two legs of the human body, both are essential.

There is no absolute meaning any word must have. The dictionary establishes only a frame of reference by recording many meanings for almost every word. At the moment of utterance you give each word its exact meaning in context. You spot the important words, let listeners know they are important and why, and communicate their meanings with precision—as *you* use them. You go below the surface of language and make clear your basic thought. This is not done by the mere utterance of words, for the mere flow of words may confuse the listener if their exact meaning and their relation to the whole thought are not made clear.

Finally, you tell listeners, "This is how I feel about these things." This is done by what we call *emotional color*. You have been using emotional color, and hearing others use it, all your life without probably knowing the term. Listen to a good speaker, and you know unerringly whether he feels determination, anger, contempt, friendship, or indifference. Each attitude is communicated by its own special tone color. The tone color of each is distinct from others, arrogance from assurance, friendship from flattery, mirth from melancholy.

How do you make voice the vehicle of thought and feeling? Shall you say, "I shall emphasize this word," or "Here I want to show determination; therefore, I shall use the emotional color of a determined person"? Not if you want to be a real speaker. If you do this, the result will be like that described (in this case a bit unjustly) by a critic of Olivia de Havilland: "She never seems to feel the part—only the importance of it. She never seems in love with Romeo—only with *Romeo and Juliet*. She recites poetry where she should radiate it; and goes through the role as though following a score marked presto or lento, *ff*. or *pp*." Listeners know whether a speaker feels what he says, or is only feigning. This is old knowledge in the human race, learned early in every life.

If you soliloquize, your voice will be a soliloquy. If you only half-grasp the thought, your voice will be perfunctory. To communicate thought you must be *thinking* on your feet, creating or recreating the full thought at the moment of utterance. To communicate attitudes you must *experience* the attitude as you speak. "Expression," said Cicero, "is always perfect." To make voice the vehicle of thought and feeling, you must think in terms of ideas, feelings, and concepts instead of mere words.

## SUPPLEMENTARY READINGS

Anderson, Virgil A., *Training the Speaking Voice,* 2nd ed. New York: Oxford, 1961. See especially "Developing Clearness and 'Correctness' of Speech," pp. 245-267.

Bronstein, Arthur J., *The Pronunciation of American English.* New York: Appleton-Century-Crofts, 1960. A good comprehensive work.

Fairbanks, Grant, *Voice and Articulation Drillbook,* 2nd ed. New York: Harper & Row, 1960. Brief tested exercises.

Grimes, Wilma H., and Mattingly, Alethea Smith, *Interpretation: Writer-Reader-Audience.* Belmont, Calif.: Wadsworth, 1961. "The Interpreter's Use of the Voice," pp. 267-296, has applications for manuscript readers.

Hahn, Elise, Lomas, Charles W., Hargis, Donald E., and Vandraegen, Daniel, *Basic Voice Training for Speech.* New York: McGraw-Hill, 1957. A good introduction is in "Critical Listening and Self-analysis," pp. 1-10, and "Why You Speak as You Do," pp. 11-23.

## EXERCISES

1. Study the following selection, get its central theme and supporting details, then in reading it communicate the full meaning:

One comfort is that great men taken up in any way are profitable company. We can not look, however imperfectly, upon a great man without gaining something by it. He is the living fountain of life, which it is pleasant to be near. On any terms whatsoever you will not grudge to wander in his neighborhood for a while.

THOMAS CARLYLE, *Heroes and Hero Worship*

2. What is the dominant mood of the following selection? Is it reverence, loyalty, admiration, entreaty, command, coaxing, anxiety, remorse, or gratitude? Decide which you think it is, and read it to communicate that mood:

And Ruth said, Entreat me not to leave thee, and to return from following after thee; for whither thou goest, I will go; and where thou lodgest, I will lodge; thy people shall be my people, and thy God my God; where thou diest, will I die, and there will I be buried: Jehovah so do to me, and more also, if aught but death part thee and me.

*Book of Ruth,* 1:16-17

3. In reading the following selection communicate its humor and suspense:

There was an old preacher once who told some boys of the Bible lesson he was going to read in the morning. The boys, finding the place, glued together the connecting pages. The next morning he read on the bottom of one page: "When Noah was one hundred and twenty years old he took unto himself a wife, who was"—then turning the page—"one hundred and forty cubits long, forty cubits wide, built of gopher-wood, and covered with pitch inside and out." He was naturally puzzled at this. He read it again, verified it, and then said: "My friends, this is the first time I ever met this in the Bible, but I accept it as an evidence of the assertion that we are fearfully and wonderfully made."

HENRY W. GRADY, The New South

4. In the following communicate the undercurrent of uneasiness:

Once upon a midnight dreary, while I pondered, weak and weary,
Over many a quaint and curious volume of forgotten lore,—
While I nodded, nearly napping, suddenly there came a tapping,
As of someone gently rapping, rapping at my chamber door.
" 'Tis some visitor," I muttered, "tapping at my chamber door:
Only this and nothing more!"

EDGAR ALLAN POE, The Raven

5. Study the meaning and determine the mood of the following selections. Then read them to communicate both meaning and mood:

I recollect a nurse called Ann,
    Who carried me about the grass,
And one fine day a fine young man
    Came up, and kissed the pretty lass!
She did not make the least objection!
    Thinks I, "Aha!
    When I can talk, I'll tell Mama."
    —And that's my earliest recollection.

FREDERICK LOCKER-LAMPSON, A Terrible Infant

In Flanders fields the poppies blow
Between the crosses, row on row,
That mark our place; and in the sky
The larks, still bravely singing, fly
Scarce heard amidst the guns below.

JOHN D. McRAE, In Flanders Fields

# 6

# Organizing the Speech

Ideas in a well-planned speech should advance "as organized platoons—in marching order." How to organize them and how to make them march are problems we shall now consider.

## MEET YOUR AUDIENCE

Customarily when you are introduced to a stranger you are given at least a short briefing: "I'd like you to know Professor Jones. He's just joined our faculty to teach in American Studies." "This is my cousin, John Hawkins, a senior in pre-law at Channing College. Since you both come from Chicago I'd been hoping to get you together." Before you say a word you have something to say—about American Studies, about law schools, or about what a small world this is. In a modest way you pursue the opening, looking for common ground, or more information: "Then you know Professor Whipple in the history department?" "What law schools have you been thinking about?" Though your "audience" is only Professor Jones, or John Hawkins, you almost automatically begin "an analysis."

We began Chapter 1 by saying that "Speaking is for listening." Here we extend that statement to say that "Speeches are for listeners." Because we believe that speech communication must be *audience*-centered, we believe that organizing a speech begins with analyzing its intended audience. Just as you want to know something about individuals you meet, so you want information before you meet your audience.

Whatever you can learn about your audience in advance will not only be useful in organizing your speech, but also in deciding how best to make your ideas clear (Chapter 7), and how to make them most persuasive (Chapter 8).

Only rarely can you wait until you actually face your audience to find out what you most need to know. Niles Dillingham, of the *Dawson Springs Progress,* reported the preacher who did just that. He announced that his sermon would be about liars. "How many of you have read the 35th chapter of Matthew?" he asked. About half the hands in the congregation went up. "Well, since there ain't no such chapter," the preacher said, "you're just the folks I want to talk to!"

Ordinarily you must start well in advance, asking for audience information from the chairman of the program, members of the organization, or friends in the community. Even for your speech class, a church group, or any other audience brought together under a common aegis, and no matter how well you may know individuals in it, there is more you will want to learn about *the audience and your subject.*

1. What is the probable significance of my subject for this audience? If any, is it casual or motivated?
2. What kind of information, and how much, is the audience likely to have about my subject? Does it want any more?
3. What beliefs, or biases, does the audience probably have about my subject? And how were they formed?
4. What is the probable audience attitude toward my subject? Favorable, neutral, or unfavorable toward my purpose-sentence?
5. What is my reason for wanting to talk to *this* audience on my subject? And why should they want to hear me?
6. What time do I have for discussing the subject? Enough, or should the subject be narrowed down?

We cannot long consider human beings without realizing how complex they are. Somerset Maugham made the point this way: "We are none of us all of a piece; more than one person dwells within us, often in uneasy companionship with his fellows." This is why we need to learn about *the audience and the speaker.*

1. What is the dominant social group represented in my audience? Students, housewives, laborers, businessmen?
2. What specific organizational group, if any, does my audience represent? Church, service club, union, college?
3. What *general* characteristics does my audience have in common? Cultural, educational, environmental?
4. What *specific* characteristics does my audience have in common? Sex, age, religious, political?
5. What are likely to be the most potent motivations of my audience? In terms of goals, expectations, aspirations?
6. What is the probable attitude of my audience toward me as speaker? A reputation for knowledge, sincerity, common ties?

As in many other circumstances, it is easier to ask the questions than to get the answers. But only when you begin to visualize your audience in some detail are you prepared to go ahead with organizing your speech.

## SELECT A DEFINITE PURPOSE

A speaker, like a traveler, should know where he is going. He ought to lay out his route in advance, and check for detours along the way. Then when he finishes his speech and arrives at his goal, no audience members will be asking, "Where was he trying to go?" They will all know.

This should be unnecessary advice, but unfortunately it is not. Many speeches are made without apparent object or aim, and we have all heard them. They start nowhere. They go nowhere. They aim at nothing—and stay right on target. When you are going to speak, avoid this waste motion; find out exactly where you want to go, and stay on the road.

### The Four General Purposes of Speaking

What alternate purposes may a speaker have? Fundamentally, there is but one basic purpose for all speaking. *The speaker wants to influence the behavior of his listeners, he wants them to respond, to do something about what he says.* But all possible responses are not equally easy to attain. Some are easier, some more difficult. Consequently we tend to divide them into four categories, arranged in order of increasing difficulty in achieving general purposes.

### TO INTEREST

What shall it profit a speaker if, no matter how good his speech, the audience is uninterested, pays no attention? Naturally a stream of interest must run through *all* speech communication. "Polite attention" given by courteous members of the audience seldom lasts, and is not usually very close attention anyway. The explanation is that the more energy a hearer spends in "giving attention" to the speaker, the less energy he has left to understand, comprehend, and consider the subject matter. Thus interest is the common denominator of all speaking.

Sometimes, though, interest is not merely a means, but the end itself. The speaker at such times has no desire to inform, to stimulate, or to change his hearers in any way. He wants only to interest them. He does this by relaxing them, turning their thoughts away from the pressures of everyday affairs. His speech has wit, repartee, anecdotes, dramatic movement, and lively style.

Most private conversations have this relatively simple purpose. So do many after-dinner speeches and toastmaster's introductions. And story-hour talks for children and "fill-in" speeches for adult organizations.

## TO INFORM

The speech to inform is next. It includes reports to organizations, group instructions to workers, pilot briefings, classroom lectures, and addresses given by specialists to lay audiences.

The purpose of those making such speeches is to tell people something they don't already know, or perhaps to explain the implications of what they do know. In either case this speech is more difficult than the speech to interest, for the information must be presented so that listeners can readily grasp, understand, and use it. Just passing out information is not enough. It must be presented so that it can be used. These are significant considerations:

1. *Arrange the information under two or three headings, hardly ever more than four.* A speech cannot be strung together like beads in a necklace. Though they be pearls, scattered bits of information will neither be appreciated nor remembered. Take all of your facts and group them under a few main headings. Two headings are best, if the facts will fit. Three are all right. But beware of using more than three, for listeners are likely to forget them.

2. *In giving the speech, fasten these headings in the hearer's mind.* When you come to the first one, say so: *"The first step in this problem is. . . ."* When you finish with that heading, make it clear to your listeners, and summarize it so they can easily remember it. Then, as you move to the next heading, be sure your audience knows it: *"We turn now to the second problem. . . ."*

3. *Always make your information specific.* Of course the speech should not be cluttered with unnecessary facts, or confusing details, but you should build it out of specifics, not abstractions. Indeed, you cannot have abstract information. An abstraction, like "freedom," is a value judgment. But "the pickets were undisturbed" is information. Avoid absurd specificity. For example, don't say "We travelled 248 and three-tenths miles," for the listener is apt to remember the unimportant "three-tenths" and forget the essential "248 miles." To help him out make it "just under 250 miles."

4. *Use charts, graphs, and diagrams for technical or complex materials.* Most persons cannot explain a complicated machine as well as a good diagram can reveal it, or describe detailed budget allocations as well as a "pie chart" can picture them. *If* you have visual aids large enough for all of your audience to see, use them to *show* in less time than you can *tell*.

5. *Make your information interesting.* Listeners can take just so much pressure at either end. You can control what happens to their heads: try not to pack in so many facts that everything becomes jumbled. Use anecdotes and illustrations, interesting comparisons, and humor if you can.

## TO STIMULATE ATTITUDES OR ACTIONS

We come now to the more complex responses that are found in two levels of persuasive speaking.

What is persuasion? *It is vitalizing a proposition so as to make it a dynamic force in the behavior of other people.* But behavior can take many forms, or be observed at different levels. Here we would like to think of behavior in terms of beliefs. Some that we hold are shallow; they may be newly acquired or temporary, and they are subject to relatively easy change. Other beliefs are deep-rooted, long-established, and very hard to change. The level of a belief, or its susceptibility to change, determines the speaker's mode of approach. For convenience we shall refer to 1. beliefs we hold in a mild form, and 2. beliefs we hold tenaciously, even obstinately.

*Speeches to stimulate latent attitudes or overt actions are concerned only with beliefs held in a mild form, or where lip service is given to a proposition but where the listener fails to act upon it.* We use "stimulate" here as the word is defined in *Webster's New International Dictionary*, third edition: "to excite to activity or growth or to greater activity or exertion." We refer specifically to exciting or arousing greater activity or exertion on behalf of mildly held beliefs.

For example, we all believe (mildly) that we should study hard, get eight hours of sleep every night, participate in public affairs, develop cultural interests—and start to prepare each speech well in advance. But so mild is our belief in some of these propositions that we *never do* what we believe we ought to do.

Most speechmaking aims at vitalizing these mild beliefs, raising them in our hierarchy. Consider, for example, commencement addresses, dedication speeches, eulogies, pep talks, inspirational talks to businessmen's groups, anniversary addresses, most sermons, and most political speeches. On the one hand these speeches are to *stimulate the listener's attitudes* (to make latent ones dominant) toward mild beliefs. On the other they are to *stimulate the listener's actions* on propositions to which they give only lip service.

Speeches intended to stimulate attitudes or actions are more difficult than speeches to interest or inform. First, such speeches must have interest and provide information, but second, they must also be fitted to the prevailing needs and desires of the listeners. The speech to stimulate must offer rewards to those who accept the speaker's proposition, *motivate* those who listen to *want* to do what they know they ought to.

## TO CHANGE ATTITUDES OR ACTIONS

*Speeches to change attitudes or actions are concerned with propositions that are not accepted by the listener; they ask the listener to alter his opinion, adopt a new belief, or to vote, buy, join, give, or do.* These speeches may be *to change attitudes* so that the listeners will say "I now earnestly accept this new belief." Or they may be *to change actions* so that the listeners will respond "I now will do this thing." In one case attitude is changed, in the other case action, and in both cases behavior is drastically modified.

To change attitudes or actions is the aim of the lawyer defending a client, the legislator arguing for a new bill on farm policy, or the speaker contending that literature is more essential to society than the broadcast media.

Speeches intended to change attitudes or actions are the most difficult of all, because they require everything called for in achieving the other three purposes, and more besides. The speaker must additionally make his hearers *want* to change dominant attitudes, or *want* to change behavior and vote, buy, join, give, or do. He must provide logical proof for his propositions and then link that proof to the highest motivational values in the listener's hierarchy.

Let us make two summary statements about speech purposes. (1) All speeches have one fundamental purpose—to gain a response. (2) Some responses are harder to gain than others, and they can be ranked on four levels (or four General Purposes of Speaking), with each successive one becoming more difficult:

1. To interest $+$
2. To inform $++$
3. To stimulate $+++$
4. To change $++++$

### Phrasing the Purpose-Sentence

You began by selecting a general subject. Then you determined your controlling purpose. Now you are ready to integrate subject and purpose in framing a single, simple purpose-sentence. It should have two distinguishing qualities. *First, it states the central idea in plain words.* It is the proposition you want to develop, amplify, and enrich with meaning. It is what you want your listeners to accept after you have presented it fully. Put it in straightaway English, striking immediately and directly at the point. Let us illustrate the process. When you first *thought* about your subject you may have been concerned about the prevalence of propagandists and "hidden persuaders" who get their ideas into print, about how many people tend to believe anything they read, and about warning people somehow not to take it all in or be taken in. But that was a circuitous path to the point and, indeed, *the* point was pretty obscure. After you have expanded and refined your thinking you should be able to write that single, simple, and direct purpose-sentence:

Learn to read skeptically.

*Second, a good purpose-sentence is distinguished by its statement in terms of the response you want from listeners.* (That's why "learn to" is in the purpose-sentence above.) By phrasing it this way you are less likely to try the impossible, more likely to limit yourself to a response you can realistically expect. For example, you can hardly expect to persuade Democrats to turn Republican, but you might hope to persuade them that bipartisanship should be stressed in making foreign policy. In effect you ask, when phrasing the purpose-sentence: "How far can I lead them in my direction?" In a single speech there will be limits, and to push beyond them may get you a backfire. Here is an example of seeking realistic response:

Though you may disagree on domestic issues, you may profit by listening to the other party's views on foreign policy.

When you get the purpose-sentence, remember that it is primarily for you. Seldom will you state it to your listeners in so many words. Certainly you will not state it didactically at the beginning of your speech. Its chief value is to help you focus your thinking and to guide your selection of materials. Like a ship's compass, it can be checked occasionally to make sure that your course is steady toward your goal.

## DIVIDE THE SPEECH INTO WELL-CHOSEN MAIN HEADS

Look at the structure of any well-organized speech and you will find that the central idea is supported, or developed, by a very few main heads or topics. A speaker does not present the central idea in one chunk, but in several easily-handled parts. Look ahead in Chapter 7 (pp. 128-136) to James Golden's speech to inform, on the idiom of political speaking since the 1920's. It is developed under four clearly distinguishable main heads. Here they are, as he spoke them (and as they are italicized in our text):

 I. First, the language which appears in a typical political address more and more represents the work of a group of collaborators who may or may not be able to produce a consistent and peculiar idiom which gives a unique stamp to the orator.
 II. An equally important trend in the style of political speaking is the present popularity of the conversational idiom.
 III. Closely related to the current emphasis on simplicity is an increased trend toward brevity and terseness.
 IV. A fourth trend in oral style—the declining effectiveness in irony and satire.

In Robert Gunderson's persuasive speech on training for an articulate democracy, reprinted in Chapter 8 (pp. 153-161), there is a similar division into four main heads, the first three analytical and the fourth one prescriptive. Look at the text and find the language he used to make these points.

I. Americans today are appalling uninformed.
II. Americans today are intellectually timid.
III. These characteristics contrast sharply with those of pioneer Americans.
IV. Teachers of speech must help train today's students for a better informed and more articulate democracy.

Had Golden or Gunderson prepared speeches twice as long, they would have had no more main heads. They simply would have added more facts, illustrations, specific instances, and other forms of support. The essential difference between short and long speeches is the amount of supporting material. Please remember this: in giving relatively short classroom speeches you will use the same speech structure as you will twenty years hence when you are called upon for a thirty-minute speech.

Is there any magic in having four main heads, as both Golden and Gunderson did? Not at all. Speakers can us *two or three main heads, occasionally four or five, but almost never more than five.* There is no magic formula in any of those numbers, either. But there are underlying reasons why in good speech after good speech the two-to-five limits are observed.

For obvious reasons there can not be *less* than two main heads in a speech. Each speech has one central idea, phrased into a purpose-sentence. Hence if main heads are to develop, elaborate, or support the purpose-sentence there must be at least two.

But why do we urge *only* two or three main heads, and almost never more than five? There are two excellent reasons: 1. A speech with too many main heads lacks a coherent thought pattern. It is a hit-or-miss arrangement. Any idea, if carefully analyzed, can be reduced to very few basic parts, usually two or three. 2. Listeners cannot remember too many main heads. If a speech has two or three, well-chosen and strongly-supported, listeners will carry them away in their heads. But seven or eight, even if well-supported, leave listeners hopelessly confused. Therefore, arrange your material into an *obvious* and *appropriate* thought pattern with few main heads.

There are five basic thought patterns for arranging main heads.

## Time Order

Marking the movement by the clock or by the calendar, you begin at a given date, period, or moment of history and move forward or backward. For example:

*The American Mind in American Literature*

I. Until early in the 19th century American literature reflected the Colo-

nial mind, or the distilled influence of American geography upon
European ideas.

II. By 1830 American frontier optimism generated an indigenous literature, crude but firmly based on a belief in liberty and the natural
goodness of man, that opened the American Romantic Movement.

III. Following the economic disillusion in the wake of the 1870 crisis
there was a period of critical appraisal of contemporary life, known
as Realism and continuing into the 20th century.

## Space Order

Any spatial pattern can serve for arranging your material. It can
be north-to-south, top-to-bottom, inside-outside, near-to-far. This pattern
serves especially the cause of simple exposition or description. See how
effectively Victor Hugo used it to describe the Battle of Waterloo, making
it nearly as clear in words as could a blackboard sketch:

*Purpose-sentence:* To form a clear idea of the Battle of Waterloo, imagine
a capital "A" laid on the ground.

I. The left stroke of the "A" is the Nivelles Road.

A. The left-hand lower point is Hougomont.

B. Rielle is there with Jerome Bonaparte.

II. The right stroke of the "A" is the Genappe Road.

A. The right-hand lower point is la Belle Alliance.

B. Napoleon is there.

III. The cross of the "A" is Mont Saint Jean; Wellington is there.

## Classification Order

According to a systematic grouping of related forms, functions, and
so on, you classify your material. Here are some possibilities.

1. *Classification according to fields of inquiry:*
   Political
   Social
   Economic
   Educational
   Religious

2. *Classification according to persons or groups involved:*
   Men and women
   Young and old
   High school graduates and college graduates
   World War II veterans and Korean War veterans
   Producers and consumers
   Northerners and Southerners

3. *Classification according to cause:*
    a.  The primary cause was . . .
    b.  Contributing causes were  . . .
    c.  The precipitating cause was . . .
4. *Miscellaneous other forms of classification:*
    Federal, state, and municipal
    Prose and poetry
    Animal, mineral, or vegetable
    Function and structure
    Earned and inherited

### Cause-and-Effect Order

When you know the result, you look backward to identify causes: "What events, factors, or circumstances caused—or caused in part—this result?" When you have identified causes, you try to determine their potency: "Which causes were primary? Contributing? Immediate?" And when you know the cause, or causes, you look forward to forecast probable results: "What will likely happen as a consequence of these events, factors, or circumstances?"

Though this kind of arrangement is often very tempting to the little bit of ex cathedra that is in all of us, two cautions should be observed.

1. *Beware of false causes.* That event or circumstance that merely *precedes* does not necessarily *cause.* Yet many persons assume the contrary: "First A happened, and then B took place, so A must have caused B." The Romans gave a label to this ancient error: *Post hoc, ergo propter hoc,* meaning "after this, therefore on account of this." Take a second look at this kind of order to be sure that you are not confusing mere accidents of time with cause-to-effect.

2. *Beware of single causes.* Few events in life result from a single cause. A complex of causes is more common, one playing on another until it is hard to disentangle or to assess them. Lack of safety features on automobiles does not *alone* cause most highway accidents, but this cause *plus* highways that are themselves unsafe, and *compounded* by careless drivers, may *in combination* account for most highway accidents.

An arrangement by causation can be cause-to-effect or effect-to-cause. The latter pattern is most common in speechmaking. It permits an initial vivid portrayal of "what happened?" and then a building of suspense over "what caused it?" Here is an example:

*Purpose-sentence:* We should understand that war causes inflation.
   I.  EFFECT: Inflation has accompanied every major war in U. S. history.
      A.  The monthly *Consumer Price Index,* compiled by the U. S. Department of Labor, has been projected back into early history. It

was revealed that during the American Revolution prices increased
at least 200 per cent.

   B. During the War of 1812, by the same measure, prices rose from
      39 to 54 (1957-1959=100).
   C. During the Civil War prices jumped from 30 to 54.
   D. During WWI prices more than doubled, from 42 to 85.
   E. During WWII and the Korean War prices almost doubled, from 60
      to 115.
II. CAUSE: The cause can be traced back to Adam Smith's law of supply
    and demand. . . .

### Problem-Solution Order

Here you first diagnose the problem and then try to find a way to
overcome it. But every doctor will testify that this process is trapped with
pitfalls. When Dr. Charles H. Mayo, of the famous medical clinic, was
asked what kind of illness was most common among his patients, he replied, "Mistaken diagnosis." The same malady plagues our analyses of
social, political, and economic ills. This two-step procedure may help
avoid faulty diagnoses:
1. What are the effects, nature, or external manifestations of this problem?
   (Sort and classify them.)
2. On the basis of this classification—what *seem* to be the causes?
The greatest help may be to remember that finding the right answers
depends above all else upon asking the right questions. And then in using
those answers to structure the right attack upon the problem.

Traditionally the steps in problem-solving, for the more complex
questions, are four in number. Here we phrase them in the usual way,
and then somewhat more vividly in the italicized versions.
1. Is there a "felt difficulty" that makes a change necessary or desirable?
   *Is the man sick?* (Actually this has been covered and you are ready for
   the next three questions.)
2. Would the change I advocate remedy the situation? *Will my medicine
   cure him?*
3. Might the change lead to new evils worse than the present ones? *Will
   my medicine make him worse?*
4. Is there another solution that would be more satisfactory? *Will any
   other medicine be more effective?*

These four steps won't, of course, convert directly into main heads.
You cannot use: I. The problem; II. The solution; III. Refuting dangers
of new and worse evils; IV. Refuting other solutions. These are only *steps
of inquiry* to help you get to the bottom of the problem and then to test
various ways of getting rid of it. Examine again the speech by Robert
Gunderson (pp. 153-161) and especially his four main heads. Note that
in effect the first three deal with the *problem* and the last one states the

*solution* (we have included some subheads under the latter to show the supporting development).

PROBLEM:
  I. Americans today are appallingly uninformed.
  II. Americans today are intellectually timid.
  III. These characteristics contrast sharply with those of pioneer Americans.
SOLUTION:
  IV. Teachers of speech must help train today's students for a better informed and more articulate democracy. Here are some possible ways of doing this.
    A. Encourage a more active role for listeners.
    B. Worry less about adjusting to and more about improving the body politic.
    C. Encourage more ideological warfare.
    D. Ensure that speakers have something to say.
    E. Insist upon a knowledge of both facts and logic.
    F. Develop greater respect for the ideas of others.

There is one rule to follow in developing speeches by this arrangement: *Beware of patent-medicine solutions.* Though men have searched for centuries, there have been no cure-all "solutions" for problems of divorce, crime, intolerance, discrimination, and war. Only quacks—medicine-men or speakers—promise sure cures. Honest men merely *keep at* the job of solving problems. Charlie Brown, a cartoon character of Charles M. Schulz, once assured Peanuts that "this world is filled with people who are anxious to function in an advisory capacity." Such persons commonly make five-minute classroom speeches that offer nothing more than patent-medicine solutions for pressing public problems.

## ARRANGE THE ENTIRE SPEECH INTO AN OUTLINE

Why have great speakers been great organizers of their materials? Because no man is skilled enough to be able, without setting down his thought pattern in plain view, to test his analysis and the order of his arrangement. Because the outline of a speech will reveal at a glance whether you have enough of the right kinds of supporting material. Yet lesser speakers still try to get by without first giving themselves the outline test. "If I were to put down the greatest weakness in most of the speeches and sermons I hear or read," concluded Bishop Gerald Kennedy in *While I'm On My Feet,* "it would be a lack of organization." Would these same speakers drive across country without a map? Do the weekly shopping without a list? Or fight a battle without a plan?

Students will find another value in outlining, and in even greater detail than some experienced speakers. For his instructor the outline is a diagnostic aid. From hearing the speech and examining the outline, the instructor can tell whether its problems derived from faulty planning, or from imperfect execution. The following are steps in composing a good outline:

1. *Prefix to the outline a clear and complete purpose-sentence.* Phrased as suggested earlier, this will pin-point your purpose and guide your selection of materials.

2. *Organize the outline into three parts: the beginning, the body, and the ending. Ordinarily these are known as Introduction, Discussion, and Conclusion, and each part should be numbered as a separate unit.* (The beginning and ending should not be confused with the thought pattern of the Discussion. Thus the numbering should start afresh with each part.)

*Introduction*

I. . . . . . . . . . . . . . . .
II. . . . . . . . . . . . . . . .

*Discussion*

I. . . . . . . . . . . . . . . .
II. . . . . . . . . . . . . . . .
III. . . . . . . . . . . . . . . .

*Conclusion*

I. . . . . . . . . . . . . . . .

3. *Use a consistent set of symbols to indicate main heads and each descending order of subheads.* The symbols used below have become almost common law through generations of consistent use. It is best to follow them.

I. Roman numerals used for main heads.
   A. Capital letters used for 1st level subheads.
      1. Arabic numerals used for 2nd level subheads.
         a. Small letters used for 3rd level subheads.
            (1) Arabic numbers in parentheses for the 4th level.
               (a) Small letters in parentheses for the 5th level.

4. *Show the logical relationship of headings also by proper indentation.*
I. Note how this symbol stands alone at the left and is instantly visible to the eye.
   A. This subhead symbol is also easily visible, standing alone and just a bit to the right of the main head.
      1. Even subheads like this stand out when the proper indentation pattern is followed.

5. *Use complete sentences only.* Though relatively few experienced

speakers use them, they may be adequately served by catch phrases; but you are *learning* and need to think through each idea and put it into exact words. Further, you want your outline to help the instructor in diagnosing your problems; and a catch-phrase outline is a poor diagnostic aid. This rule (and those that follow) is illustrated in an outline on pp. 102-107. Examine it as you read each rule.

6. *Write down each main head in a simple sentence, usually with an active verb. Beware of compound and complex sentences, circuitous sentences and dangling clauses. Preferably phrase each statement as you would speak it to the audience.* An outline is a runway for your takeoff into the speech. You don't want to have to alter sentence structure or style as you take off. (And never use the indirect "Now here I will tell them . . ." form.)

7. *Include the supporting materials in the outline.* If the outline contains only assertions—and no illustrations, factual information, comparisons, testimony, and so on—it is a skeleton, lifeless and worthless.

8. *Beware of trying to support any head by one subhead; use two or more.* An idea cannot be *divided* into *one* subhead. Just as one main head cannot support a purpose-sentence, so one subhead cannot support a mainhead. But two or more may.

9. *Include in the outline—if it seems helpful—transitions and signpost phrases.* While these are not a part of the framework of ideas, but rather signposts, they should not be numbered parts of the outline. But signposts are important, and if included here they are more likely to be used when you speak. (Insert them, without numbers, in parentheses.)

10. *Check and recheck your outline to see that it really does what you want to do in your speech:* Do the main heads as a group insure a consistent and simple thought pattern? Do the main heads support the purpose-sentence? Do the subheads at all levels develop the heads above them? *Do not think that this last admonition is too elementary for us to mention here. The hard school of experience taught us otherwise.*

We will conclude this chapter with a sample outline, illustrating the steps we have described above, and valuable in its own right for advice on how to study. This outline is on the right-hand side of each page. Though not an inherent part of the outline, we have indicated on the left-hand side of each page a *technical plot*. While the outline shows "what the speaker is saying," the technical plot shows "what the speaker is doing." It indicates where assertions appear, how well they are supported by testimony, factual information, and so on, and where humor, suspense, and general pleasantries have been usefully incorporated. The technical plot is therefore a device for helping test the outline by reflecting strengths and exposing inadequacies.

The outline following is for a six-minute speech, and contains perhaps 80 percent of the words of the final product. The main heads are stated frankly before they are developed since the speaker could assume that the listeners *wanted* to know how to study. The main supporting materials are specific instances, testimony, illustration, and restatement.

## HOW TO STUDY

*Technical plot*

*Outline*

PURPOSE-SENTENCE: Studying, thinking and remembering go hand in hand, so that the absence of one leads to the loss of all three.

### INTRODUCTION

*Getting good will by pleasantry*

I. In selecting a subject for this Monday morning's speech, I remembered that it would be the Monday after our Big Weekend.

*Getting attention and orienting the audience by direct reference to a topic of vital interest*

II. I knew that most of you wouldn't be awake yet, so I chose one that would keep *me* awake, and one that would make you wish you were awake; for final exams are just three weeks ahead, and I'm going to talk this morning on *how to study*.

*Supporting the purpose-sentence by testimony*

III. William James once said that "the art of remembering is the art of thinking," and I propose to show that studying, thinking, and remembering all go hand in hand, so that the absence of one leads to the loss of all three.

THOUGHT PATTERN:
CLASSIFICATION ORDER

### DISCUSSION

*Assertion**

I. In order to study, you must think.

*Assertion*

A. The fact that we are conscious is not proof that we are thinking.

*Hypothetical illustration*

1. We may take a train ride and at the end of the ride say to ourselves, "I've been thinking."

2. In truth, you probably have not thought for a single minute.

---

*In the technical plot usually you do not list assertions, because the purpose of a technical plot is to show the *amount and kind of supporting material being used to uphold the assertions*. They are listed here only to illustrate what assertions are as the term is used in speechmaking.

| | |
|---|---|
| *Assertion* | B. Actually you think only when you are faced with a problem. |
| *Hypothetical illustration* | 1. If your train had suddenly lurched to a stop with screaming brakes, you would have started thinking, "Is there danger?" and "How can I escape it?" because you would have faced a problem that was immediate and urgent. |
| *Restatement* | 2. But if you were faced with no problem on your train ride, you probably would not think. |
| | a. You would look at people's faces. |
| *Humor* | b. You would admire or depreciate their figure, form, and clothes. |
| *Assertion* | C. The process is the same with formal study. |
| *Specific instance* | 1. You clear your desk of *Esquire, Look,* and the letter from home—then sit down to study "How to organize a speech into concise and orderly form." |
| *Assertion* | 2. In the next half hour a parade of ideas marches through your head. |
| *Specific instance* | a. You wonder about that assignment in Math. |
| *Specific instance* | b. Your girl in Ohio gets on your mind again; "What's she up to now?" you wonder for the fifteenth time. |
| *Specific instance* | c. "What about next weekend?" you wonder. |
| *Specific instance* | d. "Those confounded exams, only three weeks away," you think. |
| *Specific instance* | 3. Also, and naturally, you talked with a couple of other people who happened by. |

| | |
|---|---|
| *Summary and climax that makes hearers wiggle uncomfortably* | 4. In short, you have not been studying at all; you have been playing mental hop-skip-and-jump. |
| *Assertion that relieves some of the discomfort* | 5. This is the *normal* way the mind and body behaves; both are restless. |
| *Explanation* | a. The human body is restless. |
| *Specific instance* | (1) I'm restless as I give this speech. |
| *Specific instance* | (2) You're restless as you listen to it. |
| *Specific instance* | (3) Even at night you turn over from 20 to 45 times while you are asleep. |
| *Explanation* | b. The human mind is quite as restless as the body. |
| *Explanation* | (1) Attention comes in "spurts" and we can think of nothing longer than a few seconds at a time. |
| *Explanation* | (2) What we call prolonged attention is simply repeated spurts of attention on the same subject. |
| *Testimony* | (3) William James once said that the only difference between his mind and any poor mind was that he could keep his spurts of attention from getting off the subject. |
| *Transition* | (So when we study, our problem is to keep our repeated spurts of attention right on the subject, and to do this we must narrow our thoughts to the point where only the problem, or point in question, is in view.) |
| *Assertion* | II. First, we should attend to the physical aspect of study. |
| *Assertion of the first principle* | A. Clean up your study area of all probable sources of interruptions. |

| | |
|---|---|
| *Analysis of A, step one* | 1. Have a definite place to study, and at that place do nothing else but study. |
| *Specific instance* | a. Don't write letters there. |
| *Specific instance* | b. Don't play cards there. |
| *Specific instance* | c. Do nothing there but study. |
| *Analysis of A, step two* | 2. Avoid disturbances. |
| *Specific instance* | a. Pictures on your desk or near-by wall can be a distraction. |
| *Specific instance* | b. A turned-on radio is certain to distract you; that popular notion that you can study while listening to a radio is wishful thinking. |
| *Analysis of A, step three* | 3. Above all, don't get too comfortable. |
| *Restatement* | a. Over-comfort is good for sleeping, but not studying. |
| *Restatement* | b. A good idea is to lean forward and put your elbows on the desk. |
| *Assertion of the second principle* | B. Follow a definite study program. |
| *Analysis of B, step one* | 1. Review the previous lesson first. |
| *Restatement* | a. This will put you in the mood to study. |
| *Restatement* | b. It will also give you something to tack your new lesson to. |
| *Analysis of B, step two* | 2. Look at the *whole* lesson before you begin. |
| *Explanation* | a. You can then plan your method of learning. |
| *Explanation* | b. The important points will thus come easier. |
| *Analysis of B, step three* | 3. Underlining the book is a good idea, but a better one is to *write* in your own words on the margin. |

*Analysis of B, step four*

4. Finally, recitation is a great help to learning.

*Restatement*

a. Recite it to yourself a few times.

*Restatement*

b. The more times an idea enters your head, the better the retention.

*Assertion*

III. Next, we should observe the mental aspect of study.

*Analysis of III, step one*

A. Study with the *intent* to remember, not just to pass an examination.

*Figures*

1. Extensive experiments show that it is possible to remember from 20 percent more to 400 percent more simply because of the intent.

*Factual information*

2. These experiments showed that those who studied to pass an exam, forgot when the exam was over; those who studied to remember kept on remembering when the exam was over.

*Analysis of III, step two*

B. Immediately apply to life what you study.

*Illustration*

1. Harry Overstreet gives a significant example of this; he asked a philosophy student studying Spinoza to go to Coney Island and see what philosophy he could find there.

a. The student stared in astonishment.

b. Respectable young Ph.D. candidates did not do that sort of thing; they got philosophy out of books.

2. This man had not learned to apply his knowledge to life.

*Analysis of III, step three*

C. Try to develop and maintain your interest in the subject.

| | |
|---|---|
| *Restatement* | 1. When you tire of one subject, switch to the study of another. |
| *Restatement* | 2. If you have no interest in a subject, you will be less likely to remember it. |
| *Analysis of III, step four* | D. Find a good reason for studying a subject. |
| *Restatement* | 1. A good reason supplies motivation for remembering it. |
| *Illustration* | 2. Everybody knows the story of the boy who was dull in physics until he learned one day that physics explained what made a baseball curve; and this boy, who wanted to be a pitcher, had no trouble thereafter remembering physics. |

CONCLUSION

| | |
|---|---|
| *Summary* | I. If you get nothing else from this speech, get these three points: 1) Clear your study area, 2) retain your interest in the subject, 3) apply your knowledge to life. |
| *Humor* | II. Follow these rules, my lords and ladies, and I'll guarantee that you'll know and understand your freshman English by the time you leave graduate school! |

Edgar Dale tells about asking a professor what he found most difficult to teach. He replied, "I have no difficulty in teaching anything in my course, but my students do have difficulty in learning it." Let us hope that the professor had a twinkle in his eye as he said that. But let us note, anyway, that he provided us with a good summing-up statement for a chapter on organizing the speech. Most recent psychological analyses of the learning process (and being informed or being persuaded *is* a form of learning) emphasize the necessity for couching what is to be taught in simple and easily perceived "structures." The "structure" of a speech, whether a classroom lecture, a political oration, or a Sunday sermon, depends upon the speaker knowing his definite purpose, dividing his topic into a clear pattern of main heads with adequate support, and organizing the whole into an orderly outline.

## SUPPLEMENTARY READINGS

Aristotle, *Rhetoric,* trans. by Lane Cooper. New York: Appleton-Century-Crofts, 1932. Treatment of arrangement, pp. 220-241.

Arnold, Carroll C., Ehninger, Douglas, and Gerber, John C., eds., *The Speaker's Resource Book: An Anthology, Handbook, and Glossary,* 2nd ed. Chicago: Scott, Foresman, 1966. Critical analyses of speeches by Thomas Huxley, Jonathan Smith, and Douglas MacArthur, pp. 264-284.

Braden, Waldo W., and Gehring, Mary Louise, *Speech Practices: A Resource Book for the Student of Public Speaking.* New York: Harper & Row, 1958. "How Speakers Organize Their Speeches," pp. 27-53, and "Types of Speeches," pp. 120-148.

Clevenger, Theodore, Jr., *Audience Analysis.* Indianapolis: Bobbs-Merrill, 1966. An original and useful treatment, with an especially helpful concept of "images in the auditor."

Mills, Glen E., *Message Preparation: Analysis and Structure.* Indianapolis: Bobbs-Merrill, 1966. A substantial presentation of the steps, from subject selection, through analysis, investigation, and outlining.

## EXERCISES

1. Use the following steps in outlining a magazine article:
a. First, determine the central idea, then phrase it into a purpose-sentence.
b. Next, study the thought movement and development until the main divisions become clear; then write these out as main heads.
c. Finally, in subhead form set down the supporting material.

2. Go to hear a speaker and make a detailed key-word outline of the speech while he is giving it. Then go home and write out the full outline, together with a critical evaluation:
a. Did the speech have a definite purpose? If so, was it stated in plain words, or only implied? Where in the speech was this done?
b. Did the speech have definite main heads? If so, were they stated clearly? Were they arranged in a clear thought pattern?
c. Was there enough supporting material? Was it the right kind of material?
d. If *you* were giving this speech how would you change the outline?

3. For one speech round make a key-word outline of each speech as it is being delivered, and later fill out enough details so you can remember the content. At the end of the round, submit a list of the two best-outlined and the two worst-outlined speeches. Give your reasons.

4. Take an outline of one of your earlier speeches. Check it against the 10 specifications of a good outline set forth in this chapter, revise it, and hand it in.

5. Outline the class lecture of one of your instructors. A good class lecture ought to move a little more slowly than a regular public speech, and you should be able to make a full outline as the lecture proceeds.

6. Use the following procedure in planning your next speech:

a. While still in preliminary form, check the outline against the 10 specifications set forth in this chapter. Revise the outline, but do not make a full revised copy.

b. Make a technical plot, and use it to test each part of the outline. Revise the outline again if necessary.

c. Make a final copy of both the revised outline and the technical plot. Use the outline for rehearsing the final extempore speech.

# 7

# Making Ideas Clear

Few public men have had a greater awareness of the power of words than John F. Kennedy. In conferring honorary American citizenship upon an acknowledged word-master, Kennedy said of Winston Churchill: "In the dark days and darker nights when Britain stood alone —and most men save Englishmen despaired of England's life, *he mobilized the English language and sent it into battle*. The incandescent quality of his words illuminated the courage of his countrymen."

Kennedy was just as sensitive to language in his own speaking. On one occasion when a Department of State team drafted a presidential message on a proposed National Academy of Foreign Affairs, Kennedy rejected it in this memorandum:

This is only the latest and worst of a long number of drafts sent here for Presidential signature. My own old-fashioned belief is that every Presidential message should be a model of grace, lucidity and taste in expression. At the very least, each message should be (a) *in English,* (b) *clear and trenchant in its style,* (c) *logical in its structure* and (d) *devoid of gobbledygook.* The State Department draft on the academy failed each one of these tests (including, in my view, the first).[1]

The quality of speechmaking in public life and in your classroom would be raised inestimably by adherence to the standards Kennedy set out. But it is hard work. It requires a sense of mission about the importance of what you have to say, and a sense of urgency about saying it just right. Pierre Salinger, Kennedy's friend and press secretary, watched at close range while Kennedy prepared his inaugural address. He spent weeks working on it by himself, he sought advice and criticism from his associates, and wrote the final draft three days before its delivery. Yet Salinger saw Kennedy at breakfast on Inauguration Day, reading and re-reading the speech, looking for possible improvements even at that late moment![2]

[1]Arthur M. Schlesinger, Jr., *A Thousand Days: John F. Kennedy in the White House* (Boston, 1965), p. 419.

[2]Pierre Salinger, *With Kennedy* (New York, 1966), pp. 108-109.

110

Whether you make presidential addresses, build houses, design computers, run a store, or study in college, your plans must first be created mentally, in words. Your ideas remain nebulous until they are put in words, whether you talk about modern poetry, ancient history, or the cost of living. Indeed, your stock of usable words limits your range of thoughts. Yet these words have no value in themselves. They are only symbols for thoughts, and for things. Like the paper and ink in a $100 bill, words have no intrinsic worth. But by good understanding and skillful techniques they can both become currency of great value.

# WORDS

First we shall look at words, then at their use in sentences. Kennedy called for a "clear and trenchant style." It is rooted in concrete words, simple words, and colorful words.

## Concrete Words

Second-rate speakers often get that way by ignoring the fact that abstract and fuzzy words signify to listeners abstract and fuzzy ideas. Listeners respond best to speakers who *create word pictures* of what they see, hear, and think. "Logicians may reason about abstractions," said Macaulay, "but the great masses of men must have images." Political speakers often begin with abstractions, like "The Great Society." The best ones try to evoke images by translating the abstract into the concrete, as Lyndon B. Johnson did at Madison Square Garden, May 28, 1964:

I ask you to march with me along the road to the future—the road that leads to the Great Society, where no child will go unfed and no youngster will go unschooled; where every child has a good teacher and every teacher has good pay, and both have good classrooms; where every human being has dignity and every worker has a job; where education is blind to color and unemployment is unaware of race; where decency prevails and courage abounds.

Even when they are aware of the virtues of being specific, some speakers are too lazy to look for the *one word* that is just right. They will remain second-raters, and they deserve to. Imagine guiding a group of strangers around your campus during commencement week. "That's our newest *building*, there on the corner," says the lazy student. But the precise student—and the best guide—knows that a building is not just a building. It's what we *do* in buildings that differentiates them, and there are concrete words to create images of each thing we do. We perform experiments in a *laboratory*, attend classes in a *lecture hall*, see plays in a *theatre*, and go to convocations in an *auditorium*. We live in a *dormitory*, eat in the *cafeteria,* work out in the *gymnasium,* read books in the *library,* watch basketball in the *field house,* and worship in the *chapel.* And so on. To be instantly intelligible our campus guide needs one of these concrete words. If he doesn't take the time to be concrete, he doesn't really want to communicate.

## Simple Words

Here is the second rule about words: *If you would be understood, talk in terms that will be meaningful to your listeners, not just to you.* Those who make special studies of topics naturally acquire specialized vocabularies pertaining to those topics. But unless they deliberately emulate the squid, they will not obscure their thoughts with murky jargon and technical terms when talking with laymen. Effective speakers of all kinds remember that they are talking to listeners and talk in listener terms. Huey Long was a master politician, and here is one of the reasons: "I try to talk to the people just exactly as I feel and in language they can understand." Supreme Court Justice Hugo Black, noted for brief and simple decisions, put it this way: "My opinions must be so clear that a man standing halfway between the educational standards of a Clay County farmer and the *Harvard Law Review* will be able to understand them." And Edward R. Murrow used to tell his CBS reporters to imagine that they were talking to a professor at dinner while the maid's boy friend, a truck driver, was listening from the kitchen: "Describe things in terms that make sense to the driver without insulting the professor's intelligence."

Big ideas don't necessarily come in big words. Erudition is not measured in syllables. Abraham Lincoln, of whom it was said he only cared how his words would fit the ears of his countrymen and "didn't care a cornhusk for the literary critics," spoke 266 words at Gettysburg: 190 were of one syllable, 56 had two, and only 20 had more than two.

If you would talk sense to your audience "speak plain and to the purpose," using simple words instead of long ones, single words instead of phrases. *Ask,* don't "make application for" an increase in *pay,* not "remuneration." *Learn,* instead of "becoming privy to," and *teach* instead of "offering instruction." Is "give voice to" something more or less than *speak?* While your listener is deciding that matter, you've gone on to the next sentence, and he may never catch up. One speaker ventured that a certain public servant "leaves something to be desired, ethics-wise." The laws of slander aside, for the moment, was the official or was he not *dishonest?* And was the speaker clear and simple, "language-wise"?

## Colorful Words

Words not only *mean,* they *suggest.* "A dead bird" means the same as "Thanksgiving turkey." And "Salisbury steak" suggests more than the "hamburger" that it is. Used car dealers are avoiding "secondhand" cars but they are selling "other owner" ones. They've taken a lesson from those who used to be "junk dealers" or run "secondhand furniture" stores, and who now advertise "antiques." Even when two terms refer to the same thing, one often has a more pleasant "feeling tone." The "mood music" record makers know the score. They sell "Music for a Sentimental Mood," "Music for Meditating," and "Music for Washing Dishes By."

We are not encouraging speakers to mislead or dissemble. Honesty in word choice is no different than honesty in weighing meat. But there is honest persuasiveness in saying "She is *slender*" rather than "She is *skinny*." Just remember the woman who stepped off the scales, scrutinized the height/weight chart, and announced that "I'm six inches underheight for my weight!"

Colorful words, because they stir up feelings as well as meanings, are more likely to linger in men's minds and move them to action. Senator Margaret Chase Smith once said about her public speaking that "I try to use the shortest and simplest words."[3] She also believes in colorful words, as this excerpt from a December, 1964, speech demonstrates:

Many years ago the word square was one of the most honored words in our vocabulary. The square deal was an honest deal. A square meal was a full and good meal. It was the square shooter rather than the sharpshooter who was admired. What is a square today? He's the fellow who never learned to get away with it, who gets choked up when the flag unfurls. There has been too much glorification of the angle players, the corner cutters, and the goof-offs. One of America's greatest needs is for more people who are square.

## SENTENCES

Out of words we fashion sentences. Some will be long, more should be short, but the experienced speaker most of all avoids falling into a pattern. Learning how to grapple with an English oral sentence is not easy, and Churchill, Stevenson, and the very few others in our time who succeeded magnificently, did so only after many years of practice. The beginning speaker cannot undertake the whole task in one semester, so let us concentrate on two basic techniques.

### Talk in the Active Voice, Not the Passive

Remember, to begin with, that the verb is a motor, propelling the whole sentence. If your ideas are to move, the verb must be worked hard. Here are three suggestions that should help you.

[3]In a letter to Sarah Pyle Bratton, March 19, 1964, and quoted with Senator Smith's permission.

1. *Use verbs, not noun substitutes.* The noun-oriented speaker has trouble facing a live verb. So he couples the inert noun "thought" with the inactive verb "is," and comes out with "It *is* my *thought* that. . . ." But the true *verb*alist flatly says "I think," and gets extra power. Examine these three statements of the same idea and see how the addition of one and then of two live verbs adds strength:

It is to be considered how the lilies grow.
*Consider* the growth of the lilies.
*Consider* the lilies, how they *grow.*

2. *Prefer active to passive verbs.* Passive verbs have a place, and are sometimes indispensable. But for every day use stick to the active verbs. This was a hallmark of the style of Lincoln and Churchill, and of Shakespeare and Shaw—who also composed for oral presentation. Certainly you can comprehend "Insufficient corporal punishment *results* in the spoiling of the child," but generations were raised on the more active "*Spare* the rod and *spoil* the child." Have you ever realized that "Precipitous action *entails the negation* of economy"? Or do you just know that "Haste makes waste"?

3. *Scrutinize every use of the verb "to be."* Backward syntax is poor in writing, worse in speaking. The "It is . . . that . . ." construction is a chief offender. The idea expressed by "is" lies in the sentence without movement. For example, "*It is* with pleasure *that* I present . . ." when it could be recast as "I *present* with pleasure. . . ." Or, "*It is* my belief that . . ." when "I *believe* . . ." is direct and vigorous. Check over adages; they are usually compactly expressed. You will never find "The advantage of timely stitching *is* ninefold," but how about "A stitch in time *saves* nine"?

## Strip Off Empty Words

Two kinds of empty words actually interfere with communication, and should be stripped from your sentences with regularity.

1. *Adjectives and adverbs.* There are two kinds of modifiers. First, there are *defining modifiers: hot* stove, *old* man, *new* book. We need these; they say something essential.

Second, there are *commenting modifiers: very* necessary, *most* unique, *obviously* harmful. In each of these cases—and most of the time—these modifiers clutter up the meaning. For example, if a thing is "necessary" can it be more or less so? If less, then perhaps the word is "desirable," anyway. Take "unique" to your dictionary and check it out; you will find that things are or are not unique, but not in varying degrees. As for "obviously," surely it must be obvious or we wouldn't be able to judge whether it is harmful. Why are these clutter words so commonly used? A good guess is that when a speaker has little to say, he at least tries to say it emphatically, and so "a good idea" becomes "a *very* good idea." If only adjectives were substitutes for ideas! Since they are not, challenge every adjective, and every adverb, that is used only for emphasis.

2. *Compound prepositions and conjunctions.* Verbs, nouns, and defining adjectives are full of meaning. But other words, and especially prepositions and conjunctions, may be only so much padding, unnecessary and hiding the full words from view. These are fit subjects for amputation. Train yourself to spot them. Here are some traditional offenders and the single words for which they are substituted:

*so*—with the result that
*for*—for the purpose of
*if*—in the event that
*of*—in the process of
*about*—with regard to
*to*—with a view to

## SUPPORTING MATERIALS

Aristotle had a way of putting things simply. "A speech has two parts," he said. "Necessarily, you state your case, and you prove it." So far in this book we have been concerned primarily with the statement of ideas, though we discussed their proof in a preliminary way (pp. 46-53). We are now ready to consider in detail the types of materials that can be used in supporting ideas.

### Supporting Ideas by Definition and Explanation

Talleyrand once remarked that language was invented to conceal the thoughts of man. It was no wonder that his frequent antagonist, Napoleon, was so sensitive to the need for clarity. To his secretaries Napoleon gave three instructions about relaying his messages: "(1) Be clear. (2) Be clear! (3) Be *Clear!*" Speakers should be under the same compulsion: *critical terms in any speech must be defined for clarity and for understanding.* There are two types of terms that especially require defining.

First are technical words, complex words, or strange words, all of the ones that listeners won't know. With increasing specialization in both theoretical and applied disciplines the output of such words races ahead of even the dictionary. These are a few terms, for example, recently used by students in classroom speeches: *emphysema* (medicine), *paradigm* (statistics), *Common Market* (international trade), *peer group* (sociology), *neo-orthodoxy* (religion), *anticipatory set* (psychology). If you must use such terms, restate them in simpler language, define them, and illustrate what you mean.

Second are familiar words that we frequently and loosely employ, but which have different meanings for different people. For example, what do *you* mean when you speak of *civil liberties, Americanism, democracy,* or *Castroism?* What meaning do *you* attach to these judgment words: *equal rights, security, antisocial,* or *honesty?* For many people these terms have emotional associations but no definable meanings. This does not mean that speakers cannot use them; indeed, often they must. But it means that by definition and explanation speakers should make clear to listeners how they are being used.

Suppose that you will use the term "democracy" in your next speech. How would you define it? To mean the same as "republic"? Can communism exist in a "democracy"? In a speech on "Who Besides the Russians?" Henry M. Wriston, former president of Brown University, defined the term by authority, comparison, classification, negation, and testimony:

... many have doubts that there is such a thing as democracy; at least they would agree with the cynical comment of George Bernard Shaw, "Democracy may be defined as a word that all public persons use and none of them understands."

Admittedly it is difficult to define. We could say of democracy what Lincoln said of liberty: "The world has never had a good definition . . . and the American people, just now, are much in want of one." The word has been utterly prostituted by the Communists at one extreme—and many ultra-conservatives, at the other end of the spectrum, tend to feel that despair expressed by Thomas Carlyle who said, "Democracy is, by the nature of it, a self-cancelling business; and it gives in the long run a net result of zero."

The difficulty arises from the fact that democracy is more than a political idea, an economic order, or a social system—it is vastly more fundamental than any of these things. Democracy is not a form of government. It exists within many forms—wherever, in fact, the consensus of mature public opinion governs public action. . . . Democracy must not be confused with ballots or any other procedural device. Instead, it is a spirit which animates political, social, and economic institutions. And the essence of that spirit is a profound respect for human dignity. . . .

Quite a different approach to definition was demonstrated by the speaker who said "Pragmatism is just a fancy word to use instead of the old crackerbox credo, 'the proof of the pudding is in the eating.'" Different still was the student who asked "What is time?" and described it by saying that "Time is so short that before you can define it the present becomes past."

## Supporting Ideas with Factual Information

Owen D. Young once observed that "facts are our scarcest raw material." It is no denigration to say that this is especially apparent in student speeches. Young people can seldom speak with firsthand authority. They need all of the power that factual information can provide.

What do we mean by a *fact?* First, we do *not* mean an opinion, a prejudice, or even a value judgment. Second, we *do* mean a statement that accurately reports something that has actually happened. We mean a statement that would be the same coming from any competent observer. It cannot be classified as positive or negative, Gaullist or Marxian, Catholic or Protestant. A *fact* remains constant, regardless of the politics, religion, or profession of the reporter. This same lack of bias is seldom found in the "selection" of facts from among those available for inclusion in a given speech. A speaker can hardly be expected to diminish his own cause, though he can be expected to interpret fairly the facts that seem to him honestly to represent his cause, and he can be expected to reveal what his true cause is.

To see an impressive massing of facts, examine the development of the first main head (pp. 128-130) in James L. Golden's speech at the end of this chapter. By our count it includes twenty-six statements of facts, ranging from the opening assertion that "Since the days of Washington, American political leaders have often sought the aid of others to assist them in speech construction" to the concluding statement that a congressman's success may depend upon his facility in finding "his way through the speeches that have been ghosted for him." Some of these statements represent Professor Golden's own observations, some are taken from the testimony of others—both lay and expert witnesses—some are revealed in an analysis of speech manuscripts, and some are summaries of an historical review.

*Figures* are an effective and special form of factual information, often helping to make generalizations more specific. You can report that "unemployment is limited today almost exclusively to the unemployables," but without some comparison of a specific current figure with the same one for a year ago, the statement may not make its greatest possible impact.

*Statistics* are really numerically expressed reports of many observed facts, presented as a method for judging phenomena collectively. Thus they usually include large quantities of data and more graphically than could otherwise be done.

In an all-networks broadcast on June 11, 1963, John F. Kennedy made what was undoubtedly one of the most effective uses of statistical evidence ever heard in a presidential address to the nation. Every American, he had just said, "ought to have the right to be treated as he would wish to be treated, as one would wish his children to be treated. But this is not the case."

The Negro baby born in America today, regardless of the section or state in which he is born, has about one-half as much chance of completing high school as a white baby, born in the same place, on the same day; one-third as much chance of completing college; one-third as much chance of becoming a professional man; twice as much chance of becoming unemployed; about one-seventh as much chance of earning $10,000 a year; a life expectancy which is seven years shorter and the prospects of earning only half as much.

### Supporting Ideas with Illustrations

Surely the story must be the oldest rhetorical device. Aesop's fables and the parables of Jesus both came originally from our oral tradition, each developed to *illustrate* a moral principle or ethical practice. Far better than didactic assertion or complicated induction is the illustration, "absolutely the only means," said Henry Ward Beecher in his *Lectures on Preaching*, "by which a large part of your audience will be able to understand at all the abstruse processes of reasoning."

Abraham Lincoln had not the advantage of hearing such formal advice, but in the laboratory of experience, after years of groping, he learned to make ideas *clear* through illustrations and how to make them *relevant* through analogies. "They say I tell a great many stories," Lincoln once observed. "I reckon I do, but I have found in the course of a long experience that common people—common people—take them as they run, are more easily influenced and informed by illustrations than in any other way, and as to what the hypercritical few may think, I don't care." That the common people have not changed much has been a discovery in our times of two superb story tellers, Alben W. Barkley and Adlai E. Stevenson. Much of their effectiveness derived from their ability to use an illustration or a witty anecdote to cast light into the dark corners of argument.

The best illustrations are short and simple, structured to move from "once upon a time" to the climax as directly as possible. Sometimes the point to be illustrated is stated first. More often, as was Lincoln's practice, both the point and the application came at the end, and then with a snap.

It may be helpful to observe that illustrations can be *factual* or *invented*. Speakers should be cautioned, however, not to confuse the two, or to mislead an audience into accepting fiction for fact. For two samples of allegedly *factual* illustrations, see the famous Roosevelt "my little dog, Fala" story from his Teamster's Union speech, and the Nixon "Tricia's dog, Checkers" story from his most famous television address. Both are included in James Golden's speech in this chapter (on p. 131).

The *invented* illustration usually takes a hypothetical form: "Let's see what would happen *if. . . .*" A classic example was Benjamin Franklin's method of opposing the notion that only men who owned property should be entitled to vote: "To require property of voters leads us up to this dilemma: I own a jackass, I can vote. The jackass dies, I cannot vote. Therefore, the vote represents not me but the jackass."

### Supporting Ideas with Specific Instances

A specific instance is a condensed illustration. It states the fact, names the person, date, place, or event, but does not develop it by details. It is not a trail, but a footprint in the wilderness. Usually a single instance is not used alone, but a battery of four or five, or even a dozen, are developed for a cumulative effect. Here are four, supporting an opening assertion, as used by Robert G. Gunderson in a speech included in Chapter 8 (on p. 154):

If citizens know little about current affairs, they know even less about the history of their country. In a widely heralded *New York Times* survey of 7,000 students in thirty-six colleges during World War II—

Eighty-four per cent were unable to cite two of the many contributions made by Thomas Jefferson.

Twenty-five "scholars" . . . managed to get through college with the erroneous idea that George Washington was president during the Civil War.

Only two in a hundred could identify Alexander Stephens.

A third of them thought Alexander Hamilton distinguished himself as president; some—and these were college folks, remember—thought he was famous because of his watches.

A speaker may lead off with a battery of specific instances and then follow up with some other form of support, such as an illustration or comparison. Or he may begin with some other form of support, and then use a battery of specific instances to reinforce it. This was what the Rev. Martin Luther King, Jr. did in accepting the Nobel Peace Prize on December 10, 1964: first, a description and an illustration, then a transition and five specific instances, and a conclusion phrased as a figurative comparison.

The deep rumbling of discontent that we hear today is the thunder of disinherited masses rising from dungeons of oppression to the bright hills of freedom, in one majestic chorus the rising masses singing, in the words of our freedom song, "Ain't Gonna Let Nobody Turn Us Around." All over the world, like a fever, the freedom movement is spreading in the widest liberation in history.

Something within has reminded the Negro of his birthright of freedom, and something without has reminded him that it can be gained. Consciously or unconsciously, he has been caught up by the Zeitgeist, and with his black brothers of Africa and his brown and yellow brothers in Asia, South America and the Caribbean, the United States Negro is moving with a sense of great urgency toward the promised land of racial justice. Fortunately, some significant strides have been made in the struggle to end the long night of racial injustice.

We have seen the magnificent drama of independence unfold in Asia and Africa.

In the United States we have witnessed the gradual demise of the system of racial segregation.

The Supreme Court's decision of 1954 outlawing segregation in the public schools gave a legal and constitutional deathblow to the whole doctrine of separate but equal.

Then came that glowing day a few months ago when a strong civil rights bill became the law of our land.

Another indication that progress is being made was found in the recent presidential election in the United States. The American people revealed great maturity by overwhelmingly rejecting a presidential candidate who had become identified with extremism, racism, and retrogression.

The problem is far from solved. We still have a long, long way to go before the dream of freedom is a reality for the Negro in the United States. To put it figuratively in Biblical language, we have left the dusty soils of Egypt and crossed a Red Sea whose waters had for years been hardened by a long and piercing winter of massive resistance. But before we reach the majestic shores of the promised land, there is a frustrating and bewildering wilderness ahead. . . .

## Supporting Ideas with Comparison and Contrast

*Comparison* measures similarities, connecting the known with the unknown, the more familiar with the less familiar. *Contrast* measures opposites, improving our vision of one thing by looking at the converse. Both are methods of making ideas more clear, more vivid, or more interesting.

Sometimes they are brief and pointed, like these three taken from student speeches:

You may not be able to make all nations good, but a strong international organization can make them behave.

A citizen who fails to use his vote is like a combat soldier who fails to use his gun. He risks not only his own safety but the lives of his fellow men.

General Stillwell was the "G.I.'s" general, soft spoken, and kind to all. General Patton was the "spit and polish" general, demanding and getting the utmost in discipline and obedience.

At other times the development is longer, more detailed. In the quotation from Dr. King above was such a figurative comparison. Here is a much longer comparison *and* contrast, developed to describe Tallulah Bankhead by John Mason Brown, America's best known popular lecturer on the lively arts:

No one on our stage is quite like Miss Bankhead. . . .

She is of a species, if not a race apart. . . . Miss Bankhead's personality is all fire. She smoulders and erupts, where others smile and ogle. There is as much heat in her laughter as there is in her frowns. She is a furnace no less than a woman. As I once pointed out, in her presence we understand why theaters need asbestos curtains.

She is a patrician and a lion-tamer; a tragedian and a comedian; a Polly Peachum on speaking terms with fate and a Medusa who laughs. . . . Her face can at one moment be almost Cordelia-soft; at the next, harder than Goneril's. Its volatility is endless. It can bubble with vivacity, and freeze with hate. . . .

Miss Bankhead's voice is something that in its range outdistances the express elevators at the Empire State. She can make bassos look to their laurels, and sopranos mind their high C's. She can cajole or mock, entice or terrify, grind nails on her tonsils, or outroar Leo. Her laugh is so volcanic a force that, if she released it on the streets of Herculaneum, startled citizens would not unnaturally take to their heels. . . .

The truth is Miss Bankhead is a show in herself—and something of a side-show, too. She has enough temperament to share with whole stagefuls of more tepid performers; enough energy to permit Niagara to take a well-earned rest. . . . Beyond any question she is one of the few genuine virtuosi our theater boasts.

## Supporting Ideas with Testimony

Listeners may not reject your unsupported word, but they usually appreciate confirmation of it by acknowledged experts. You may know very well that the cost-of-living has risen two percent in the last month (because *you* got it on good authority), but your statement will carry more weight if you cite the Secretary of Labor as your authority. Student speakers especially need the supporting testimony of others. Few of them have, after all, had the same experience in judging art works as the Director of the National Gallery, know as much at first hand about economic problems on the reservations as the Commissioner on Indian Affairs, or have read as widely in physics journals as the chairman of your college department.

Even experienced speakers often support their own ideas with testimony. Notice how Professor Golden (on p. 134) quotes historian Arthur M. Schlesinger, Jr., on the long view of political debating, and how Professor Gunderson (pp. 153-154) cites George Gallup on matters of public opinion.

Testimony is used largely for proof. But it is also used for vividness. There are times when the statements of others are so lucid and memorable that you can reinforce *your* arguments simply by quoting *them*. Among these sources for testimony are great men, great literature, or great bits of folklore. Winston Churchill was especially fond of quoting the English poets to support his causes. Lyndon B. Johnson has been referred to as the "Bible-quotingest President since Lincoln." Here are a few examples of vivid phrasemaking. Can you do better than these quotations?

Whether there will be another war is known only to God and Drew Pearson.

BISHOP FULTON J. SHEEN

A church is a hospital for sinners, not a museum for saints.

ABIGAIL VAN BUREN

An American university is an agglomeration of entities connected only by a common plumbing system. A university faculty is a group of independent entrepreneurs held together by a common grievance over parking.

CLARK KERR

## Supporting Ideas with Restatement and Repetition

Though listeners may think they are "paying attention every minute," experimental evidence reveals that they actually listen in spurts, perhaps no more than thirty seconds at a time. Key ideas, or key words and phrases, may therefore be missed. To assure recall by everyone, concerned speakers reinforce the initial statement of key concepts by restatement and repetition. It appears that *after* three or four such efforts retention is not appreciably increased. Here is an example of *restatement* (same idea, different words), in "The American Scholar," a speech given by Ralph Waldo Emerson at Harvard in 1837:

We will walk on our own feet; we will work with our own hands; we will speak our own minds. The study of letters shall be no longer a name for pity, for doubt, and for sensual indulgence. . . . A nation of men will for the first time exist, because each believes himself inspired by the Divine Soul which inspires all men.

Count the restatements of his basic idea. He uses no illustrations, comparisons, or specific instances. He simply says the same thing five times, using different words. If the idea is such that an audience is unlikely to grasp it the first time, even though attending, restatement gives listeners time to mull it over. When it becomes clear it may also be acceptable.

The following five sentences undoubtedly constitute the best known example of *repetition* (same idea, same words) in the modern English tongue. They were spoken by Winston Churchill as he rallied his countrymen after the tragedy at Dunkerque.

We shall defend our island, whatever the cost may be. *We shall fight* on the beaches. *We shall fight* on the landing grounds. *We shall fight* in the fields and in the streets, and *we shall fight* in the hills. We shall never surrender.

Four times the Prime Minister repeated his defiant phrase, driving home the idea, reinforcing it in memory, and ensuring its viability. Shakespeare had long since lent his support to the notion that repetition is persuasive: nine times in a short speech he has Marc Antony ironically refer to Caesar's murderers as "honorable men." At length the citizens "hear" the intended contrary meaning, and they race to "burn the house of Brutus."

## Supporting Ideas with Description

Description is a recreation in words of places, things, and people for the listener's personal inspection. He can learn how a thing looks, feels, tastes, smells, or how it acts. For two brief examples of this kind of supporting material see James Golden's description of Gerald L. K. Smith's use of vilification in speaking for "Share the Wealth" (p. 134), and Robert Gunderson's description of Davy Crockett as "a refreshing contrast" to the contemporary "beat" generation (pp. 156-157).

Here is a somewhat longer example, relying heavily upon dialogue, and creating a sharp mental image of each participant. The speaker was Dr. John A. Schindler, a physician in Monroe, Wisconsin, and one of the first to be concerned with psychosomatic illnesses.

As regards the layer of c.d.t. [*cares, difficulties,* and *troubles*] that people have in their lives, there are three divisions. There is the first division. . . . Those are the people who are habitually crabby. They get up in the morning grumpy; they're mean all day; they don't crack a joke; they don't have a smile; and they go to bed the same way. I have a friend who illustrates that group. He has a farm, a beautiful farm, and a couple years ago in our country we had a wonderful crop of oats. I drove past his farm one week early in July and I saw this field of oats and I thought to myself, "This ought to make Sam happy." Now, I had inquired among his relatives and friends as to whether they had ever heard Sam say a happy, pleasant word. None of them ever had, excepting his wife, who thought that he had the first year they were married, but that was so long ago that she wasn't sure. So I drove into Sam's yard and saw Sam, and I said, "Sam, that's a wonderful field of oats," and Sam came back with this, "Yes, but the wind will blow it down before I get it cut." But I watched his field. He got it out all right, he got it threshed, and I know he got a good price for it—'twas the year before last. Well, I saw him one day and I thought, "Now I've got Sam where he just can't get out of this!" So I said, "Sam, how did the oats turn out?" And he said, "Oh, it was a good crop, and I guess the price was all right, but you know a crop of oats like that sure takes a lot out of the soil." Some time later in October—it was a beautiful October—on a nice, warm afternoon I saw him on the street and I said, "Sam, it's a wonderful day, isn't it?" I said it real enthusiastically, to try to make it contagious. But not Sam, he didn't catch. He just said, "Yes, but when we get it we'll get it hard."

Now, people like Sam invariably get a psychosomatic illness before they get to be a hundred. Usually it's in the late 50's or the 60's or the 70's, and when they get it they get it hard.

Dr. Schindler reflects four practices that make description effective. 1. He had a specific purpose, describing one type of psychosomatic illness. 2. He kept the description relatively brief, and sustained interest by the use of dialogue. 3. He omitted most of the cluttering adjectives that less skillful speakers enjoy, and let the nouns and verbs carry the load. 4. He followed a systematic plan, from start to finish.

## Supporting Ideas with Narration

The power of narration is great, and experienced speakers use it freely. Students often neglect it, partly because they fail to recognize its power. They also feel that in telling who did what, where, when, and how, and for what reason, they are not really grappling with an argument. They could not be more wrong. The narrative forms, such as extended illustration, story, fable, historical incident, and anecdote, make moving pictures in words. They create suspense, arouse laughter, and depict tragedy, in concrete, interesting, and active terms. While they create no controversy in themselves, they are potent engines of persuasion.

Like description, good narration is developed with its own techniques: 1. Report the events in the order in which they occur. 2. Describe them in the form in which the listener might have seen them. 3. Organize the narration so that it starts somewhere, moves clearly to somewhere else, and terminates. Check for these qualities in the following narration from a speech dedicating an interfaith chapel at West Georgia College, in May, 1964. The speaker was Robert F. Kennedy, then Attorney General of the United States.

. . . I thank you for the many kindnesses Georgia extended to him [the late President Kennedy], beginning in November, 1960.

His candidacy and election exemplify tolerance. This chapel is an expression of the same spirit of tolerance. And that is a spirit which is as old as Georgia.

The charitable groups in England which sponsored settlement of the colony of Georgia saw it as a haven for the persecuted and the poor. Contributions poured in from all classes of people. The clergy, for example, gave thousands of books. One of the notable titles was *A Friendly Admonition to the Drinkers of Gin, Brandy and Other Spirituous Liquors,* a volume whose message, I am certain, is still being taken to heart.

Your first settlers were warmly received by the other colonies. South Carolina sent horses, cattle, hogs, rice, and 2,000 pounds in cash. Thomas Penn sent 100 pounds in cash. In my home state, however, the opponents of foreign aid prevailed; the Governor of Massachusetts sent his best wishes.

Georgia flourished nonetheless. Its promise for religious refugees was so great that before the colony was six years old, it had as varied a population as any, with Swiss, Salzburgers, Moravians, Germans, Jews, Piedmontese, Scotch Highlanders, Welsh, and English.

Yet not even in the New World, not even in Georgia, did all the early settlers find freedom of faith. Catholics, for example, were not admitted to Georgia for seventy years. In other colonies, they were harassed, Quakers were jailed and Protestant sects were hounded.

It was in the South, in Virginia, that resentment against these practices flowered into religious freedom. With Madison and Jefferson in the vanguard, the Virginia Bill of Religious Liberty was enacted, to be followed by the First Amendment, separating church and state. Official intolerance thus ended. Religions were free to preach, to grow, and to multiply. . . .

## VISUAL AIDS AS SUPPORTING MATERIALS

It may not be quite true, as the Chinese proverb has it, that "one picture is worth more than a thousand words." It all depends—upon whether the subject lends itself to, or needs, this kind of support; and if it does, the appropriateness of available aids, and the skill with which the speaker can use them.

Highly technical or complex subjects may be clarified by charts, diagrams, maps, models, and pictures. Other subjects may be illuminated by films or slides that bring distant scenes to the audience. We shall describe briefly a number of such aids, those that are prepared in advance and those that are created in front of an audience, and comment on how to use them. But first, the governing rule: *never use a visual aid unless it can make a point more clearly than words alone, and never forget that even in this case it is an* aid *and not a* substitute *for speech.*

## Previously Prepared Aids

*Pictures, cartoons, maps, and posters* may convey specific bits of information in ways more vivid than spoken words. A photograph of a local slum, or a map showing the site of a proposed flood control project, provides a "you are there" orientation. The major problem in selecting from available aids of this type is to get them large enough, detailed enough, and with enough contrast in color or form, to be seen clearly from all parts of the lecture hall. Without any projection, it is not likely that more than 200 people can see clearly this type of aid. Sometimes these aids may be usefully exposed during an entire speech, but they are more likely to illustrate a single point, or segment of the speech, and should be saved until then. Freshness is part of their value.

*Graphs* are usually black-and-white presentations of statistical data and designed to make it easier for the listener to see relationships: *comparisons* of the quantity of several things at once, such as educational facilities for rural and urban children; *trends* in the quantity of several things over a period of time, such as gross annual incomes for farm and industrial workers in the past decade; and combinations of both comparisons and trends. These may take the form of *bar graphs* with a horizontal stripe extended along a base yardstick for each item being compared. They may be *pie graphs,* showing "cuts of pie" proportionate to quantities of a whole, such as various categories of expenditure in a state budget. Similar is the *pictograph,* using a series of human figures, with larger ones representing larger amounts, and so on. Finally, there is the *line graph,* used to show trends or curves, usually against a grid of coordinates, as in annual sales figures.

*Charts* are used to clarify complex organizational structures (such as the multiple United Nations agencies), standard procedures (as parliamentary law), or movement (as in a flow chart showing each step in the complete process of counseling-registering-fee paying, and so on).

Neither *graphs* nor *charts* are likely to carry a great amount of detailed information, and audiences will be tempted to puzzle over them rather than concentrate upon the speaker. To prevent this, keep the aids out of sight, or covered up, until you are ready to use them. If you can, dispose of each one in a series before revealing the next. Like other aids, graphs and charts must be large enough and boldly drawn, to be visible to the entire audience. If listeners are straining to *see* they are unlikely to be listening.

### Aids Created Before the Audience

Many of the same aids that can be prepared ahead of time may be created in full view of the audience, and while you are speaking. Generally this is less desirable: you may not draw well, it will take extra time or time away from what you have to say, and you must undertake the mastery of a special skill. And do not be beguiled—handling a speech and at the same time handling a piece of chalk is not easy!

On a blackboard, or a sketch pad mounted on an easel, a speaker can create *charts* and *graphs* of various kinds (though the lines that represent quantities are likely to be approximate when drawn freehand), and he may be able to draw *maps, cartoons, floor plans,* and so on.

Whether using prepared aids or creating them on the spot, here are four cautions:

1. Don't try to crowd too many details into your visual aid; "stick to the skeleton" if you would make complex things simple.
2. Don't be fussy about artistic details and thus take the audience's attention off the main point; use circles, straight lines, squares, stick-figures, and other shorthand methods of presentation.
3. Do make the items in your visual aid large enough to be seen by everyone; use large lettering and large symbols, even in exaggerated proportions if necessary.
4. Do use contrast, by size of figures, color of chalk or paint, and variety in style, in order to add emphasis and clarity.

Whether you use prepared aids or ones created on the spot, here are four cautions about using them:

1. Don't let yourself "doodle" on the blackboard or sketch pad; use it when you need it, and then erase it or cover it up: unused but exposed charts *distract* attention.
2. Don't talk to your visual aid instead of to the audience. It is awkward to try to project your voice to your listeners over your shoulder, so practice using the aid just as you practice your speech.
3. Do let the audience see the aid; stand to one side when commenting on it, using a pointer if necessary.
4. Do practice making chalk sketches, if that is your supporting aid, so that you can do it with some finesse; and check them out from the back of the room ahead of time, to be sure about their visibility and clarity.

### Films and Slides

As with any other aid, so with a documentary film giving background for a topic to be discussed: it must be viewed as an animated, interesting, even exciting introduction to, but not a substitute for, direct oral discourse. Slides or filmstrips, however, may be utilized during a speech in the same way as graphs, charts, and so on. Indeed, with a large audience the projected slide may be the *only* way to use such supporting material.

The use of films and slides requires projection, and this introduces a new set of cautions:

1. Use a screen large enough for the image to be easily seen.
2. Have the room adequately dark and use a projector that throws plenty of light.
3. Do not seat members of the audience directly behind the projector.
4. Pay special attention to making yourself heard and understood over possible projector noise, and from a possibly disadvantageous position behind the listeners.

In this chapter we have concerned ourselves with one of the key problems in speech communication, the selecting and phrasing of supporting materials necessary for making ideas clear. Effective speakers are resourceful ones. They keep adding constantly to their reservoir of facts, illustrations, specific instances, and testimony. They know that the only answer to "How much should I know about my topic?" is "More!" They know that just talking isn't enough. Abraham Lincoln said all there was to say about a speaker who was not really *master* of his subject, but talked anyway: "He can compress the most words into the smallest ideas of any man I ever met."

---

*The following speech makes a vital contribution to the text of this chapter.* Because speechmaking is its subject it both amplifies and exemplifies many of the principles we have discussed about making ideas clear. In its own right it is a significant and scholarly study. Finally, it demonstrates splendidly what a good speech to inform is like; in this respect it is a "model."

We are grateful to James L. Golden for permission to reproduce the speech here, and we are pleased to be able to include the citations to the sources he used in building it. Student speakers should read this speech as they would listen to a classroom speech: 1. to learn about the subject—happily, in this case, speechmaking, and 2. to observe the techniques employed by someone else in making ideas clear.

The speech was given at the annual convention of the Speech Association of America, held in Denver, Colorado, August 20, 1963. The speaker was then head of the Department of Speech, Muskingum College, and is now Professor of Speech, Ohio State University.

## POLITICAL SPEAKING SINCE THE 1920'S:
## CHANGES IN THE IDIOM

James L. Golden

In 1949 Harold Lasswell and his associates observed that "the language of politics is the language of power" and "of decision."[1] Twelve years later, at the close of his first year in office, President Kennedy gave new meaning to the Lasswellian thesis when he said: "Words can do more than convey policy. They can also convey and create a mood, an attitude, an atmosphere—or an awakening."[2] The truth of these premises has long been recognized by dynamic and persuasive political speakers ranging from Demosthenes and Cicero to Wilson and Churchill. Yet there is an alarming body of evidence to suggest that the quality of style during recent years has deteriorated and that the decline, in turn, has contributed significantly to what Dean Richard Hunt of Harvard University calls "The Mid-Century Eclipse of Political Eloquence."[3] Moreover, it has prompted the Archbishop of York to conclude, somewhat regretfully, that a speech holds "but a tiny place among the many new media of persuasion and debate."[4]

Of the numerous changes in the idiom of political speaking which indicate a steadily decreasing effectiveness in style since the 1920's, four are of particular significance. *First, the language which appears in a typical political address more and more represents the work of a group of collaborators who may or may not be able to produce a consistent and peculiar idiom which gives a unique stamp to the orator.* Since the days of Washington, American political leaders have often sought the aid of others to assist them in speech construction. But it was not until the early phase of the New Deal Era that this practice came into full flower. Historians have frequently referred to Roosevelt's Commonwealth Club Address delivered during the 1932 campaign as a clear statement of the meaning inherent in the early New Deal philosophy. Not only was this speech written in full by Adolph Berle and Rexford Tugwell, but was not seen by Roosevelt until the time before delivery.[5] After his election the President cre-

[1] Harold Lasswell, Nathan Leites and Associates, *Language of Politics* (New York, 1949), p. 8.

[2] John F. Kennedy, *To Turn the Tide* (New York, 1962), p. xvi.

[3] Richard M. Hunt, "The Mid-Century Eclipse of Political Eloquence," *Virginia Quarterly Review*, 38 (Autumn, 1962).

[4] *The Times Literary Supplement* (February 17, 1961), p. 105.

[5] Carl N. Degler, "The Ordeal of Herbert Hoover," *The Yale Review*, LII (Summer, 1963), p. 583.

ated a "Brain Trust" including such intellectuals as Harry Hopkins, Robert Sherwood, Raymond Moley, and his longtime speech advisor, Judge Samuel Rosenman. Sometimes Rosenman, surrounded by other collaborators, began work on a Roosevelt manuscript with these words: "Well, gentlemen, there comes a time in the life of every speech when it's got to be written."[6] Many of Roosevelt's most significant declarations came from this group of talented scholars. It was Hopkins who wrote the line: "We must be the great arsenal of democracy."[7] After the sinking of the Bismarck, Sherwood and Rosenman penned the following proclamation which appeared in one of the President's speeches: "I hereby proclaim that an unlimited national emergency exists." Despite the fact that this assertion represented an abrupt departure from the earlier American policy of viewing the war in Europe as a "limited" emergency, Roosevelt let it remain in the manuscript.[8] Although he usually revised and approved the drafts, and on occasion changed them during delivery, Roosevelt, as Gunderson aptly points out, presented speeches which, "in every sense of the word," were "a collaboration."[9]

The contributions of the collaborators are similarly evident in the manuscript addresses of Stevenson, Eisenhower, and Kennedy. Stevenson, a former ghost writer himself, exemplified in 1952 a brilliant and scintillating style which was largely his own. In 1956, however, he employed a staff of fifty men who helped him in his research and writing. The purpose of these assistants, observed Arthur Schlesinger, Jr. who served as chairman and coordinator, was to assist a "modern presidential candidate" who cannot possibly be expected to write all of the speeches required of him.[10] Eisenhower's reliance upon collaborators was even more remarkable. On one occasion, embarrassed by the praise he had received for one of his addresses, the Chief Executive wrote a letter to his ghost writer expressing regret that the real author of the speech did not have the opportunity "to take over also its delivery."[11] As a writer and experienced speaker, Kennedy, like Roosevelt and Stevenson, is fully capable of utilizing language that is eloquent and distinctive. But like his predecessors, he has become indebted to a group of collaborators, not the least of whom is Theodore Sorenson. If Nixon's analysis is correct we are forced to conclude that the philosophy of many of Kennedy's aides is this: "We don't care where the good line comes from as long as the guy at the top puts it out."[12]

Nor is the cold imprint of the ghost writer seen in presidential oratory

[6]Robert Sherwood, *Roosevelt and Hopkins* (New York, 1950), p. 184.
[7]*Ibid.*, p. 226.
[8]*Ibid.*, p. 297.
[9]Robert G. Gunderson, "Political Phrasemakers in Perspective," *Southern Speech Journal*, 26 (Fall, 1960), p. 24.
[10]Arthur Schlesinger, Jr. and Seymour Harris, "Introduction," in Adlai Stevenson, *The New America* (New York, 1957), p. xxi.
[11]*Life Magazine* (March 16, 1959).
[12]Alan Levy, "Richard Nixon's Biggest Crisis," *Redbook*, 119 (July, 1962), p. 105.

alone; it is also present in the utterances of congressmen, governors, and mayors. Convinced—rightly or wrongly—that they are too busy to write their own addresses, these officials have appointed others to perform the arduous task of extensive research, analysis, and speech construction. The time normally required for speech preparation may then be used for committee assignments, appeasing constituents, meeting pressure groups, entertaining delegations, answering mail, and attending to "pork barrel" legislation.[13] Whether or not a typical congressional or state leader is to succeed, observes V. O. Key, depends not only upon his ability to perform social amenities but upon his ease in finding "his way through the speeches that have been ghosted for him."[14]

*An equally important trend in the style of political speaking is the present popularity of the conversational idiom.* Partly because of television and partly because of a world-wide shift in audience sentiment, we have become preoccupied with clarity and the understatement and scornful of vivid, vehement, and heroic images which move rhythmically toward a climax. The speaker's language, therefore, is easily understood but is often trite, pedestrian, and dull. As a writer for the *Times Literary Supplement* recently put it: contemporary speaking style has descended "to the everyday, matey sort of level."[15] Even Roosevelt was happiest, points out Sherwood, when he could use such homely and banal phrases as "rule of thumb," "clear as crystal," "neither here nor there," and "simple as ABC."[16] Truman was also proud of his "off the cuff," plain, blunt style which he cultivated during the 1948 campaign. Delegates cheered as he leaned forward from the convention rostrum and, waving his hand vigorously up and down, asserted: "Senator Barkley and I will win this election and make these Republicans like it—don't you forget that." Workers responded with equal enthusiasm when they heard the President say: "If you get an Administration and a Congress unfriendly to labor, you have much to fear, and you had better look out."[17] Moving from whistle stops in the large metropolitan areas to those in the small cities and farm regions, Truman carried out his promise to "fight hard" and "give them hell." The President in 1948 had, suggests one eyewitness, "acquired a style where it was not at all as if he were making a speech, but as if he were leaning over the back platform chatting in a man to man fashion."[18]

Standing squarely in the tradition of Truman are two other prominent Democratic orators—Lyndon Johnson and Hubert Humphrey. The "grassy jokes," "snapped phrases" and "corn-ball" style of Johnson, observes Theodore White, are more appropriate for a dinner held in a Masonic Temple

[13]Jerry Landauer, "Debate's Decline," *Wall Street Journal* (February 7, 1963).

[14]V. O. Key, *Politics, Parties and Pressure Groups* (New York, 1958), p. 514.

[15]*The Times Literary Supplement* (February 17, 1961), p. 105.

[16]Sherwood, *op. cit.*, p. 213.

[17]Harry S. Truman, *Memoirs*, Vol. II (New York, 1956), pp. 207-210.

[18]*Fort Wayne Journal Gazette* (June 16, 1948), cited in Cole S. Brembeck, "Harry Truman at the Whistle Stops," *Quarterly Journal of Speech*, 38 (February, 1952), p. 42.

in a small Southern town than they are for a hotel banquet sponsored by a group of New York Democrats or for a national television audience.[19] Similarly the simplicity, clarity, and homely sparkle which are the trademarks of Humphrey's style give him a rapport with his listeners. But they also give him what one critic calls a "too folksy folksiness."[20]

If the extemporaneous style of the Democratic orators—with the possible exception of Stevenson—is undistinguished, so too is that of the Republican speakers. The syntax of Eisenhower's impromptu remarks is too well-known to recount here. One of his most ardent admirers confessed that the General often "murders the English language."[21] Nixon, on the other hand, consistently speaks with accuracy and clarity. But his words not only lack the rhetorical embellishment of a Lincoln or Churchill, they frequently fail to surpass the eloquence of an interoffice memo. As a case in point consider Nixon's bold and deliberate attempt to imitate Roosevelt's clever and highly amusing story concerning his dog Fala. Roosevelt, you may recall, alluded to his pet in the following vein:

The Republican leaders have not been content with attacks upon me, or my wife, or my sons—they now include my little dog, Fala. Unlike the members of my family, he resents this. Being a scottie, as soon as he learned that the Republican fiction writers had concocted a story that I had left him behind on an Aleutian island and had sent a destroyer back to find him—at a cost to the taxpayers of two or three or twenty million dollars—his Scotch soul was furious. He has not been the same dog since. . . . I think I have a right to object to libelous statements about my dog.[22]

This effective use of ridicule, cutting with the impact of a two-edged sword, produced raucous laughter, turned the tables on the opposition, and breathed new energy into an otherwise indifferent campaign. As a close student of practical politics Nixon could not help but be impressed with Roosevelt's skillful attack. But when he told the story of his dog "Checkers" as a mean of answering his critics in the celebrated fund case of 1952, he used a conversational idiom which fell far short of the distinction in style.

A man down in Texas heard Pat on the radio mention the fact that our two youngsters would like to have a dog and, believe it or not, the day before we left on this campaign trip we got a message from the Union Station in Baltimore, saying they had a package for us. We went down to get it. You know what it was? It was a little cocker spaniel dog, in a crate that he had sent all the way from Texas—black and white, spotted, and our little girl Tricia, the six-year-old, named it Checkers. And you know, the kids, like all kids, loved the dog, and I just want to say this, right now, that regardless of what they say about it, we are going to keep it. . . .[23]

[19]Theodore White, *The Making of the President, 1960* (New York, 1961), p. 132.
[20]*Ibid.*, p. 90.
[21]Levy, *op. cit.*, p. 105.
[22]Franklin D. Roosevelt, "America Has Not Been Disappointed," in Wayland M. Parrish and Marie Hochmuth, *American Speeches* (New York, 1954), p. 516.
[23]Richard Nixon, *Six Crises* (New York, 1962), p. 115.

That Nixon had understood the folksy idiom and undisciplined emotions of the general populace there can be little doubt. But his appeal, while effective, was contrived and maudlin. Competent critics in England viewed it as "a classic example of American huckstering. . . ."[24]

The plain, factual, and conversational language which characterizes the extemporaneous speeches of modern political orators is likewise present in many of the manuscript addresses. There have been occasions, to be sure, when recent speakers, with the help of their collaborators, have succeeded in clothing their ideas in words that are clear, vivid, graceful, and moving. Most of the addresses which Roosevelt delivered as President epitomize these traits.[25] So, too, did MacArthur's stirring speech presented at the Joint Session of Congress following his return from Korea. At times, as in the case of Kennedy's Inaugural Address, the style, rich in sentiment and graphic in description, reaches the level of the sublime.[26] But these moments of eloquence are rare. The statistical average is a boring commonplace. Truman and Eisenhower, more than Roosevelt, demonstrate in their manuscript speeches the mid-twentieth-century political idiom. Unfortunately, it is an idiom which is rooted in mediocre prose, seldom rising above factual statements or pious platitudes. If, as Dean Hunt suggests, these two Presidents, because of style and delivery, "could be counted among the less successful orators in history,"[27] they can take comfort in the fact that they are at least as eloquent as the Rockefellers, the Goldwaters, the Nixons, the Deweys, the Scrantons, the Romneys, the Humphreys, the Symingtons, the Russells, the Clements, the Churches, and the Johnsons.

Of the living American orators only one political leader—Adlai Stevenson—ranks as a stylist in the classical rhetorical tradition. But his reputation derives primarily from his noble attempt in 1952 to raise the level of pedestrian and contrived political oratory to the plane of persuasive and enduring rhetoric. For his efforts he was praised by the intellectuals, but condemned by the average man who found the style "too fluent" and "literary."[28] At the close of the contest Stevenson denied his critics' charge that he had spoken over the heads of his audience.[29] It is significant to note, however, that the Governor, according to his chief assistant Arthur

[24]David Butler, "An Englishman's Reflections on the Change of Administration," *American Scholar*, 30 (Autumn, 1961), p. 518.

[25]See Earnest Brandenberg and Waldo Braden, "Franklin Delano Roosevelt," in Marie Hochmuth, ed., *History and Criticism of American Public Address*, Vol. III (New York, 1955), p. 505-515.

[26]A leading newspaper referred to the speech as "one of the most eloquent" Inaugural addresses in history. *Washington Post* (January 21, 1961). Also see Donald L. Wolfarth, "John F. Kennedy in the Tradition of Inaugural Speeches," *Quarterly Journal of Speech*, 47 (April, 1961), p. 132.

[27]Hunt, *op. cit.*, p. 674.

[28]*Ibid.*, p. 673.

[29]Adlai E. Stevenson, *Major Campaign Speeches of Adlai E. Stevenson, 1952* (New York, 1953), p. xxviii.

Schlesinger, Jr., deliberately used a style in 1956 which was more simple and less rhetorical.[30] In commenting on Stevenson's change in language control, Hunt points out: "After his defeat in the first election, the quality and style of Stevenson's speeches gradually diminished; in his 1956 campaign he was rarely capable of rousing audiences out of their deepening lethargy."[31] The contemporary political orator has, in short, substituted a homely and unadorned idiom for a virile and vehement style which ennobles as well as persuades.

*Closely related to the current emphasis on simplicity is an increased trend toward brevity and terseness.* The 1930's which began with a two hour keynote address by Alben Barkley and lengthy appeals by Huey Long and Gerald L. K. Smith ended with short speeches exemplifying economy and precision in style. In later decades, under the influence of Madison Avenue publicity experts, this economizing tendency led to the condensing of symbols into key slogans. The Republican chant of the 1950's was brief and pointed: "Communism and Corruption"; "I shall go to Korea"; "I like Ike"; and "Peace, Progress and Prosperity." Disturbed by these catchwords and slogans, Adlai Stevenson, after pointing out that Jefferson would have been dismayed at this type of language control which serves only to "smother debate," predicted that the 1960 campaign motto would perhaps be "seven wonderful years!"[32] Stevenson apparently had good cause to be piqued with his Republican opponents who, he had come to believe in 1956, countered all of his arguments with the words, "Trust Ike."[33]

The incisive quality which sometimes comes from brevity and terseness is often an indispensable characteristic of speeches delivered in times of crisis when the outlook is pessimistic. In an age of nuclear power, electronics, and international diplomacy there is not much time for prolixity and diversity. A more important force responsible for the trend toward shorter speeches is the development of mass communication media. And herein lies a threat to present-day political oratory—the tendency to avoid discussion of essential issues. Standing in front of the radio microphone or the television camera, the candidate, hard pressed to finance the exorbitant fee for a broadcast which has become necessary, is seriously limited by time.[34] The policies and arguments which he should discuss are, in many instances, more technical and complex than those of his predecessors; yet he has less time to do it. Arthur Schlesinger ably describes the far-reaching significance of this problem:

[30]Schlesinger and Harris, *op. cit.*, p. xxvii.

[31]Hunt, *op. cit.*, p. 673.

[32]Adlai E. Stevenson, "Jefferson and Our National Leadership," *Virginia Quarterly Review*, 36 (Summer, 1960), p. 343.

[33]Stevenson, *Major Campaign Speeches of Adlai E. Stevenson, op. cit.*, p. 269.

[34]One of the contributing factors responsible for Humphrey's defeat in the West Virginia Primary was his inability to finance television speaking engagements. See White, *op. cit.*, p. 110.

A hundred years ago we had the Lincoln-Douglas debates. Fifty years ago, audiences listened enthusiastically while a Bryan or a LaFollette held forth in detail on . . . the problem of monopoly. Then the radio came to shorten political speeches, first to forty-five minutes and then to half an hour. Television has further abbreviated political communication. TV experts contended in 1956 that half an hour was too long, that fifteen minutes should be the maximum for a political speech, and that five-minute or one-minute spots were the most potent of all. Obviously no one can make a very thoughtful or extended analysis of any very complicated subject in fifteen minutes.[35]

This enforced brevity not only renders intricate questions incomplete and unclear, it prevents the speaker from employing subtle distinctions, rhythmical patterns, and lengthy, resounding periods. Variety, nuances, and amplification, in short, are all but eliminated, thereby depriving the speech of a style which is rich in connotative power.

Along with the increased emphasis on speech preparation through collaboration, the widespread popularity of the conversational idiom, and a strong devotion to brevity and terseness is a fourth trend in oral style— *the declining effectiveness in irony and satire.* The rapier thrusts of a Richard Brinsley Sheridan, a Benjamin Disraeli, or a Winston Churchill have in the hands of the typical contemporary American political orator become bludgeon attacks. Apart from Roosevelt and Stevenson there are few political leaders who know how to use the clever phrase, the poignant analogy, or the pun in order to turn the tables on an opponent. Not inclined to use such subtleties, the mid-twentieth-century orator strikes back at his enemies with scathing denunciations and half-truths. The particular weapon of Huey Long, observes Schlesinger, was vilification which took the form of "blistering frontier invective."[36] Long's great supporter in his "Share the Wealth" Movement was Gerald L. K. Smith—a former evangelical preacher and master of name-calling and innuendos. Describing the Kingfish's foes as "thieving drunkards," Smith frequently asked his audience: "All of you that ain't got four suits of clothes raise your two hands." As arms were lifted in the air, he would then ask: "Three suits?—two suits?" With deep emotion in his voice, he then pleaded: "Not even two suits of clothes! Oh, my brethren, J. P. Morgan has two suits of clothes. He has a hundred times two suits of clothes!" Satisfied that he had made his point, Smith concluded with these words: "Share, brother, share, and don't let those white-livered skunks laugh at you."[37]

The outsized rhetoric, with its highly calculated grammatical structures and libelous charges, so frequently used by Long, Smith, and other frontier orators yielded in the 1940's and 1950's to a new type of invective which was more sophisticated and polished, but equally devastating and

---

[35]Schlesinger and Harris, *op. cit.*, p. xxii.
[36]Arthur M. Schlesinger, Jr., *The Age of Roosevelt: Politics of Upheaval* (Cambridge, 1960), p. 51.
[37]*Ibid.*, p. 65.

unfair. From the time of his entry into politics in 1946 until the close of the congressional campaign in 1954, Nixon relied heavily upon this method. During the presidential contest of 1952 Acheson, Stevenson, and Truman were his major targets. The Secretary of State was indicted for his "spineless school of diplomacy," and for his "color blindness—a form of pink eye—toward the communist threat in the United States." Then, leveling his attack upon Stevenson, he charged that "side saddle Adlai the appeaser," "whose feet stick out to the left," has a degree all right—"a Ph.D. from the Acheson College of Cowardly Communist Containment." The American people do not want to elect as President, he continued, "a weakling, a waster, and a small caliber Truman." This reliance upon question-begging terms expressed in alliterative language which has strong emotional overtones took a different form in the 1954 campaign. Here Nixon devised the clever, shocking formula called "K-1, C-3—Korea, Communism, Corruption and Controls." Although the Vice President shifted his style in subsequent years to a moderate, almost nonpartisan tone,[38] He never succeeded in altering the image which he had created. Democrats and not a few Independents remember him as "Tricky Dick," while the English, despite their predilection for satire and irony, view him as a harsh, strident champion of "holy-war anticommunism."[39]

When the McCarthy era of American history officially came to an end in 1954 with the censure of the Wisconsin Senator, a more innocuous form of ridicule began to appear in our political speeches. In a strained and obviously contrived manner Governor Frank Clement, in his keynote address at the Democratic National Convention in 1956, needled his Republican opponents with the prediction that the American people would reject their "double-faced campaign," led by "the vice-hatchet man slinging slander and spreading half truths while the top man peers down the green fairways of indifference."[40] Perhaps no incident, however, better typifies the present decline of effective satire than that which occurred in the Senate a few months ago. Senator Thomas Kuchel, alarmed by the "fright" mail which he regularly receives from the "superpatriots of the far right," read to his colleagues a few excerpts from the letters.

The United States today has no Navy, no Army, no Air Force!

The United Nations is training thousands of foreign troops in Georgia, including barefoot savages, as a prelude to a takeover of the United States.

Thousands of Chinese Communist troops are poised on the Mexican border for an attack on California.

[38]Nixon worked hard to avoid personal attacks during the 1960 campaign. He even argued that Truman was "in some respects a strong president." See *Christian Science Monitor* (March 29, 1960); The *New York Times* (January 17, 1960); *Washington Star* (February 7, 1960).

[39]Butler, *op. cit.*, p. 519.

[40]Frank G. Clement, "Keynote Address, The Democratic National Convention, Chicago, August 13, 1956," in *Vital Speeches* (September 1, 1956).

How did the California senator—one of the more popular minority leaders in the Congress—answer the ridiculous charge that America has become the victim of a gigantic, incredible, and unprecedented conspiracy? "The only reasonable reply I can give them which they understand," said he, "is the honorable 100 percent red, white, and blue expression: 'Nuts' "[41] Kuchel's preference for a trite, blunt colloquial expression as a device for deflating his critics points up the present low estate of the art of satire and ridicule.

Since the 1920's more political speakers have addressed larger audiences on a wider range of topics than at any time in history. Yet so marked is the decline in the quality of style that the majority of speeches are pedestrian, prosaic, and impotent. During those infrequent moments when sublime and heroic rhetoric occurs we cannot be sure which of the noble sentiments and well-turned phrases were conceived in the mind of the speaker. In the nineteenth century Clay, Calhoun, Webster, Lincoln, Grady, and Ingersoll wrote history and literature with their speeches. From 1900 to 1940 the two Roosevelts, Wilson, Bryan, LaFollette, Borah, and Churchill also profoundly influenced national and international politics and contributed to the English language through the spoken word. "Much of the crucial history of the American nation during the past sixteen years," however, "could be written," argues Dean Hunt, "without reference to the effect of its leaders' speeches."[42] Literature, moreover, has been written without help from a contemporary political oratory which, according to the Archbishop of York, has failed to achieve distinction in style. If the trend toward decadence in the idiom of political speaking is to be reversed, speakers must stop hiding behind the rationalization that they are too busy to engage in thoughtful preparation, and listeners must refrain from rewarding mediocrity. Most of all, the political speech must strive to go beyond the mere dissemination of facts and charges expressed in a conversational idiom. It must on occasion, as President Kennedy suggests, create a mood and atmosphere which awakens the spirit. Only in this way can the political address earn a permanent place in literary history.


## SUPPLEMENTARY READINGS

Aristotle, *Rhetoric*, trans. by Lane Cooper. New York: Appleton-Century-Crofts, 1932. Treatment of style, pp. 182-219.
Berquist, Goodwin F., Jr., ed., *Speeches for Illustration and Example*. Chicago:

[41]*Washington Post* (May 3, 1963).
[42]Hunt, *op. cit.*, p. 673.

Scott, Foresman, 1966. Three speeches illustrating "the problem of presenting specialized material," by a doctor, a clergyman, and a diplomatic adviser, pp. 101-131.

Bosmajian, Haig A., ed., *Readings in Speech*. New York: Harper & Row, 1965. Relevant to making ideas clear are Gilbert Highet, "The Gettysburg Address," pp. 240-247; Aldous Huxley, "Words and Behaviour," pp. 211-223; Ralph L. Woods, "This Euphemistic Age," pp. 235-239.

Braden, Waldo W., and Gehring, Mary Louise, *Speech Practices: A Resource Book for the Student of Public Speaking*. New York: Harper & Row, 1958. Directly related to making ideas clear are "The Speaker Expresses His Ideas," pp. 94-119, and "The Speaker Supports His Proposition," pp. 70-93.

Linkugel, Wil A., Allen, R. R., and Johannesen, Richard L., eds., *Contemporary American Speeches: A Sourcebook of Speech Forms and Principles*. Belmont, Calif.: Wadsworth, 1965. Seven speeches to inform (to impart and to augment knowledge) representing students, public figures, and one corporation "stock speech" prepared by public relations staff, pp. 21-105.

## EXERCISES

1. List the violations of language techniques found in the following passages. Then rewrite and improve them:

a. It is with very great pleasure that I address you on this most auspicious occasion.

b. Special emphasis has been placed on miniaturization and ruggedization of new equipment.

c. It is advisable that one makes an examination of what is ahead before committing oneself to moving forward precipitantly.

d. It is a very unique book that I have just read, a book in the nature of a biography of Thomas A. Edison. It shows how Edison, even as a boy, was most unusual. It shows how Edison as a man developed into a genius who was most exceptional.

2. Examine one of your old outlines; or, if you have recorded a speech in this course, listen to the playback. Write a brief report on your skill in using each of the five word and sentence techniques discussed in this chapter.

3. In preparing your next speech, check whether you are using language techniques with reasonable skill. In the technical plot, left margin of the outline, note where you are making deliberate use of these techniques.

4. Give a two-minute speech of definition in which you classify, compare, illustrate, and if possible use testimony, in making clear the meaning of a technical, complex, or strange word.

5. Give a two-minute speech of definition on some common word or phrase

used loosely by different people, such as *Americanism, freedom, the common man, apple-polisher, straight-laced, civil rights, extremism.*

6. Give a two-minute speech in which you compare or contrast such ideas as: (a) art and science, (b) prose and poetry, (c) town and gown, (d) education and training, (e) comedy and melodrama, (f) honesty and integrity.

7. Give a two-minute speech supporting an idea with one of these:

a. factual information.

b. one good illustration.

c. half a dozen specific instances.

d. acceptable testimony from two or more sources.

e. restatement or repetition, or both.

f. description, and decide in advance whether you want to make it factual description, imaginative description, etc.

g. some form of narration.

8. Read James L. Golden's speech (pp. 128-136) to get answers to these questions:

a. Can you draw up lists of words and phrases to show whether his language was concrete, simple, and colorful?

b. Can you find instances when he justifiably violated the principles of sentence structure set out in this chapter?

c. How many of the customary forms of supporting material did he use? Enough? Varied enough?

d. Were there any main head assertions that you felt to be inadequately supported?

e. After examining the footnotes, what generalization can you make about the sources he used?

f. How would you evaluate his introduction? His conclusion?

g. What kind of summaries, transitions, and other signposts did he use?

h. How would you rate his overall effectiveness in achieving his purpose?

# 8

# Making Ideas Persuasive

Throughout almost this whole book we have been concerned, directly or obliquely, with making ideas persuasive. Chapter 3 (The First Steps in Managing Ideas), Chapter 6 (Organizing the Speech), and Chapter 7 (Making Ideas Clear) have been directly and almost exclusively concerned with the *process* of persuasion. In this chapter we shall discuss the *system* of persuasion by which the procedures covered previously can be used most effectively to influence human behavior.

We can best begin by agreeing that people are filled with all sorts of beliefs and attitudes that were not produced by reason, logic, or critical thinking. Plato wanted men always to see things as they are, but modern psychologists know that "we see things not as they are but as we are." The eighteenth century liberal philosophers believed that men are rational creatures who will recognize and accept the truth once they find it. All that was needed for enlightened democracy, therefore, was free speech and free press, untrammeled discussion, and majority rule. But social psychologists report that "belief is rarely the result of reasoning," and that much so-called reasoning is actually rationalization, the construction of "socially acceptable rather than real reasons for behavior."

It would be delightful, of course, to say—especially to college students —that higher education will change all that. Less well-educated persons may be undiscriminating, uncritical, even whimsical in "making up their minds," but surely educated persons need only to be given the facts and shown the logic in order to make rational decisions. Alas, even your college education may not achieve this. As Oliver Wendell Holmes wrote, after nearly thirty years on the Supreme Court: "As I grow older I realize how limited a part reason has played in the conduct of men. *They believe what they want to.*" That is exactly the point: men generally believe what they want to. This means that *persuasion is largely a matter of making men want to believe.*

In speech communication—whether it be in formal public speaking, or

139

even the fragmented speeches of group discussion—there are four constituent elements in a systematic effort to persuade.

## SEIZE AND HOLD THE LISTENER'S ATTENTION ON THE SUBJECT

John H. Glenn, Jr. addressing the American Astronauts Alumni Association, or Mrs. Indira Gandhi talking to an India Congress Party meeting, would have little concern about getting attention. With these audiences each already has high status. This is not true for George Spelvin when he makes a speech in class. He must *earn* his status, and perhaps by late in the semester he will. But now he gets a *"ho hum!"* response from his audience, as do thousands of relatively unknown speakers who address thousands of Rotary, Kiwanis, Exchange, and Lions Club audiences each week. ". . . and Mr. Spelvin will speak to us about geriatrics" draws the *"So what?"* response.

So what Spelvin faces is the formidable task of "crossing the interest deadline," seizing the attention of the audience, and with no help from his status in the group ("he's a nice fellow, I guess") or from his topic ("Jerry who?"). He needs to do it in the *first* sentence or his audience may be lost forever. How can he kindle a quick flame? Mostly by knowing what attention is and how it operates.

Attention is a kind of mental activity we cannot see. But we know that when we focus our sensory receptors (we *listen* for words and we *watch* for action) on a stimulus (a speaker, in this case) we are attending, momentarily committing ourselves. We also know that the state of attending is not constant. *Attention comes in spurts and lasts for only a few seconds at a time.* We say that a classroom lecture should not last more than fifty minutes, that fifty minutes is about as long as we can expect to hold a student's attention. Indeed, we cannot hold his attention for fifty *seconds,* if we believe the psychologists who measure these things. Perhaps we get attention for as long as thirty seconds (time enough for the average speaker to say about 75 words), but then it turns off and then comes back on again. The speaker's challenge is to keep those repeated spurts of attention on his subject so that the listener's mind won't hop-skip-and-jump.

The listener is not half as concerned about the off-again, on-again nature of his attention as is the speaker. From force of habit the listener may take a second look at any new speaker who walks on the platform, but he does not *naturally* continue to attend. His mind can wander while his body is seated. He may daydream. He may make up shopping lists, plan his evening, or just sit. If he attends only for a few moments at a time he will go away remembering only a few bits from your speech, and they may not fit together. In sum, he must be compelled to direct his repeated spurts of attention to the speaker and his subject. The chief ways of holding attention are surely as old as human nature. Here are two that we have already discussed in connection with other fundamentals of speech-making.

1. *First are the techniques for making ideas clear, including the more vivid forms of support.* The most compelling of all means for holding attention is to give the listener moving pictures in words—by illustrations, specific instances, comparisons, testimony, description, and narration (see pp. 118-124). These supports make an idea vivid. They keep it moving. Like a magnet they pull the listeners' repeated spurts of attention back to the subject.

2. *Second is to arrange ideas into a simple, unsubtle, and sensible pattern* (see pp. 94-99). This will keep listeners from getting lost, or just wandering away. They can tell where you (and they) have been, and where you are now, and foresee where you are going. Your pattern is a road map. And like all maps, it helps to maintain interest in the road. Here are three additional methods of holding audience attention.

3. *Suspense.* Detective fiction writers know that suspense leads us to continue reading to the climax of the story. This is no different in kind, though it is in degree, from the suspense we feel when our football team has the ball on the one-yard line. The feeling of uncertainty, or of anxiety, quickens our pulse and tightens our muscle set. Speakers can build suspense in many ways. One form of "keep 'em guessing" is the titillative title, such as "How Long Should a Wife Live?" Another ploy—common in political conventions—is to make a nominating speech that describes the qualities of the candidate but without revealing his name until the final sentence. On a smaller scale, of course, is the use of suspense in building sentences. For example, a loosely constructed sentence would say "He was relieved of his command for what amounted to gross and persistent insubordination," but the meaning is suspended briefly when it is rephrased: "For what amounted to gross and persistent insubordination . . . he was relieved of his command."

Note that Robert G. Gunderson, in the speech reported near the end of this chapter, used the first method with his title, "Davy Crockett's Tongue-Tied Admirers." And not until he was more than a third of the way through the speech (see p. 156) did he relieve the listener's curiosity by making an extended reference to Crockett.

4. *Activity.* "Take me where the *action* is," says the teen-ager. "My boys may strike out pretty often, but they're *always swinging* for the long ball," says the baseball manager. "Get some *animation* in the TV com-

mercials," says the advertising manager, and so beer foams, tanks are full of tigers, and digestive tracts are in turmoil. We *"go for"* activity, directly or vicariously.

Speakers can capitalize upon the natural attention values of activity by incorporating it in descriptions of lively scenes, reports on living characters, portrayals of conflict, and so on. Professor Gunderson not only does this in a long, lively word picture of Davy Crockett, but also scatters throughout his speech other "activity phrases" such as, ". . . they may die laughing," "wallowing thus in a morass . . ." "taken a kick-at-the-cat . . ." "speakers displayed a remarkable laryngeal stamina."

5. *Humor.* It has been said that nothing describes a man better than his sense of humor. Even those who are themselves humorless, tend to respond to a speaker's wit. They pay attention to humor (because it is often in narrative form, building suspense to the final punch line). They remember ideas reinforced by humor. They are impressed by the speaker whose wit is displayed by a clever and seemingly impromptu turn of phrase. They appreciate the incongruous application of a quotation or well-known maxim. But they are generally *not* impressed with stories dragged in by the heels and relevant to nothing at all, with hackneyed jokes, or with flippancy in general.

Here are some examples of humor, not necessarily funny stories in the Tom Corwin tradition, but witty observations naturally arising out of the occasion. First, refer back to the ironical account by Franklin D. Roosevelt of his dog Fala's resentment at unfair political attacks (p. 131). Second, here is Adlai E. Stevenson, in the 1955 commencement address at Smith College:

While I am not in favor of maladjustment, I view this cultivation of neutrality, this breeding of mental neuters, this hostility to eccentricity and controversy with grave misgiving. One looks back with dismay at the possibility of a Shakespeare perfectly adjusted to bourgeois life in Stratford, a Wesley contentedly administering a country parish, George Washington going to London to receive a barony from George III, or Abraham Lincoln prospering in Springfield with nary a concern for the preservation of the crumbling Union.

Third, is four sentences from a 1960 campaign speech of John F. Kennedy in Albion, Michigan.

I want to express my thanks to all of you, particularly those of you who are college students and can't vote, who came down here anyway. I recognize that the sacrifice is not extensive as I am doing the work this morning and you are not in class. I am glad that you are participating actively in the political process. Artemus Ward, fifty years ago, said "I am not a politician and my other habits are also good."

Lest these examples give the impression that wit is confined to one political party, let it be recorded that it was Barry Goldwater who said of the legendary articulateness of Hubert H. Humphrey, that "Hubert has been clocked at 275 words a minute, with gusts up to 340." And it was Senator Margaret Chase Smith whose impromptu drollery once broke up a press conference. A questioner wanted to know about the possibility of a woman becoming President, but the way he put it was, "What would you do if you woke up one morning and found yourself in the White House?" Mrs. Smith said, "I would go to the President's wife and apologize, and then leave at once."

## GET LISTENERS TO ACCEPT YOUR COMPETENCE AND CHARACTER

Listeners don't accept or reject ideas merely from the way they are presented. They also accept or reject *because of the person who advocates them*. Experimental studies indicate that your manner of delivery, the level of your diction, your poise, and your apparent straightforwardness, all affect your credibility and the acceptability of what you have to say. That's what Emerson said, over a hundred years ago: "The reason why anyone refuses his assent to your opinion . . . is in you . . . you have not given him the authentic sign." To be accepted, and believed, *you must give listeners "the authentic sign."*

First are two "signs" to be avoided. Neither is "authentic."

1. Don't say, or even imply, that you are favoring the uninformed audience with your wisdom: "Since you don't know much about this subject, let me tell you about it," or "None of you have probably realized that. . . ." Some *will* know much, and others have *long since* realized. Silently, but viciously, they will tell you so. A persuasive speaker takes the opposite tack: "You remember so-and-so," or "I'm sure you realize that. . . ."

2. Don't criticize your audience without including yourself. Even though it may be true that your listeners have neglected their obligations, and they realize it, they will resent any holier-than-thou attitude. Instead of implying that *you* are judging *them*, say "*We* have neglected this," or "*We* must all share some blame."

Now let us examine the truly "authentic" signs. Of these there are four.

1. *Listeners trust the speaker who shows intellectual integrity and sound judgment*. Never give your hearers a chance to call you a chronic exaggerator, or to brand you as being careless with the truth. Defend yourself against going beyond the evidence by staying within the limits of reasonable objectives. In public speeches, as Lincoln said of courtroom arguments, "it is a good policy never to *plead* [promise] what you *need* not, lest you oblige yourself to *prove* what you *can* not." You want to pre-

sent your case in such a way that even those who are doubtful or who disagree will say, "He speaks honestly." But more than that, you want to keep your *self*-respect, win or lose. This standard has been no better expressed than by Adlai Stevenson in what might well be his epitaph. On election eve, 1952, before the votes were cast, he summed up: "I have said what I meant and meant what I said. I have not done as well as I should like to have done, but I have done my best, frankly and forthrightly; no man can do more, and you are entitled to no less."

2. *Listeners trust the speaker who seems to know what he is talking about*. They like to know that a speaker is qualified to discuss the subject because of his firsthand experience or because he has investigated it thoroughly. The implication that "some of this I saw myself," or "for this I am personally responsible," pleases them. Billy Graham sensed this audience desire for speaker assurance when he admonished participating clergymen before the Indianapolis Crusade of 1959: "Preach with *authority*, with simplicity, with urgency, and for a decision."

Inexperienced speakers are often hesitant about suggesting that they *are* speaking with *authority*. They need not be *if* they have objectively examined their own experience, or have conscientiously processed trustworthy information provided by others. Their problem may really be how to say without seeming boastful that they have earned the right to speak. There are ways to do it. For example, "When I was gathering materials for this speech, I came across an unusual book. . . ." Or, "I got only a corporal's view, but last summer while on maneuvers. . . ." Or, "This morning I want to talk about 'How to Study.' Last year my grades told me I didn't know much about it, so this year I have tried to find out what psychologists know about it."

3. *Listeners trust the speaker who shows moderation, restraint, and good will*. Nothing may be more important to your hearers than their beliefs and attitudes. After all, they have spent a lifetime cultivating them. Now they are deep-rooted, they satisfy deep-felt wants. Speakers who try to tear up these beliefs or attitudes by the roots must resign themselves to probable failure and certain resentment. Effective speakers, instead, water and cultivate ideas to produce growth and change, just as they would water and cultivate crops to promote growth and harvest. The best persuader follows the proverb literally: "Make haste slowly."

For like reasons, don't *indiscriminately* praise or damn, whether your target is the President, the Congress, labor, management, or anything, or anyone. No question is too controversial to discuss, *if* you make sure of your facts, present your case, and let the facts speak. As H. L. Mencken used to say, "I simply record the facts, in a sad, scientific spirit."

4. *Listeners trust the speaker, above all, who seems sincere*. So long as you are obviously trying to generate light, not heat, listeners are often amazingly tolerant even though they are skeptical about your views. But

let them have any reason to suspect your motives, experimental studies have shown, and they conclude that you haven't enough facts, that the facts are not sound anyway, and that you are "too one-sided." Lawyers, who admittedly speak only for one side, are especially conscious of the strength of sincerity. Francis L. Wellman, a famous jury pleader of a few years ago, spoke this way about the lawyer in *Success in Court:* "He must be himself. He cannot assume a character in the courtroom which he is not. If he customarily wears red suspenders and snaps them as he talks, he can do it in the courtroom because the mannerism is part of him. If he is customarily well-groomed and demeans himself as a person of refinement, then he cannot play the tramp before the jury and get away with it."[1] And Louis Nizer, perhaps the best known lawyer of today, and author of *My Life in Court,* put it in a capsule: "Persuasion does not come from affectation or from charm and wit. It is derived from sincerity."[2]

## REST REASON ON LISTENERS' IMPELLING WANTS

Many people assume that a speaker has only two choices—he must either "appeal to emotion" or "appeal to reason." Along with this assumption there is usually an implied corollary, that "appeal to emotion" is unethical, or at least that it panders to human weakness. Such people ought to know better. If they have not caught up with twentieth-century psychology and the study of human motivation, they should at least have studied themselves. Human nature has not changed for centuries, and man is moved by the same *basic wants* as always. He is not consistently, or even primarily, rational in the way he satisfies his wants and solves his problems. But under specific conditions of motivation, and on particularly pressing problems, he can think analytically. When there is no other way out, and as a last resort, man does turn to reason, or turns to someone else who can use it.

*Man does use reason, then, not as an intrinsically satisfying activity, but as a means of solving his problems and satisfying his needs and wants. In a system of persuasion, therefore, reason has a role in showing man how to get what he wants, how to reach his goals, how to lift himself toward his ideals. Thus, he who would persuade must rest his reason—his evidence and his logical argument—upon those deep-seated wants that have for centuries been man's chief motivations.*

In such a system of persuasion there is neither common sense nor profit in separating "appeal to emotion" and "appeal to reason." Let us nail this idea down tight.

[1]( New York, 1941 ), p. 280.
[2]( New York, 1961 ), p. 269.

First, there is no "either-or" about emotion and reason. Man's mind has no pigeon-holes for segregating the two, and psychologists tell us that even if he wanted to he could do no better than chance in classifying them. Furthermore, reason and emotion are not at opposite ends of the same continuum. Just because a person has a lot of one he is not necessarily short on the other.

Second, that word "appeal" can be misleading in this context. We should not, and effective speakers do not, "appeal" to or for an emotion or a reason. We ask for a *response*, some sort of behavioral answer, and we know that emotions (needs and wants) reinforce reasons (evidence and argument). We know that one rests upon the other. It was in this sense that Harry A. Overstreet wrote in *Influencing Human Behavior*, that "no appeal to a reason that is not also an appeal to a want is ever effective." He knew that many of us, indeed, *want* others to appeal to our *reason*.

Finally, the use of the term "emotion" can also be misleading. To be sure, people have emotions. They are essential in each individual's psychological makeup. But speakers don't usually deal with emotions as such. Rather they deal with wants, motives, goals, drives, needs, ambitions, and those social habits called culture patterns. And these, not emotions, are what effective speakers think of and what they address themselves to.

If we have made our point, and destroyed the false dichotomy, you now understand that in persuasion you show people by reason how to satisfy a want, reach a goal, or move toward an ideal. *In short, in persuasion you rest reason upon the listener's impelling wants.*

To do this, of course, you must know what those impelling wants are. This should mean constructing a complete catalogue of men's needs, hopes, ambitions, and fears. But that isn't easy. You cannot really collect the information in a public opinion poll by asking people what their impelling wants are. Even if they knew they might not want to tell you, and many simply wouldn't be able to sort out one from another. The best we can do is to study behavior systematically, and observe and classify behavioral patterns that have apparently been set off by strong motivational drives. Eisenson, Auer, and Irwin, in *The Psychology of Communication*, have identified six basic, unlearned drives, universally present in all human beings, and intended to satisfy impelling wants.[3] From their treatment we borrow the six generalizations, and add our own comments.

1. *Human beings direct their activities toward the satisfaction of physical wants and general well-being.* At bottom this is a desire for survival, and under optimum conditions. Positively it refers to food, clothing, and shelter. In terms of avoidance it includes any physical deprivation, such as pain, hunger, thwarting of sex impulses, and the need for sleep. It is significant to note that individuals are willing temporarily to forego satisfaction of some of these wants if they believe that ultimately there will be greater satisfactions of some kind.

[3] ( New York, 1963 ), pp. 245-246.

2. *Human beings normally behave in ways that will lead them toward success, mastery, and achievement.* And, of course, they try to avoid situations that would threaten or thwart these aims. Formal education, self-study, book clubs, participation in community affairs, special lessons from a golf pro, hard work at the office, and one kind and another of self-improvement nostrums, are some of the ways men and women choose to help satisfy this want. If, within reasonable periods of effort along one of these lines, they do not achieve success or mastery, they are likely to seek alternate means.

3. *Human beings tend to behave in ways that will help them to gain recognition, admiration, respect, and approval.* Action that brings disapproval, or that results in being ignored, will of course be avoided. No one really wants to be cast in a production of "the common man." As a consequence people tend to identify what, in a given society, is most praiseworthy, and then set out to cultivate it. This is called a drive for "status." Sometimes status comes with intellectual achievement or creative work, but more commonly it comes with the acquisition of material things, even on the installment plan.

4. *Human beings generally act in ways that will lead toward their being loved, and the realization of a feeling of being wanted.* There is a strong feeling about "belonging" or being "accepted," in a variety of business and social peer groups. People are sometimes led into behavior that is not for them intrinsically rewarding—attending concerts, playing bridge, joining particular clubs—in order to strengthen group ties. Most people seek the company of familiar persons, but prefer even unfamiliar ones over being alone.

5. *Human beings usually act in ways that will bring about peace of mind, security, and a feeling of release from worry and anxiety.* Those situations that potentially involve fear, anxiety, or insecurity, are of course avoided. These motivations affect security in terms of employment, social relationships, and family ties. And they affect not only individual behavior, but the behavior of social and ethnic groups, regional and national groups, and nations. In any of these contexts, the most complex decisions involve choices where each alternative carries some security risks.

6. *Human beings indicate by their behavior that they seek some adventure, new experiences, and zestful living.* This also means, of course, that they tend to avoid boredom and monotony in their jobs, their family and social relationships. More than with most other wants, there is individual variation here, since family circumstances, personal inclinations, and group commitments, may require more security than is compatible with new experiences. This desire is also variable because some people can find adventure vicariously, by reading, television-watching, or even daydreaming.

These six patterns of behavior, each reflecting an impelling human want, are the foundations of persuasion. If attention is the *channel* for the flow of persuasive communication, then these impelling wants constitute its *headspring*.

We turn now to the ways and means for applying in a convenient system and strategy of persuasion all of the procedures and techniques of speechmaking we have so far studied.

## DEVELOP EACH IDEA ACCORDING TO THE LISTENERS' ATTITUDE

In Chapter 6 we suggested a method for an audience analysis (pp. 88-89). It was pertinent there to the overall process for organizing the speech. It should be reviewed now for its critical bearing upon your strategy of persuasion. For we are now ready 1. to consider the attitude of the most significant part of your listeners toward *each part of your speech*—in effect, toward each main head, and then 2. to develop *each part of your speech* so as to relate it most effectively to the impelling wants of these listeners.

For convenience we shall identify four levels of attitude (actively favorable, indifferent, doubtful or uninformed, opposed), and appropriate strategies of persuasion for each.

1. *Is the audience actively favorable?* Then develop the topic by the **impressive or dynamic method.** This consists of telling people what they already know—familiar facts, old stories, tested ideas. People like to relive events of the past, figuratively returning to "the good old days" (and the good old ways of doing things). College graduates return to the campus after many years. Societies meet to renew memories. Nations commemorate great events of their past. Consequently a large amount of speaking consists simply of telling people old things in new ways.

When you put "old wine in new bottles" you are not trying to *prove* what your listeners already actively believe. Instead you are reviving cherished memories and associations. You vitalize them, enrich their meanings, and perhaps surcharge them with a drive for action. In adopting this strategy of persuasion the following forms of support will be especially effective:

|                    |                    |
|--------------------|--------------------|
| Illustrations      | Narration          |
| Specific Instances | Suspense and Climax |
| Comparisons        | Testimony          |

2. *Is the audience indifferent?* Then use the **motivative method** to show why the topic is important. Is it an unanticipated problem, or one now dimly seen that will soon become acute? Is it a neglected problem that is about to catch the listeners unaware? Is it a once-settled prob-

lem that now returns to life? Is it a perennial or unpleasant problem that we want to forget or "let George do it"? The strategy of persuasion for these circumstances may take one of two possible forms of development:

*Motivate it* by showing the involved wants, needs, hopes, and ideals. Possible forms of support for this are:

|  |  |
|---|---|
| Facts and Figures | Explanation |
| Testimony | Restatement |

*Vitalize it* by making the ideas vivid. For this the following forms of support are most effective:

|  |  |
|---|---|
| Illustrations | Description |
| Specific Instances | Narration |
| Comparisons | Suspense |

3. *Is the audience doubtful or uninformed?* Then develop the topic by the **instructive method.** Uninformed listeners, or doubtful ones, require a development different from that for those who already know a good deal about the topic or who have already approved it. For the uninformed you must present information—accurate information, clear information, systematic information, and interesting information. We do not change our minds as the result of logic and refutation, said Matthew Arnold, but *as we learn more, the ground gently shifts beneath us, and we no longer look at things as we formerly did.*

The speechmaker plays a vital role in this process. Most people do not want for available information, but much of it is not in usable form. Some information that reaches them is false—propaganda manufactured to mislead or to serve hidden purposes; other available information may be accurate, but it only comes as raw facts, unprocessed and unrelated to people's needs. One of the functions of speech communication is to give form to this information, and to organize it so as to establish alternative solutions for problems.

In presenting information, a speaker will not categorically state his conclusions at the outset, as if to say: "I'm going to prove that these are the only relevant facts in the case, and anyone who doubts me is stupid." A good speaker does not think that way, and he does not talk that way. Rather he asks listeners to consider the problem with him: "What are the facts on this issue?" or "What caused this problem to become acute?" When he has caught and focused his listeners' interest, he then proceeds to make clear the answer. Especially useful are these means of making ideas clear:

|  |  |
|---|---|
| Definition and Explanation | Facts and Figures |
| Narration | Illustrations |
| Restatement and Repetition | Specific Instances |
| Comparisons and Contrasts | Testimony |

4. *Is the audience opposed?* Then develop the topic by **conciliation**

**plus impelling argument.** If someone asks, "Why try such a thing? Whoever heard of anyone changing his mind because of a speech?" the answer is written boldly by hundreds of experimental studies and centuries of experience. In this changing world people *do* change their minds. And not just on minor matters, but upon major issues that vitally affect their lives. Reversals of opinion, to be sure, seldom come from reading a single book or listening to a single speech, but rather from continuous watering and cultivating of ideas. Bull-headed argument is poor strategy for persuading those who oppose your ideas, but a conciliatory manner and an adaptation to your listeners' impelling wants can win the desired response.

People who understand the psychology of communication have always sold goods, won votes, made converts, lifted men's faces toward new ideals, and inspired them to battle for humanity. But they have done it by knowing and harnessing the drives that impel men to action. The steps in this process are easily set down in print, but exceedingly difficult to follow in practice. Here are four basic principles.

*Don't provoke argument.* An opposed listener is like a cocked gun. It takes only slight pressure on the trigger to set it off. Take no chances: keep your finger off the trigger. Don't call names. Don't deliberately irritate by such terms as *"selfish* business interests," *"irresponsible* labor leaders." Students often find it hard to resist name-calling. They hold back until the pressure mounts, then relieve it by letting go one lusty epithet that they hope won't do any harm. But one is plenty. Like Mercutio's wound, it may not be as wide as a church door, or as deep as a well, but it will do the business in the end. Face it frankly. Strong character is required to keep from name-calling, from igniting a forest fire just to get illumination. With favorable audiences it is regrettable, but may do no harm. With an opposed audience it will be the speaker whom the flames consume.

*Seek at the outset to get a Yes-Response.* One rash speaker says "Campus politics are rotten. No one gets elected without secret bargains." Every listener who voted for a winner will, in his own mind, retort "Nonsense! That's not true!" This reaction is more than a simple negative response; it sets the whole personality of the listener against the speaker, and his pride will keep it set. Now shift focus to another speaker. "I am proud of this college," he says. "Like you, I'm glad I came here. There is no better place to be." Everybody agrees—*he gets a Yes-Response.* "I want to talk with you about campus politics," he continues. "Of course we must have campus politics. We can't have officers without candidates, or candidates without organized supporters." Who can disagree?—*more Yes-Response.* "To illustrate this sequence, let's look at the last campus election. I wonder if we won't find alarming the report of a student-faculty committee that investigated it. The report says. . . ." So far not a listener has had a chance to say "No." In the long run the listeners may not agree with the second speaker, but at least he will get a hearing.

*Beware of being ingratiating.* Listeners cannot long be fooled, and they will not be mocked. They will find insincerity as transparent as a picture window. They will discover both faces of a two-faced speaker. And they will have a name for what he does: apple-polishing, a snow job, or less printable terms known to most students. To seek common ground with your listeners through Yes-Response is an honest way of attacking differences of opinion by talk. It is the way that permits us to live together despite our differences. But talking out of both sides of your mouth is something else again. It may not take much intelligence to distinguish between them, but it does take character to separate them in practice.

*Follow up by developing the subject so that hearers either 1. forget their objections, or 2. have them removed by logical processes.* It is a curious commentary on human nature that some people can be persuaded simply by causing them to *forget* their objections, or at least to *suspend judgment.* The forgetting process is accelerated by focusing the hearers' attention onto sustained narratives, moving illustrations, or vivid descriptions. But frankly, this is not the best method. Far more effective is the method of following up a Yes-Response with impelling argument. Don't confuse this with "provoking an argument." Indeed, this impelling argument is not "argument" at all. Rather it is well-ordered *information:* systematic, reliable, and pertinent, *and* related to the wants, hopes, aspirations, and ideals of the listeners.

From a character in *Number One,* by John Dos Passos, we take our summary about making ideas persuasive: "People's minds are full of mean lil barbwire fences. . . . The thing to do when you are trying to talk folks into somethin' is to kinder fool around till you find a gate or a break in one of them fences. . . . If you try to storm through a barbwire fence you'll git your pants tore."

---

*The following speech contributes vitally to the text of this chapter.* Because it was addressed to teachers of language arts and was about training for an articulate democracy, it bears directly upon our discussion about making ideas persuasive. As a study of contemporary problems of communication it is both significant and scholarly. And not least, it is clearly a "model" of what a good speech to persuade is like.

We are grateful to Robert G. Gunderson for permission to reproduce the speech here, and we are pleased that we can include a set of citations to specific sources he used in developing it. Student speakers should read this speech as they would listen to a classroom speech: 1. to learn about the subject—fortunately, in this case, it deals with communication, and 2. to observe the techniques employed by someone else in making ideas clear.

The speech was given at the University of Virginia Institute for Teachers of English, Speech, and Drama, in Charlottesville, Virginia, August 8, 1955. The speaker was then chairman of the Department of Speech, Oberlin College, and is now Professor of Speech, Indiana University.

## DAVY CROCKETT'S TONGUE-TIED ADMIRERS: TRAINING FOR AN ARTICULATE DEMOCRACY

Robert G. Gunderson

A lecturer, says the bitter lexicographer, Ambrose Bierce, is one who has "his hand in your pocket, his tongue in your ear, and his faith in your patience." The process of lecturing is, in fact, designed to induce that heroic euphoria which psychiatrists now call, with appropriate apologies to James Thurber, the Walter Mitty syndrome. "No one can imagine what dreadful hard work it is to keep awake and listen to what's said," confessed the restless Coonskin Congressman, Davy Crockett, after a term in Congress. "Splitting gum logs in August is nothing beside it." Over one hundred years have passed since the King of the Wild Frontier uttered these immortal words, and during that time Americans have distinguished themselves as genuinely lazy listeners. Indeed, public opinion polls prove that people resist serious talk, as Davy would say, just as a coon dog fights fleas. So determined are they to be amused that Dr. George Gallup, in all seriousness, worries publicly for fear that they may die laughing.

According to the best evidence of our pollsters, we devote but little time to serious reading and listening. An analysis of 131 television programs last Sunday reveals that twelve programs, less than ten percent, were devoted to subjects which might, with some stretch of the imagination, be called informative or educational. Twelve were religious broadcasts, and the remaining seventy-two percent strained manfully to keep listeners amused. Sunday, of course, is a day of rest and relaxation. But on Monday, a week ago today, there was even greater opportunity for amusement. Ninety-one percent of the broadcast time went for hot-weather entertainment fare—or handy-dandy know-how and uplift. In a total of 149 listings, there were eleven short news broadcasts and only two manifestly significant programs. Well, it's August, you may say, and the educational Sahara of last week end is atypical. This, however, is unhappily not the case. During all of 1953, Americans devoted more man-hours to "I Love Lucy" and "Show of Shows" than to all the educational programs broadcast.

It would be comforting to discover that those not listening to Lucy were busy reading *Harper's* or *The New York Times*—or perhaps some recent best seller. Again, public opinion surveys demonstrate that Americans look at the printed page primarily for amusement. Many adults don't even have a kinesthetic appreciation of books. "Despite the fact that we have the highest level of formal education in the world," says Dr. Gallup, "fewer people buy and read books in this nation than in any other modern democracy." The average American—and when pollsters use the term *average* they evidently mean what they say—spends less than four minutes a day reading about national or international news. A survey of metropolitan newspaper readers reveals that more people read the most popular comic than read the most important news item.[1]

These reading and listening habits might logically lead one to suspect that Americans run a good chance of being ignorant. Several polls do indeed confirm this suspicion. In his presidential address at the Seventh Annual Convention of the American Association for Public Opinion Research, Bernard Berelson concluded that from twenty to forty percent of the public is "totally uninformed" about specific issues of the day.[2] On tests of simple information results are appalling. After the biggest radio, television, and news coverage of the nominating conventions in history, one citizen in four was still unable to name the two vice-presidential candidates. Lest you think this is an even greater reflection on the vice-presidency, let me add hurriedly that one in ten had never heard of the atomic bomb, two in every ten were unable to identify the United Nations, and only one in four had a "reasonably accurate" idea of what the Bill of Rights was about. Three out of every four were unable to identify Nehru or Molotov.[3]

If citizens know little about current affairs, they know even less about the history of their country. In a widely heralded *New York Times* survey of 7,000 students in thirty-six colleges during World War II, eighty-four percent were unable to cite two of the many contributions made by Thomas Jefferson. Twenty-five "scholars"—though certainly no Virginians —managed to get to college with the erroneous idea that George Washington was president during the Civil War. Only two in a hundred could identify Alexander H. Stephens. A third of them thought Alexander Hamilton distinguished himself as president; some—and these were college folks, remember—thought he was famous because of his watches. In a more recent survey, high-school students demonstrated that they knew more about current events than did most adults; but both groups, to quote *The New York Times*, were "shockingly ignorant." Last month, the Gallup poll proclaimed that the "average college graduate has a knowledge of

[1]George Gallup, "Mass Information or Mass Entertainment," *Vital Speeches* (May 15, 1953).

[2]Bernard Berelson, "Democratic Theory and Public Opinion," *The Public Opinion Quarterly*, XVI (Fall, 1952), p. 318.

[3]Gallup, *op. cit.*, p. 473-4; Rensis Likert quoted in Quincy Wright, ed., *The World Community* (Chicago, 1948), p. 282; Bernard Berelson and Morris Janowitz, eds., *Reader in Public Opinion and Communication* (Glencoe, Illinois), p. 487; Ralph O. Nafziger, Warren C. Engstrom, and Malcolm S. Maclean, Jr., "The Mass Media and an Informed Public," *The Public Opinion Quarterly*, XV (Spring, 1951), p. 106.

geography unworthy of an eight-year-old."[4] More people than ever before are graduated but not educated.

Worse still, we are scared as well as ignorant. *Time* calls this the "silent generation"; a survivor of the Korean War calls it the "beat generation"; and President Eisenhower worries because we are becoming a nation of spectators in sports, too timid, apparently, to take the field— even at play. Projected into the more unfamiliar realm of ideas we feel our way timorously like a barefoot boy on a cinder path. At a Madison, Wisconsin, Fourth-of-July celebration several years ago, only one stalwart patriot out of 112 was brave enough to affix his signature to the Declaration of Independence. A leading Protestant clergyman testifies that ministers today avoid basic social and moral issues in sermons which are studiously "inoffensive."[5] Robert M. Hutchins, one of the boldest of our educational leaders, and certainly not one to be easily intimidated, is quoted as saying that it's dangerous to join any organization, "even one whose sole objective is merely to preserve and perpetuate Mother's Day in America." After bewailing this sorry kind of "hostility to eccentricity and controversy," Governor Adlai Stevenson begged the girls at Smith to be more "ornery," while noting that our century needs more "idiosyncratic, unpredictable" characters.[6]

Wallowing thus in a morass of intellectual timidity, those of us yet free enough to lift a finger point it quite appropriately at demagogues, witch-hunters, and other cowardly neurotics who are, in fact, the most frightened folks of all, for they are afraid to let us decide things for ourselves. In our dismay over these antediluvians, however, we forget that we are, after all, the ones who educated those who support them. Aren't we in some measure, at least, to blame for the prevailing fear of deviationism? By preachment and assiduous practice we prepare an intellectual atmosphere in which it is more comfortable to be docile. Who among us can say in candor that he has not taken a kick-at-the-cat of eccentricity lately? Oh, to be sure, the less vigorous among us may perhaps have only clucked our tongues to advertise the horrors of being different; but, in general, we pay a studied obeisance to sacred cows of fashion in art, architecture, dress, grammar, literature, pronunciation, and parlor games. Preoccupied with the tattle-tale gray of social irregularity, we find little time for new ideas. From nursery school to graduate seminar our favorite expression is, "We don't do that." The massive disapproval of society is thus marshalled against even the most incipient tendency to stray from tribal mores or ritual.

Ignorance and intellectual timidity look bad on a Rorschach ink-blot

[4]*New York Times* (April 4, 1943), and (March 22, 1953); *Time* (July 4, 1955).

[5]Roy A. Burkhart, "Action from the Pulpit," *The Annals* of the American Academy of Political and Social Science, Vol. 250 (March, 1947), p. 80.

[6]*New York Times* (June 7, 1955).

test of democratic society. There is, as Delbert Clark has warned, "danger in what we don't know." Scared, uninformed people inevitably inspire cynicism and demagoguery in others, who, as Ambrose Bierce says, find it convenient to exploit "the conduct of public affairs for private advantage." Annoyed by the remote, impersonal operation of government, the uninformed citizen all too easily loses his faith in democratic processes. When I tell students to write their Congressman, for example, they laugh with the same cynical laugh of the G.I. when told to "go see the chaplain."

Unfortunately, this kind of cynicism is subtle, pervasive, and fashionable. Brisk young advertising men in charcoal-gray suits on Madison Avenue, tired no doubt of recommending the proper taste in toothpaste, now talk knowingly about "the engineering of consent."[7] Viewing the uninformed mass mind as merely a goose-like vacuum for them to stuff, they feed it capsulated wisdom predigested in the capacious gizzards of the great public-relations agencies. A better educated public can successfully resist this forced feeding, but we should start educating fast for as Alistair Cooke has pointed out, "We can keep hydramatic drive and still lose our democracy."[8] Our liberties are safe, said the founder of this University in a far less complicated day, only in the hands of people with a certain "degree of instruction." "If once they become inattentive to public affairs," Mr. Jefferson warned, ". . . Congress and Assemblies, Judges and Governors, shall all become wolves."

Pioneer Americans provide a refreshing contrast to the "beat" generation of today. They admired vigor in speech, bombast in oratory, hyperbole in humor, and no-holds-barred in politics. "I'm David Crockett, fresh from the backwoods, half horse, half alligator, a little touched with snapping turtle," proclaimed the newly-elected Congressman on his first trip to Washington. "I can wade the Mississippi, leap the Ohio, ride a streak of lightning, slip without a scratch down a honey locust, whip my weight in wildcats, hug a bear too close for comfort and eat any man opposed to Jackson." The irrepressible Representative from West Tennessee hardly needed to add, "I'll wear no man's collar." Like many Westerners, our hero was suspicious of the kind of pussyfooting now popular with many who today sing his praises. "Always suspect a man," he said, "who affects great softness of manner, or unruffled evenness of temper, or an enunciation studied and slow. These things are unnatural. . . . The most successful knaves are usually of this description, as smooth as razors dipt in oil, and as sharp. They affect the softness of the dove, which they have not, in order to hide the cunning of the serpent which they have." When a White-House functionary cried, "Make way for Colonel Crockett," Davy re-

[7] Edward L. Bernays, "The Engineering of Consent," *The Annals, op. cit.,* pp. 113-20.

[8] Alistair Cooke, *Vital Speeches* (November 15, 1951).

sponded with a vigorous independence now alas out of fashion: "Colonel Crockett can make way for himself."

Foreign travelers invariably testified that nineteenth-century citizens were bold, articulate champions of democracy—convinced of their own stake in the American experiment—and of their own important role in it. Charles Dickens was dismayed because politics was the "national amusement." Count Adam Gurowski noted that "the thirst for knowledge" was a major "characteristic of the American mind." Though admittedly most citizens lacked formal education, de Tocqueville found "hardly a pioneer's hut" which did not "contain a few odd volumes of Shakespeare." Philip Hone, onetime mayor of New York, observed that an American blacksmith "would think meanly of himself if he could not argue a point of law with the village lawyer." James Bryce reported a kindly sense of "human fellowship" in which citizens valued the integrity of others and felt that citizenship itself constituted "a certain ground" for respect.

Though respecting each other as individuals, our ancestors did their own thinking. Since they enjoyed controversial talk, they spoke frankly— and often at great length—even when sometimes they had little to say. So eager were they for speechmaking that they preferred it even to drama. "Lectures," complained the aristocratic Philip Hone in 1841, "are all the vogue, and the theaters are flat on their backs." Speakers displayed a remarkable laryngeal stamina, and listeners rewarded them with an even more remarkable patience, if not to say interest. A commentary of thirty minutes or an hour was hardly worthy of being called a speech. During the famous hard-cider canvass of 1840, for example, William C. Rives of Albemarle County made many speeches, some of which were over four hours' duration. A detailed analysis of these verbal marathons proves that they were informative as well as lengthy; a few, in fact, were outstanding. The solid intellectual content and the frequent classical allusions testify to the respect which speakers once accorded their listeners. As always, of course, there were those who said a lot about nothing. "Their tongues," said Congressman Crockett, "go like windmills whether they have grist to grind or not."

With the passing of the Frontier, Americans evidently lost something of their independence, something of their bold coonskin self-assurance, their articulate capacity for talk, and their willingness to listen. In the present age of mass production and specialization, individuals speak collectively through pressure groups. We hire a public-relations mouthpiece to do our talking for us; and most debate takes place at the summit, if one can call it that, between special-interest-group spokesmen. Where once politics was truly the national pastime, the engrossing subject for conversation around every village pump and cracker barrel, it now finds itself far subordinate to baseball, and way out in the deep left field of national interest. According to a recent survey, fully half of our adult population rarely if ever talk politics—and then only when activated by dramatic events. Twenty-five to thirty percent do not engage in political discussion at all.[9] The old-fashioned general store is gone; and in the jostle of the super-market, there is no room for the pot-bellied stove which once fostered an articulate democracy.

Mass production has spread from industry to art and communication. Industrial workers, bored by their routine operations, quite understandably seek escape in passive entertainment. Frustrated after eight hours with spot welder or soldering iron, they crave to be amused—thus a passionate preoccupation with the frivolities piped out of New York and Hollywood—amusing spectaculars requiring no mental effort, only a bovine capacity to endure commercials. The political programs that do find their way into our communications channels are usually concerned either with the carnival aspects of politics or with cliches—comforting verbal massage carefully designed to ease intellectual labor pains.

Yet never before have we been so well equipped to develop an enlightened electorate. In a land completely wired for sound and picture, the discouraging revelations of the pollsters are hardly credible. Our means of communicating enlightenment are unexcelled. "You are," as the Bell Telephone advertisement confidently says, "now in touch with more people and more people are in touch with you than ever before." Last year, fifty million homes had radio; the knobs of thirty-three million television sets dialed feverishly for Sullivan, Gobel, Godfrey and the rest. Meanwhile, a Ford Foundation study at the University of Toronto demonstrated that instruction by television was "as effective in teaching as classroom lectures."[10] At last, we have the technical capacity to bring enlightenment into every home—to achieve the kind of responsible and responsive democracy heretofore possible only in the small Greek state, the Swiss canton, and the New England town meeting. If we would insist, our public officials could be forced to thrash out current issues in our living rooms; but instead we apparently prefer the saturnalia of national conventions and the fanfaronade of investigations, rituals certainly more designed to debase than to enlighten.

The commercial-minded executives of our mass media will of course continue the present imbalance in favor of the frivolous and the spectacular only so long as we continue to show a taste for it. Thus it's not so much a question of will our politicians talk sense to the American people as it is a question of will we listen if and when they do. Obviously this is our problem and not one for UNIVAC.

There of course are those who say "why bother." In a genuinely pro-

[9]Berelson, *Public Opinion Quarterly*, XVI (Fall, 1952), p. 323.
[10]*World Almanac*, 1955, pp. 789-90.

vocative book, *The Lonely Crowd*, David Riesman musters his brilliant Freudian mumbo jumbo to ridicule "indignants" who are so Draconian as to demand that mass media project "civic affairs and other serious matters" into the already crowded airwaves. Though Riesman hints darkly that such "inner-directed" middle-class moralists are motivated by "a Puritanical dislike for leisure," I nevertheless should like to suggest that our mass media might well devote more than one hour out of every ten to educational broadcasting. If this informational hair shirt is too uncomfortable for a civilized citizenry, I'll purge myself of that "neo-Puritanic hygienic feeling" by scrawling "I Love Lucy" five-hundred times on a *Variety* billboard, while recalling Alistair Cooke's heartening assurance that "the piety" of Queen Victoria "depressed the English sinner for sixty hopeless years."[11]

Teachers, as Henri Peyre of Yale has said, should be bold intellectual leaders, not "retiring recluses." We should lead, not follow, public opinion. Our freedom to criticize is not a privilege granted magnanimously by a tolerant public; it is a duty and a responsibility. The Riesman doctrine of relax and enjoy TV is merely a hedonistic determinism which in practice gives the country over to the hucksters of imbecility.

More specifically, what can we do to train a better informed and more articulate democracy? Professor Harold Lasswell says we need "a new way to talk." Public discussions need a new functionary, Mr. Lasswell says, a "clarifier" who abruptly interrupts the continuous drone of sound in order to force intelligibility into talk.[12] He would operate as a kind of Mr. Quiz not too unlike the amiable but skeptical professor on Herb Schreiner's program, who speaks up when there's a communications failure. By calling the speaker back to order, the clarifier might also rouse listeners from their chair-bound Walter Mitty exploits and reveries. In practice, this means less old-fashioned oratory and more face-to-face discussion, more cross-examination, more meet-the-press kind of interrogation. It also means a more active, if not to say aggressive, role for listeners. Our students should be encouraged to ask why and when—and the rest of the stock questions required of all good reporters. Public officials need the vigorous give-and-take of cross-examination. In a free country, they are our servants, as Davy Crockett and his contemporaries frequently reminded themselves. They are not our masters, nor are they our inquisitors. We are the ones who should be asking the questions. Students should discover, as a colleague of mine once said, that they are free—not just at large.

In training a more articulate democracy, we should worry less about adjustment and more about what can be done to improve the body politic.

11David Riesman, *The Lonely Crowd* (New Haven, 1950), pp. 210-24; Alistair Cooke, *Vital Speeches* (November 15, 1951).

12Harold D. Lasswell, "Democracy through Public Opinion," in Berelson and Janowitz, eds., *Public Opinion*, pp. 469-83.

Democratic living of course requires adjustment and compromise, but it also demands the mastery of troublesome human problems—problems to which we should not become adjusted. In the past, we have talked too much about adapting the individual to his surroundings and not enough about adapting the surroundings to the individual. If a member of the current silent generation were perchance to find himself transported across the Stygian creek to Hades, he would hurriedly recall our advice, toss a bone to Cerberus, shake hands with the Prince of Darkness, and try to acclimate himself as best he could to his uncongenial surroundings. This is not, as we have often kept repeating, training for democratic living; it's the softening-up process for George Orwell's *1984*.

In an articulate democracy there should be more ideological warfare, a kind of conflict which needs our vigorous encouragement. The whisper in the Voice of America overseas is in part caused by an acute aphonia around the domestic cracker barrel. We can't export a clear conception of our way of life unless our citizens are capable of phrasing their convictions. If students learn by doing, as of course we all believe, then there should be more training in discussion and debate, the essential tools in a democratic society. Here, as Professors Henry L. Ewbank and J. Jeffery Auer point out in *The Bulletin* of Secondary-School Principals, we have the ideal laboratory method for training in the solution of "social, political, and economic problems."[13]

Mere talk, of course, is not enough. Students must have something to say. Part of the prevailing cynicism about politics arises from a popular feeling that speech-making consists largely of saying nothing well. Max Eastman writes of "the lost art of oratory," and Professor William G. Carleton of the University of Florida bemoans the "deterioration" in the "intellectual content" and "literary style" of even those leaders who "by reputation stand in the first rank."[14] The stockpile of quotations ("commonplaces" Aristotle called them) which American leaders glean from their schooling is so inadequate that of course they must rely upon ghost writers. Recognizing this, the Harvard Committee on *General Education in a Free Society* urges more memorization of "poems and passages of lasting significance." The British debaters who tour our campuses each year have given American debaters a profound sense of inferiority for they clearly demonstrate that they are at home with ideas; they have wit, and a classical culture to draw upon for their illustrations. In short, they are articulate, and we, for all our file boxes of information, are tongue-tied. A part of this Oxford erudition comes from a regimen of memoriza-

[13]Henry L. Ewbank and J. Jeffery Auer, "Decision Making: Discussion and Debate," *The Bulletin* of the National Association of Secondary-School Principals, XXXII (January, 1948), pp. 4-50.

[14]Max Eastman, "The Lost Art of Oratory," *Saturday Review*, XXXVI (March 6, 1954), pp. 11-12, p. 36; William G. Carleton, "Effective Speech in a Democracy," *Vital Speeches* (June 15, 1951).

tion, a practice abandoned here as unrealistic; yet the same generation which rejected this as too artificial, now accepts the inherent dishonesty of the ghost writer without blush or embarrassment.

An articulate citizenry must know both facts and logic. Facts are what people think with; consequently, it's impossible to teach thinking in a factual wasteland. The most pointless, yet often the most acrimonious, arguments develop over questions which might be settled quickly by shuffling a few pages in the *World Almanac*. Arguments arising from faulty logic, however, are less easily settled because most of us are unable to find the right page in Aristotle's handbook. More time can well be spent specifically on the labyrinthian mysteries of the reasoning process itself. As Professor Arleigh B. Williamson suggests, we might well add a "T" to the three "R's," reading, writing, arithmetic, and *thinking*.[15]

By emphasizing facts and logic we can perhaps encourage a corresponding lack of respect for successful sophistry. When leading rabble-rousers pay eloquent tribute to their academic training in public speaking, we all cringe in collective embarrassment for obviously an ethical X-factor has been neglected, even though a success-mad society is no doubt more blameworthy than the educational system which reflects it.

Finally, students in an articulate democracy must have more respect for ideas—particularly for the ideas of others. Lord Bryce listed this as an American characteristic in the 'eighties, and isn't it indeed a basic ingredient of true democracy? Despite their self-canonization as apostles of Americanism, those who would silence us by inquisitorial strategems are Arch-enemies from an Underworld of Authoritarianism. "In America," wrote two distinguished foreign observers a century ago, "the spirit of progress is bold, and often encroaching . . . new ideas easily get a fair chance of being practically tried; the public at large does not shrink from testing . . . different solutions of a political problem, and the Sovereignty of the States affords great opportunity for it." The University of Virginia was established in this bold spirit as a testing ground for ideas. "This institution," said Mr. Jefferson of the newly founded University, "will be based on the illimitable freedom of the human mind. For here we are not afraid to follow truth wherever it may lead, nor to tolerate any error so long as reason is left free to combat it."

Training for an articulate democracy, as John W. Studebaker, former Commissioner of Education said of teaching, is not "a task for timorous or feeble souls; nor for the complacent and uncertain. It requires Americans whose faith in democracy does not waver or falter because they know whereof they speak and are convinced that the values they defend are eternally right and true."[16]

[15]Arleigh B. Williamson, "Safeguarding Channels of Communication," *The Annals, op. cit.*, p. 10.

[16]*Congressional Record*, 80th Congress, 2d Session, Vol. 94, Pt. 10, pp. 2205-06.

## SUPPLEMENTARY READINGS

Aristotle, *Rhetoric,* trans. by Lane Cooper. New York: Appleton-Century-Crofts, 1932. Treatment of the nature of rhetoric and persuasion, pp. 1-89.

Berquist, Goodwin F., Jr., ed., *Speches for Illustration and Example.* Chicago: Scott, Foresman, 1966. Interesting collection of four speeches illustrating "the problem of speaking on behalf of a group," pp. 17-99.

Braden, Waldo W., and Gehring, Mary Louise, *Speech Practices: A Resource Book for the Student of Public Speaking.* New York: Harper & Row, 1958. An emphasis upon the use of ethical and pathetic appeals in "The Speaker Meets the Audience," pp. 54-69.

Eisenson, Jon, Auer, J. Jeffery, and Irwin, John V., *The Psychology of Communication.* New York: Appleton-Century-Crofts, 1963. A summary of research studies and their applications to the speech-building process, in "Psychology of Public Address," pp. 271-309.

Linkugel, Wil A., Allen, R. R., and Johannesen, Richard L., eds., *Contemporary American Speeches: A Sourcebook of Speech Forms and Principles.* Belmont, Calif.: Wadsworth, 1965. Twenty-two speeches to persuade, with some each on propositions of fact, value, and policy, and some on general problems, pp. 21-105.

## EXERCISES

1. From *Vital Speeches,* or some of the collections of speeches listed in the Supplementary Readings, study the introductions to three speeches. Imagine yourself sitting in each audience, and decide whether the speech would get your attention at the beginning if effectively spoken. Don't be discouraged if most, or all, of these introductions seem to fail. Remember that most speeches today (though conspicuously not all) are given by people who may be experts on their subjects, but who have never learned the techniques of speaking.

2. Make an outline of Robert G. Gunderson's persuasive speech (pp. 153-161). Make also a technical plot (see p. 101 for an explanation of technical plots) in which you set down in detail the steps and procedures in persuasion that were used by the speaker.

3. Go to hear a speaker, and while he is speaking make a key-word outline of his address. Later, but while the speech is still fresh in mind, expand this into a full-content outline. In the technical plot set down the steps and procedures in persuasion that were used. Also note any essential ones that were missing.

4. Make a full-content outline including the technical plot for one or more

of the speeches given in class. After studying the speaker's method, as revealed by this outline, write a brief critique of the speech that *will be helpful to the speaker in future talks.*

5. Prepare and deliver a speech to persuade. As you know (see pp. 92-93) there are two levels of persuasion: (1) to stimulate, and (2) to change. You may attempt either one, depending on the listeners' attitude to your proposition, but you should know which you are attempting. The following suggestions may be helpful:

a. Choose a subject about which you are concerned, and on which you have thought for a long time.

b. Reinforce your own ideas and experiences with material gathered from the library. Talk with others. Be alert to materials that always come to a speaker who is on the lookout.

c. Follow the steps and procedures of persuasion set forth in this chapter.

d. Don't try to be an authority on government, politics, or world affairs. If you need it, get authority, and tell when and where authority testified.

e. Don't use this speech as an excuse for airing thinly veiled prejudices. Don't damn or praise indiscriminately Russia, China, Congress, the President, Labor, Management, or anything or anyone.

f. Instead, if you discuss a controversial issue, get your facts (and be sure they *are* facts), assemble your ideas, rest them on impelling wants, and present them to listeners. Hit as hard as you want with the facts, but do not name-call or sing a hymn of hate. No question is too hot to handle, but mud-throwing does not solve problems.

g. Don't pretend to have proved more than you really have proved. In short, don't give listeners a chance to call you a falsifier or exaggerator. So present your case that even those who disagree will say willingly, "He was honest and fair."

6. Read carefully the speech by Robert G. Gunderson in this chapter (pp. 153-161), and discover answers for these questions:

a. Judging only from the text of his speech, what do you think must have been the speaker's preliminary analysis of his audience—the general and specific characteristics of its members, their attitudes toward him, and toward his subject?

b. What examples can you list of how the speaker used words and sentences to get attention and hold interest throughout the speech?

c. In what ways, if any, did the speaker's organization depart from the principles set forth in this chapter?

d. What use, if any, did the speaker make of suspense, activity, or humor?

e. What evidence can you cite in the text of the speech suggesting that the speaker attempted to develop audience confidence in his competence and character?

f. Taking into account what you can generalize about an audience of Virginia high school teachers of English, speech, and drama, which of their impelling wants would be significant for this speech? What evidence is there that the speaker similarly identified their impelling wants and rested his reason upon them?

g. Again taking into account the general character of the audience, how would you characterize their probable attitude: favorable, indifferent, doubtful or uninformed, or opposed? What evidence is there that the speaker similarly identified their probable attitude and developed each part of his speech to meet it?

h. What is your overall evaluation of this as a persuasive speech?

# 9

# Speaking in Group Meetings

Sometimes it seems that committees are for comics: "A committee is a group of the unwilling selected by the unfit to do the unnecessary," "A camel is the product of a committee that started out to design a horse," or "Search all the public parks and you'll never find a monument to a committee." But those responsible for the world's work know better. Rollie Tillman, Jr., reports in the *Harvard Business Review* that business executives spend approximately fourteen hours a week in committees and informal conferences.[1] That means almost two working days each week, without counting conversations with staff members, sales training meetings, and other occasions for informal talk. This pattern is repeated in government agencies, college administrations, labor unions, and organizations of all kinds.

Those who talk over their common problems, informally and purposefully, in committees and other small group meetings, are not *public* speakers. But, as we shall see, they nonetheless rely upon the common principles of all speech communication: definiteness of purpose, clarity of organization and language, adequacy of support, persuasiveness in matter and manner.

## TYPES OF GROUP MEETINGS

Discussion in the sense of purposeful talk intended to exchange information and ideas, critically evaluate them, and then to evolve from them solutions for common problems, takes place in many types of group meetings.

### Informal Group Discussions

Here no more than twenty people converse rather than make set

[1] 38 (May-June, 1960), pp. 7-12.

speeches, in a face-to-face setting, about a subject of mutual interest. It is assumed that members share equally in the meeting and in responsibility for its outcome. It is also assumed that members will come with information to share, and expect to learn from each other. Their talk may be informal, but it should be informed; if the group appears to have done no homework in gathering facts or drawing inferences, it should be adjourned to remedy the defect.

Although an informal group has no audience and a minimum of organization, it usually functions under the guidance of a discussion leader, selected in advance and prepared for his task by developing a tentative outline (usually in the form of questions to be addressed to the group) to get the conversation underway and to keep it on the track.

Discussions do not always achieve their goals. Sometimes the goals are too high. Not every discussion should aim at solving its basic problem; just identifying and exploring it may be enough for one session. Sometimes members have not learned the steps of logical problem-solving, and become impatient with the process or anxious to dominate it. And sometimes the leader is inept. But when conditions are right and conferees are conscientious, informal group discussions can profitably cultivate and apply good ideas.

## Cooperative Investigations

The procedure for this type of group function is more formal, as its purpose is more sharply focused. It is designed for situations where group members have little information on the topic, and no expert is available to lecture on what they need to know. There are usually eight steps in this "do-it-yourself" exercise.

1. The group meets in advance to elect a leader and to divide the subject into a number of subtopics. Each member then undertakes to investigate at least one subtopic.
2. So that members can know what each has accomplished, the leader calls one or more meetings to review assignments and make final plans.
3. When the discussion meeting is held the leader begins by analyzing and defining the problem.
4. Each member then presents his information in a brief report. The report contains no argument, but only information, and that in concise and orderly form.
5. When these reports have been completed, the leader calls for any other pertinent information that members may have.
6. The leader then concludes the first portion of the meeting by succinctly summarizing the fresh pool of information, and then opens the second half by inviting discussion in light of the facts presented. Members should not now debate possible solutions for the problem, but focus

only on this goal: *How can we settle this problem so that it is settled right, and will stay settled?* Possible solutions are scrutinized carefully for disadvantages, and then these are explored to find ways of overcoming them. If too much information has been presented for easy digesting in one meeting, the leader should suggest concentrating only upon one segment of it. If a particular item in the discussions tends to stir up members' emotions, the leader may—figuratively—want to refrigerate it. He should know that a minimum of emotionalism and a maximum of logical analysis is necessary for any longtime settlement of problems. (For this reason Quaker meetings and some corporate boards of directors effectually refrigerate problems for years, waiting for tensions to subside.)

7. Finally, if the nature of the problem permits, ways and means for putting an agreed-upon solution into operation are discussed.

8. At the conclusion of the discussion the leader may want to summarize the points of agreement, identify any problems that may still need attention, and evaluate the process by which the group reached its understandings.

City councils, boards of education, adult education groups, church boards, and similar groups, use approximately this method in their deliberations.

## Committees and Conferences

We appoint a committee to represent all of the members of an organization and to perform a task they could not efficiently undertake. (A *conference*, in the way we use the term, is operationally the same as a committee, but those who confer are delegates from different organizations.) Congressional tax bills, board of education employment policies, or fraternity bylaws are thus formulated by committees of the parent groups. All members of the organization, of course (or organizations in the case of a conference), may file suggestions with the committee, and debate its recommendations when they come before a full meeting.

To facilitate decision-making, committee or conference groups should include an odd number of members. When the task is analyzing a problem and suggesting solutions, seven or nine members may be desirable. But three are more effective in detailed tasks such as drafting reports, collective bargaining agreements, or constitutions.

The atmosphere of a committee or conference meeting should be that of an informal group discussion, and the chairman's role should be that of a good discussion leader. The information-gathering process may resemble that of a cooperative investigation, but of course many committees, such as legislative ones, may gather facts and opinions from those who testify in public hearings.

### Business Meetings

At stated intervals, clubs and voluntary associations hold business meetings. All members are urged to attend, and it is assumed that those who do not will acquiesce in decisions made by those who do. The president, or some other elected officer, presides, and the structure of the meeting traditionally includes minutes of the last meeting, reports of officers and standing committees, reports of special committees, new business, and old business. A standard code of parliamentary procedure, previously adopted by the organization, governs the conduct of business, including rules of debate, voting on motions, and so on.

Because most speaking in business meetings is for or against a specific motion it usually differs in important ways from speaking in other group situations: 1. it is aimed at persuasion more than exploration, 2. it is governed by established parliamentary rules (each member must be formally "recognized" by the presiding officer before he "has the floor," his remarks must be germane to the question "before the house," and he may be limited in how long or how often he can speak on a single motion), and 3. it customarily has the hallmarks of formal discourse (introduction, body, and conclusion), albeit commonly a short "one-point" speech.

The presiding officer functions more formally than the discussion leader or committee chairman. He follows a traditional *agenda* (we listed the sequence of business a paragraph ago), he recognizes speakers in some order (choosing between two who seek recognition simultaneously, usually alternating those for and against a motion, and giving precedence to those who have not spoken previously), and he enforces the organization's parliamentary rules in such matters as submitting motions, debating them, and voting upon them.

Business meetings need not always be so sharply structured. One proper motion asks for "informal consideration" of a subject, and another permits group discussion without most parliamentary rules (in "committee of the whole"). When the time comes for ultimate decisions, however, some degree of formality must be resumed in order to determine in a fair and orderly way the will of the majority. (For a handbook on parliamentary procedure see the references at the end of this chapter.

## CHARACTERISTICS OF GOOD GROUP MEETINGS

There are many ways of looking at discussion—as a tool in the democratic process, as a channel for human relationships, and as an educational method. No matter the point of view, good discussion meetings have essential characteristics, reflected in this definition: *a planned, but relatively informal, meeting in which those who attend are invited to join in purposeful talk about a topic or problem of mutual interest, under the guidance of a leader, chairman, or presiding officer.* Let us look at each element.

1. *Planning* will do more for a discussion than spontaneous combustion. Like any other form of discourse, discussions need to progress from point to point with some order. Practically the leader may do much of the planning, but ideally he will get all of the help he can from group members.

2. *Informality* is a way of creating an atmosphere that encourages maximum participation. The number of participants, the flexibility of seating facilities, and the nature of the meeting place will all contribute to the discussion climate.

3. *Participation* should be as broad as possible, assuming that each group member has something significant to contribute, and that the frank and full exposure of all points of view is the best way to come to the right solution.

4. *Purpose* is a prerequisite for any kind of profitable talk. Talk that is pleasant only, "here I come, relevant or not!" lends color but not content to discussion.

5. *Leadership* of some sort is necessary in any successful group meeting. While the discussion leader or committee chairman may customarily provide much of the leadership, his failure to do so should result in other members sharing the responsibility.

These characteristics alone will not make a good discussion meeting, but a good one is most unlikely without them. Part of the occasional breakdown in the discussion process can be charged to expecting too much of the method, or misusing it. For example, discussion is a slow process, no way to decide whether to call the fire department if the library is ablaze. Discussion is a poor method for resolving questions of fact: you check out Casey Stengel's managerial record in the *World Almanac*, not in a committee. And discussion applied to a new problem may lead only to a pooling of ignorance, whereas selected readings or pertinent lectures can provide the necessary facts. Perhaps the most common errors are 1. stating the question for discussion in such a way that it does not focus sharply on one specific problem, and 2. stating the question in such a way that each group member can automatically respond "yes" or "no." The first error leads to a diffused discussion—like the short, short skirt, it covers almost nothing completely. The second error leads to a divided discussion—like kids playing cops and robbers, members are on one side or the other before the dicussion really starts.

# HOW TO PARTICIPATE EFFECTIVELY

Those who are inexperienced with the discussion method may think that little preparation is required if "we're just going to talk things over," and that any experienced public speaker will surely be a good discussion participant. Nothing could be more erroneous. Effective participation in discussion is rooted in an understanding of basic communication skills. But they must be adapted, just as a public speaker must adapt them with different audiences, subjects, and occasions.

### Get the Facts and Get Them in Order

Even the quickest wit is no substitute for information. Only a substantial base of facts will support a structure of trustworthy opinions. And facts and opinions are the building blocks of good judgments in discussion meetings as they are anywhere else. When you are to take part in any kind of discussion, therefore, you must first prepare yourself by studying the subject. Review what we said in Chapter 2 in more detail, and with these adaptations:

1. *Take stock of what you know.* Try to organize your information, your recollections, and your feelings into an orderly outline. This will not only help you see what you know, but show what you have yet to find out.

2. *Investigate by talking, listening, and observing.* Remember that in discussion there is free give-and-take, a greater opportunity for modifying and explaining ideas while they are still in process, and a more highly individualized response to anything you say than would be so in a public speech. Therefore think in terms of individuals—those who will be your fellow-participants, if you know them—as you gather information. Close human relationships are inherent in discussion, and the wider range of examples, illustrations, and other specific and vivid instances you can collect, the better your chance of relating to each other group member. Because discussion topics are often problems "close to home" (such as local school policies, recreation programs, student government affairs, and social welfare projects), there may be little library material on them. First-hand observations and conversations with those intimately involved in the problem thus become of prime importance.

3. *Investigate by reading.* Discussions are also held on national or international problems with few local counterparts (such as balance of trade, containment of aggressor nations, industrial depreciation tax allowances, and United Nations activities), and on these traditional library research is essential. Thus all that we have said earlier about checking

standard sources, reading from the general to the specific, and so on, applies here.

4. *Organize what you know into an expanded outline.* Your search for information should help you fill gaps in your earlier outline. It may also raise new questions, suggest new dimensions of the problem, and indicate critical relationships with other problems. All of these matters should appear in your expanded outline. As a guide to final outlining, remember that most problem-solving follows this kind of pattern:

1. What is the nature and extent of the problem confronting the group?
2. How did the problem come into being?
3. What possible solutions have been proposed?
4. What are the advantages and disadvantages of each?
5. Which solution, or combination of solutions, seems best?
6. How can this solution be put into operation?

### Develop an Attitude of Inquiry

A very wise woman, Bonaro W. Overstreet, recently observed that "I've long felt that our educational system rather fails to help young people be graciously ignorant and perplexed—so that they are tempted to retreat into some oversimplification in order to feel that they can speak confidently."[2] Discussion is no cure-all for this problem, but it does provide a method for repairing ignorance and an atmosphere where perplexities are welcomed. Discussion is *"thought in process."* Participants must approach it in a spirit of inquiry, a tentativeness of position, and willingness to follow where the evidence leads. Discussion is not a contest: there are no "sides" and you cannot score points off the opposition. The desire to excel, to dominate, or to scintillate are out of order in discussion.

Instead, cultivate a concern for the welfare of the whole group, especially those who are uninformed and in doubt. Their questions can lead you to re-think your own ideas. Remember that an idea isn't necessarily good just because it is your own—and that even if it is good it may become better after you have explained it to others. Conversely, remember that ideas that have never occurred to you may still be good ones. Be willing to appraise ideas, not their sources. You are looking for strengths and weaknesses in ideas, advantages and disadvantages, not "Brownie points" for the proponents.

A large element in successful participation is *learning to participate by listening.* Irving J. Lee, an astute observer of troubles that come when people talk together, wrote in his *How to Talk with People* that a major problem arises when discussion participants "talk past each other." They aren't really listening to each others' comments, he says, but just thinking about what they'll say when they can break into the conversation. Indeed,

[2]In a letter to Richard L. Weaver, II, April 5, 1966. Quoted with Mrs. Overstreet's permission.

in this sense, there is no developing and cumulative conversation, only a verbal ping-pong game. The remedy? Listen to what others have to say, work with them in improving their ideas by asking questions and making suggestions. As nearly as is humanly possible, rise above your biases and avoid emotional tensions. The end product is worthwhile. The Quakers long ago set it down as a truism in their Book of Discipline, and it has been confirmed in dozens of experimental studies: when the purpose of discussion is to make decisions, groups usually make better ones than any individual member can.

## Test the Things You Hear

A healthy skepticism is one hallmark of a well-educated man. Don't confuse the skeptic with the cynic. A cynic announces that he believes nothing; a skeptic says he *may* be willing to believe, but not until after he asks a few questions.

In group discussions skepticism should be encouraged. The little bit of Socrates that is in every man should be brought out. We cannot here write a textbook on fallacies and how to detect them, but we can suggest four of the chief ways they arise in discussion and how to ask questions to test them.

1. *The nature of testimony and testing "authorities."* It is good practice when we are in doubt to get information from those who are not. Thus we commonly employ evidence by testimony, given by a man whose special qualifications to know or to judge lends special weight to his words. Sometimes, however, persons with impressive credentials in one area may be cited as "authorities" in areas quite outside of their competence, or persons with dubious credentials may be passed off as "authorities."

Participants in discussion need to know what testimonial evidence is and be prepared to test alleged "authorities." Here are some stock questions with which to start: Is the testimonal reference specific and relevant to the point at issue? Is the authority generally qualified—physically, mentally, morally—to testify? Is he really in a position to know or to interpret the facts? Is he aware of the signficance of his testimony? Is he reluctant to testify, as against his own best interests? Is he free from hidden bias? Is he supported by known facts, by other authorities?

2. *The process of generalizing and testing "examples."* The art of generalizing makes life easier for all of us. We should be forever making up our minds even on routine matters if we had to review individually each relevant experience or bit of knowledge. Instead we save time by generalizing that the United States lies in the temperate zone, that icy roads require caution, that creativity can be cultivated, that the overall

trend of the stock market is up. At the base of each of these generalizations lies one or more "examples," facts, opinions, or phenomena that are
allegedly typical of a whole class of like instances.

Discussion participants should know how generalizations evolve and
how to test the basic "examples." These questions will help. Have the
examples been selected to support a preconceived conclusion? Are they
really typical of their class? Have contrary examples been deliberately
or inadvertently ignored? Are the examples numerous enough to make a
truly representative sample of their class? Are the generalizations based
upon examples supported also by other kinds of evidence?

3. *The argument by analogy and testing "similarities."* "Once before
I was in a bind like this, and what I did that time was . . ." is a thought
that precedes many personal decisions. It is a way of shortcutting; instead
of making a fresh analysis of the new problem we assume its "similarities"
with other situations where we know all of the details. Thus we assert
that because two things resemble each other in certain known respects,
the resemblance will persist into unknown aspects. "The thirteen colonies
were able to establish a federal government, and certainly the democratic
nations of today should be able to do the same."

Those who prepare for discussion should understand the structure
of arguments by analogy and also how to test the presumed "similarities."
Begin with: Is the analogy relevant to the point at issue? Does the
analogy over-emphasize "similarities" and disregard fundamental differences in the two situations? Are all aspects of the two situations accessible
to observation and analysis? Does the analogy rest upon a valid generalization based on many "similarities" or only upon a single example? Do other
forms of support lead to the same conclusion as the alleged analogy?

4. *The argument by causality and testing "coincidences."* When we
know that two events are associated, one invariably and indispensably
occurring *before* the other, and we assume that therefore the first is the
*cause* of the second, we are arguing by causality. "Excessive nationalism
—as in Kaiser Germany and Hitler Germany—led to war. So Chinese nationalism will do today." The problem here? It is that when we allege
causations we deny the possibility of simple "coincidences." Some things
just *happen* to happen pretty close together in time, but are otherwise
unrelated.

Participants in discussion ought to study the logic of causality (cause-
to-effect, effect-to-cause, and effect-to-effect) and know some tests for
"coincidences." For example: Can it be demonstrated that the alleged
cause really brought about the effect? Is it reasonable to assume that the
alleged cause could produce the effect? Does the alleged causality ignore
other equally possible causes? Could the alleged cause produce still other
effects? Do other methods of reasoning support the alleged causal relation?

## Practice the Right Techniques

A constant hazard in any form of discussion is that it becomes profitless talk. It can become profitless by ignoring the processes of thinking, forgetting the virtues of a spirit of inquiry, and by failing to develop a healthy skepticism. Related to all three of these sins of omission, and significant in their own right, are demonstrated patterns of effective behavior. The following are reminders developed by experienced leaders of discussion:

1. Remember you are cooperating in serious conversation. You should feel free to join in whenever you have something to say. Help the leader keep the discussion moving forward.
2. Listen thoughtfully to others. Ask for explanations if you are unclear. Always be clear before you reply.
3. Speak up when you can make a contribution, but don't try to monopolize the discussion.
4. Try to speak no more than one minute at a time, except under unusual conditions.
5. If you don't understand something just said, say so, for there may be others like you. Ask for an example.
6. If you disagree with what is said, be candid and say so, but in a friendly fashion.
7. Don't wait to be called on before you speak, especially early in the discussion.
8. Stay seated while speaking, address others informally, but speak up so you can be heard.
9. Remember to practice what you know about effective speech communication—be clear, be simple, be coherent, be specific.
10. Come to every discussion meeting intending to take part. If you don't have information to give, have questions to ask.
11. Don't expect one meeting to resolve an important and controversial problem. There is no such thing as "instant wisdom."

# HOW TO BE AN EFFECTIVE LEADER

Yes, it's easier to write about than to be one. And it's easier to say how *not* to be an effective leader. A discussion leader guides but does not steer the discussion meeting. He is not simply a chairman. He is neither a teacher nor a lecturer. He is not a persuader. He is not an autocrat who dominates the discussion. Instead he personifies the spirit of democratic inquiry by helping group members work toward their own solutions, yet without directing or controlling their thinking.

## The Leader—in General

In general, the effective discussion leader has a complex of personality attributes, knowledge, and skills. If you weren't born with them, be assured that they can be learned.

1. *Be steady and stable.* The unexpected is the most likely thing to happen in a discussion, and the leader must be able to think and act quickly. The man who always needs a map to go by will be in trouble. Leaders will also be in trouble if they are not emotionally stable, for they must sometimes deal with members who are not.

2. *Be courteous and fair.* In a turbulent discussion heated arguments and angry words can best be cooled by a courteous and restrained, though firm, leader. He must be eminently fair and tactful, but not to the point of abdicating his responsibility for seeing that every member has his chance to speak, and that the main focus is kept on problems, not people.

3. *Keep the spotlight on the members.* The leader who calls attention to the mistakes of others, or parades his own knowledge of the topic, will be about as popular as the quarterback who assigns himself the ball for every touchdown play. The spotlight is for the members, and the background for the leader, so long as the discussion moves forward, no matter how slowly.

4. *Know the rules of the game.* He should know about the discussion process, what to expect and some of the ways for encouraging it; about how to sort out assertions from truths, evidence from speculation; about his group, the qualifications and potential contributions of each member; and about communication, with an ability to talk the language of the group, a facility for asking questions, and a voice that can be heard.

5. *Know the topic.* The leader should possess a good general knowledge of the topic, but behave like the layman who asks questions about it, not the expert who answers them. If he really is an expert, he would be more useful as a member, or as a resource person, with someone else in the leader's role.

## The Leader—in Action

To help a group establish its own goal, and then to help it keep moving toward that goal, requires the patience of a saint, and the persistence of a sinner. But even those who fall somewhere in between should be able to learn from experience, and these admonitions.

1. *Plan the meeting.* First, learn all you can about the group. Is this its first meeting? Do members know each other? What do they know about

the discussion method? How much about the topic? Second, consult with members when you can in setting up the meeting, determining the scope of the discussion, assigning special subtopics for investigation, and so on.

2. *Prepare a discussion outline.* "The best laid plans . . . ," and so frequently do outlines made in advance. But if the group might need an overview of the whole topic, or the leader might need a checklist of the discussion process as applied to *this* topic, or if pump-priming questions are needed to keep the discussion going, then an outline can be a life saver. Even if it has to be modified as the discussion progresses, because members see new dimensions the leader didn't anticipate, or because he over- or underestimated their knowledge, it is better than having no plan at all. Modifying it according to all the circumstances of the discussion, the leader can use the six-step problem-solving outline that appeared a few pages back.

3. *Get the meeting started.* Whatever he says, the leader's opening remarks should be brief and direct, and set an example for the group. He may himself want to define the topic, state its development in current thinking, or just toss out a provocative question or two. Or he may ask in advance some member with first hand experience to comment on the topic. Or have a "situation story" read about how someone else dealt with the same problem, or illuminating it with a brief case study. Whatever he does, the leader should plan it. Even rehearse it.

4. *Keep the discussion moving down the track.* This is really a twin problem. Keeping the conversation moving at all may sometimes be a challenge. If it's because the members are all talked out, have nothing new to say, and need more information, then by all means move it to a quick close. Keeping a lively discussion on the track may be harder. The problem is to find the golden mean. On the one hand, don't be too sure that a seemingly irrelevant comment or two may not prove to have real significance. And on the other, do discourage clearly frivolous, extraneous, repetitious, or stupid remarks. Especially with the latter type the leader's tact should be showing.

5. *Make occasional summaries.* One of the ways of halting a runaway discussion, or retrieving one that is stalled on a siding, is to summarize "where we are now." The summary should be brief, impartial, and honest in not trying to force agreement where none exists. It is a useful device for completing the talk about some subtopic, or for finding out if the group is ready to complete it.

6. *Encourage general participation.* Real genius may be called for if the leader is to involve every member of the group in discussion, but he should try. Except, of course, for the one who has nothing to say and is willing to keep it to himself. He also needs to keep the discussion, if he can, from being one-sided. If need be to restore balance, he may play the

devil's advocate. Or he may specifically encourage those whom he knows to have divergent opinions. He need not be a mind reader to know who to call on, for members will show in their faces whether they are in agreement or disagreement with a speaker. To achieve these ends, and most others, he needs a mental storehouse of questions: "Has anyone thought about . . ." "What reasons do we have . . ." "Can anyone tell me what . . ." "Can you give us a specific example . . ." "Would anyone else like to . . ." and so on.

7. *Round out the meeting.* We deliberately say round out rather than conclude the meeting. More than a simple summary is needed, though that is part of the leader's responsibility. Where there has been consensus, he should recognize it, and do the same for any unresolved difference of opinion. Beyond summing up the leader should, assuming that it is so, leave the members with a feeling of having progressed toward a goal, of having learned something about the spirit of inquiry, and about looking before leaping. These achievements can be as important as finding a solution for the original problem.

Walter Bagehot long ago observed that "one of the greatest pains to human nature is the pain of a new idea." It is still true today. But it is also true that the highest tolerance for new ideas is most likely to be found in discussion groups, committees, and conferences where people can work together on their common problems and for the common good.

## SUPPLEMENTARY READINGS

Auer, J. Jeffery, *Essentials of Parliamentary Procedure*, 3rd ed., New York: Appleton-Century-Crofts, 1959; paperbound, 58 pp. Compatible with Robert's *Rules of Order*, but only the essentials for taking part in or presiding over clubs and voluntary associations.

Chase, Stuart, *Guides to Straight Thinking; with Thirteen Common Fallacies.* New York: Harper & Row, 1956. A sprightly analysis of the most common fallacies, with examples from political speeches, advertisers, broadcast commentators, and propagandists of various kinds.

Eisenson, Jon, Auer, J. Jeffery, and Irwin, John V., *The Psychology of Communication.* New York: Appleton-Century-Crofts, 1963. A summary of research studies on behavior in communication groups by participants and leaders, in "Psychology of Group Discussion," pp. 253-270.

Harnack, R. Victor, and Fest, Thorrel B., *Group Discussion: Theory and Technique.* New York: Appleton-Century-Crofts, 1964. A modern treatment of discussion, drawing generously upon small group contributions to traditional rhetorical concepts.

Lee, Irving J., *How to Talk with People: A Program for Preventing Troubles*

*That Come When People Talk Together.* New York: Harper & Row, 1952. An analysis of committee, conference, and board meetings and practical suggestions for overcoming their communication difficulties.

## EXERCISES

1. Listen to a radio or television discussion and report on the following: (a) Which of the six steps of discussion were covered. (b) Whether in your opinion any steps left out should have been covered, or any covered should have been left out. (c) How you would have discussed the problem differently if you had been a participant.

2. The class will select a topic for cooperative investigation, then elect a leader. The leader, of course, will lay careful plans: (a) Appoint a special committee to give the topic preliminary consideration and to divide it into subtopics (or the leader may do this himself, or in conference with others). (b) Appoint members of the class to investigate each of the subtopics. (c) Conduct the cooperative investigation with the entire class taking part.

3. The class will organize itself into a Legislative Assembly and set up a group of committees so that each person in the class is a member of one committee. Class members can then introduce bills into the Assembly, as many as they want. When all bills have been presented, the Assembly will vote on which bills it wants to consider, and the Speaker of the Assembly will refer these bills to the proper committees, taking care to see that every committee has a bill referred to it. The committees will then meet and discuss the bills. This discussion, of course, ought to follow the regular discussion steps and ought to represent cooperative group thinking. Out of the discussion each committee will prepare a report. If committee members cannot agree on a single report, then two reports may be prepared—a majority and a minority report. The committee chairman will present the report at the next class meeting; and if there are both a minority and a majority report, another committee member can report the second one. After the bills have been reported, the Assembly can discuss them further and vote on them, but this is not necessary for the purpose of this project. The real purpose is to give committee members experience in working on a problem by thinking and talking together.

4. Analyze the discussion heard in one of your classes (or in a campus organization, the Student Council, or a conference of some sort): (a) Which kind of discussion was it? (b) To what extent did it measure up to the qualities of good discussion as set out in this chapter, and where did it fail? (c) To what extent did the leader have those qualifications described in this chapter, and wherein was he deficient? (d) To what extent did the other participants take part, and how could they have been more effective?

5. Listen to a discussion and identify and evaluate testimony, generalizations,

analogies, and causalities that are presented by the participants. How do they stand up under the tests suggested in this chapter?

6. Select a topic for discussion appropriate to an informal group: (a) Modify the six suggested steps in discussion to fit this topic; (b) Develop a series of questions that would enable the leader to probe but not pronounce on each of the subtopics.

# 10

# Speaking in Public Meetings

The editors of *Life*, a few years ago, speculated that in the October to April season over 100,000,000 Americans heard at least one public lecture on some topic from the Mohole Project to Mandalay. "Today's platform pundits," they reported, "try for a factual, flexible tone, wrap a dose of learning inside a dollop of laughter. World affairs lectures draw largest interest with the lively arts second." *Time* also recorded that "a significant 20th Century characteristic of U. S. life is the revival of public discussion . . . lectures, forums, panel discussions. Busy and learned men give their time to these gatherings in the American belief that an informed and alert citizenry is the basis of democracy."

Such activity has much in common with the increased reliance, among small groups, upon informal discussions, committees, conferences, and business meetings, also a notable characteristic of this century. The philosophical basis is much the same for all these forms of speech communication. And the same principles and techniques apply basically in all human relationships. The differences are largely adaptations to specific situations. Here are some peculiar to speaking in public meetings.

## CHARACTERISTICS OF PUBLIC MEETINGS

1. In the group meetings described in Chapter 9, relatively few people are involved, everyone literally has an opportunity to participate, and there are no on-lookers. In public discussion meetings, however, the speaking is done by not more than three or four persons, and before a large audience, a very few members of which can really participate actively. Thus those who speak in group meetings talk for each other, those in public meetings for an audience.

2. In group meetings we have urged a climate of informality as the

most productive. In public meetings, however, everything is necessarily more formal. Those who speak are customarily on a platform where they may be visible to several hundred or even several thousand persons. Instead of speaking in small snippets of talk, they make extended addresses (except in panel discussions) and are truly solo performers. This obviously means that those who take part in public discussion meetings are truly *public speakers*, not the conversationalists of the small groups.

3. In group meetings, where there is no audience, there are no audience questions. The questions that are asked—and they may be many—are put to each other by the participants in the group, and they are asked at the time they seem most pertinent. They are not saved up to be asked in the closing minutes of the meeting. Except for such applause as it may give along the way it is only in the last segment of a public meeting that the audience can participate overtly. Even then the time available relative to the audience size is probably such that not more than a dozen or two persons can be recognized during the forum period. Mostly they ask questions to get additional information or speaker opinions, but sometimes they are also encouraged to state their own views.

4. Finally, in group meetings one person plays a very active role as discussion leader, committee chairman, or presiding officer. He may, with varying restrictions, participate directly in the discussion, and usually does. In public discussion meetings, by contrast, the man in charge is a *moderator* (except in panel discussions) whose main function, aside from introducing whoever is to speak next, is to ask for audience questions during the forum period. Unlike small group meetings, generally unharried and exploratory, public meetings are expected to begin and end on time, and to keep moving along in between. This thankless task is also assigned to the moderator. Common sense, poise, a good voice, and a sense of humor are his best attributes.

More than in group meetings, public meetings are organized into formats that significantly influence both speaker-participant and moderator-leader. It is thus expedient to discuss each form separately and completely, and saving only the forum period for a generalized treatment. Assuming that the forum is an essential aspect of all public meetings, these patterns for presentation are called panel-forum, symposium-forum, lecture-forum, and debate-forum.

## THE PANEL-FORUM

A panel discussion is designed to increase audience understanding of a problem or to help it weigh advantages and disadvantages of possible courses of action. It is especially effective as a means for introducing a totally new problem.

Essentially a panel is a group of three to five persons, including a chairman who usually functions much like the leader in a small group meeting. The panel members are persons with special knowledge of the topic. Before an audience that can see and hear them they carry on a public conversation, albeit one more rigorously structured than what the same participants might have in front of your living room fireplace. Like any other model oral discourse, a panel discussion has an introduction (attention-getting and subject-orienting), an organized body or main development of the topic (built around a central idea and supporting main heads and materials), and a conclusion (summarizing and perhaps motivating). Customarily a panel includes persons with divergent views, and thus the audience not only hears an exposition of the topic, but also witnesses good-tempered and orderly disagreement.

## Preparing for Panel Discussion

The first step is the selection of the chairman. His general qualifications are the same as for the discussion leader described in Chapter 9. Next, the panel members must be chosen. They should be knowledgeable about the topic and represent different sources of information or opinion about it. Because a public audience will expect a fairly cohesive, lively, and skillful presentation, members must be carefully selected for sustained conversational ability. Willie Wisecracker may prove a liability. Ponderous Paul will be a disaster. If the participants are inexperienced, they will need a briefing. These are points that might be covered:

1. Don't expect to make a formal talk, not even an opening statement. Good conversation, held in public, is the pattern of the day.
2. Keep individual contributions brief, as you would in any other conversation. Anything over 200 words, or one minute, should be exceptional.
3. Address your remarks to each other, but speak up so that you can be heard everywhere in the hall.
4. Listen as well as speak; let your manner and facial expression show that you are attending to your colleagues.
5. Don't sit back and wait to be called on. Get involved. If two try to speak at once, the chairman will designate a priority.
6. Be clear. Use transitional comments and quick summaries. Label three points "1, 2, 3," and otherwise help the listeners to follow you.
7. Direct your remarks to other panel members by name occasionally: "What I can't see, Fitzhugh, is how. . . ." Remember you are talking in a dialogue.

8. Help establish each other as authorities when it is appropriate: "Peters, you're our labor expert. . . ." "Out of your experience, Knight. . . ."
9. Stick to the agreed upon outline generally, but don't be afraid to follow up a truly significant new idea.
10. Keep on the ball. Listeners may identify with you, and they will want you to be alert, lively, and intelligent, as they wish *they* could be.

Old hands will know how to put a panel discussion outline together. First-timers can learn quickly if they are experienced at constructing speech outlines. As we indicated above, panels have introductions, bodies, and conclusions, similar to speeches. Indeed one speaker *might* say everything in a speech that the panel will say collectively, but he would lack the authority that its members have when they speak for their own views, and he certainly would not have the dynamic give-and-take of discussion. There are two differences between the typical detailed speech outline and a panel discussion outline: 1. While the sequence of topics may be similar (a good pattern would be the six-step analysis in Chapter 9) *one* of the panelists agrees to take the lead in discussing each subtopic (not make a little speech about it, but perhaps make the transition to it, suggest the first question, or provoke the first response), and thus a shift of focus is built into the plan. 2. Some general decision is made in advance about the total time for the panel before opening up the discussion to the audience, and each subtopic is given an approximate allowance. The leader and the members put the outline together jointly, perhaps in a sequence of two meetings.

## Conducting the Panel Discussion

Here we are on familiar ground. The leader, with three or four panel members, behaves about the same way he would in an informal group discussion with fifteen or twenty. He gets the meeting underway with a planned remark or two about the nature and significance of the topic, identifies the panel members, and tosses out the first question. He sees to it that each member gets to say something in the first two or three minutes so that he can be clearly identified by the listeners.

A copy of the agreed upon outline should be before each member as the group sits around three sides of a table, and it will remind him not to get off the track. Beyond that concern, the leader's main task is to keep up with the approximate time schedule so that the whole subject can be covered. He also asks questions: to clarify points for the audience, to secure emphasis, or to maintain the structure of the analysis. As nearly as he can, he should draw members into equal participation.

At the conclusion of the discussion the leader should make a brief summary of the main points, and then invite the audience to enter in.

With audiences up to 200 it may be possible to create the illusion of merely enlarging the conversation to include everyone, rather than moving to a formal forum period.

# THE SYMPOSIUM-FORUM

The symposium differs from the panel primarily in the formality of the opening presentation. A moderator and three or four others take part, but while the panel is essentially conversational, the symposium is a public speaking program. It is particularly effective in providing a lot of information about a subject from a variety of experts, and cohesive expositions of different viewpoints on controversial questions.

The speakers should be well-informed about the aspect of the topic they discuss, or about the viewpoint they espouse. More information can probably be transmitted in the same amount of time by a symposium than a panel, but perhaps with less novelty. Symposium participants are likely to make thorough preparation since they stand alone in the spotlight for the duration of their time. It will help if they are first-rate speakers, for listeners have the same rights as in any other circumstance to expect interesting and substantial content, clear organization and style, and lively delivery.

## Preparing for a Symposium

The possible breakdown of the topic into subtopics must be considered when speakers are invited. Or, the availability of qualified speakers and their interests may determine the structuring of the topic. The simplest illustration of the basic pattern would be a symposium on "Who is the best qualified candidate for the Presidency?" with each of three speakers presenting a different nominee in about 7 minutes each. "What can we do about juvenile delinquency?" as a general topic might permit four speakers to divide the answer in terms of the home, the school, the juvenile court, and the neighborhood club. Allowing the chairman 3 minutes to introduce the topic and the speakers, about 10 minutes apiece for the speeches, 2 minutes to launch the forum period, and 30 minutes for audience questions and comments, would make a 75-minute program.

Once each speaker understands clearly the overall plan for the program, and his specific assignment, the rest is up to the individual participants. They should be cautioned to keep in mind, as they prepare, that stump speeches are not in order, that they are obligated to help the listeners think through the whole problem, and that thoughtful and temperate exposition will be most helpful.

### Conducting a Symposium

The chairman's opening remarks should be brief and focused upon the program topic. His introductions of the speakers should also be brief, but since they were selected because of special qualifications, these should be made clear to the audience. Depending upon the topic and the speakers, there may be a brief summary before moving into the forum period. Another useful procedure is to omit that summary, but to conclude the forum period by giving each speaker a minute or so to summarize his own views in the light of what others have said.

# THE LECTURE-FORUM

Recall the more than 100,000,000 people who *Life* editors believe hear public lectures each year (and add to it the 5,500,000 college students who hear academic lectures regularly in more than half of their classes). This should make listening to lectures one of the most widely practiced, and one of the most popular, indoor sports, since, for one reason, it is the easiest form of public meeting to arrange. The planning committee names a chairman, lines up a single speaker, puts up a few posters, and that's it. In part it is so because most observers agree that in an orderly and thorough analysis of a problem, uninterrupted by hostile questions or comments, even a 30 to 45-minute lecture is undoubtedly the most efficient way, minute for minute, of presenting new material to an audience.

The lecturer is asked to speak because he is an expert on the topic, either from serious study or firsthand experience. This very expertness may handicap him, however, in making a contribution to "thought in process." Because he is an expert, particularly on controversial problems, he has undoubtedly developed convictions about the right thing to do. It may be difficult, and sometimes impossible, to so far remove himself from his judgments as to make a balanced consideration of other alternatives. Indeed, unless he is carefully briefed on the purpose of the meeting, he may conclude his lecture with motivational appeals that preclude any serious forum period and even discourage post-meeting discussion among listeners.

### Planning for a Lecture

It is important that any speaker know as much as he can about his audience before he prepares his speech. Getting appropriate information to him is the responsibility of the chairman or of the planning committee.

In particular, the lecturer should be given some idea of how much the audience probably knows about the topic, and how much it has already been discussed. If the lecturer is closely identified with one point of view on the problem, and it is hoped that he will present a variety of views, even as a devil's advocate, he should know and agree to this when he is invited to speak.

### Conducting the Lecture Meeting

With a single speaker to introduce, some chairmen are tempted to make his speech for him. Resist it. If the audience already knows the chairman, then he needs no moment of glory for himself. If they don't know him, then whatever time he steals from the speaker, no matter how glowing the introduction, will only irritate the audience. Start with a straightforward presentation of a few general credentials, and close with those that specifically seem to qualify the speaker to talk on *this* subject, to *this* audience, *tonight*.

If there is some concern about a speaker concluding his speech with a rousing appeal for action, when only information was expected, the chairman may want to damp down the fires with a brief and noncommittal summary. Or he may ask a few pointed questions to restore the balance before opening the forum period. Best of all, of course, is to persuade the lecturer to conclude his speech with a question or two that suggests a continuing inquiry for the truth of the matter, and indirectly provokes audience reactions.

# THE DEBATE-FORUM

Said John F. Kennedy, "The give and take of debating, the testing of ideas, is essential to democracy." Because it is a final step before discovering where the majority lies on any public issue, we have saved it for last in describing public meetings. Unlike the panel, the symposium, or even the lecture, the debate moves from inquiry and exposition into *advocacy*. Though new information may be presented in a debate, its primary function is to provide an intensive scrutiny of the pros and cons of one specific proposal or suggested solution.

As for every public discussion meeting, participants should be selected from among the well-informed, not just those who volunteer. This is especially important in debate, for here there should be a confrontation —in equal and adequate time—of matched contestants, on a stated proposition, and to gain an audience decision. Inevitably there is an element of competition in such a situation, and this usually appeals to audiences.

But to match debaters who are unequal in prestige, knowledge, or speaking skill, is as unfair as scheduling a prize fight between a welterweight and a heavyweight.

### Planning for a Debate

If the debaters selected are extreme partisans they may provide more heat than enlightenment. But a bigger audience may be attracted by partisans. The chairman should be primarily concerned that the problem at issue be given a thorough analysis and that each point of view receives a fair hearing.

Although school debates commonly use two-speaker teams, public discussion meetings are better with one speaker on each side. Thus the chairman might make a 3-minute statement about the topic and about the debaters, the affirmative speaker (who proposes or supports the resolution) could talk for 20 minutes, the negative speaker (who opposes) for 25 minutes, the affirmative in a 5-minute rebuttal, and still finish in less than an hour, plus the forum period. (For classroom debates, of course, these times may have to be cut considerably.)

### Conducting a Debate

The moderator's duties here are the same as for a symposium: quickly highlight the topic in an opening statement, introduce the speakers succinctly, and let them get on with their business.

# THE FORUM PERIOD

It is often assumed that attending a public discussion meeting is a pretty passive enterprise. Not so at all. If the speakers are effective they get good listeners, and listening is an active process. As one person has the floor active listeners are "talking back," formulating ideas into sentences they would speak if they had a chance. The forum period following a panel, symposium, lecture, or debate, gives at least some listeners that chance. "There is no such thing," says Norman Thomas, "as a good public speech without audience participation." A great public speaker himself, he should know.

Most listeners who are recognized by the chairman want to ask a question. It may be for more information, or a request for the speaker's opinion. Sometimes it is a friendly question that gives the speaker a chance to amplify something he said previously. Occasionally it is a challenging question, asking the speaker to defend what the listener thinks is a weak position. Most forum moderators will also accept statements of the listener's own views, or statements refuting the speaker's, but they will insist on relevancy and brevity.

Special qualifications for the moderator of a public meeting forum period are what you would expect in a situation that involves people: warmth, sincerity, tact, firmness, and a sense of humor. The audience member who enjoys being on his feet may want to give a full length speech. The one who has a pet theory to explain everything is usually irrelevant. And the one who launches a personal attack upon the speaker is rude. The moderator must be resilient enough to deal with them all.

Some experienced moderators begin the forum period by a pleasant statement of simple rules for the forum game: Rise and be recognized before you speak. Be brief (one minute, or two at the most). Be clear. Be loud. Be courteous. Be seated.

What happens next depends upon the vagaries of the listeners—and the moderator's ingenuity. He cannot control the former. Here are some ways he can exercise the latter: 1. He may plant a few questions in advance with people he knows in the audience. These will be pump-primers, especially for audiences not familiar with the discussion approach. 2. He may invite symposium speakers or debaters to question each other. 3. Whenever he feels certain issues in the topic are neglected by questioners, or when most of the questions are addressed to one speaker after a symposium or a debate, he may restore the balance by asking questions himself. 4. He may plan in advance to have a special panel of interrogators come up onto the platform and quiz the speakers before inviting general participation.

Whatever he does about prompting questions and comments in the forum period, the good moderator will close it on the upswing, rather than just quit because everyone seems worn out. Perhaps he has a special and critical question saved for a climax. Or he may ask each speaker for a final one-sentence comment.

Public discussion meetings are more than merely interesting variations from traditional rounds of speeches in the classroom. They represent one of the important ways for people to acquire the information they need before making decisions. As Harold Laski put it, "the art of public discussion . . . is central to the achievement of the democratic purpose."

## SUPPLEMENTARY READINGS

Crowell, Laura, *Discussion: Method of Democracy*. Chicago: Scott, Foresman, 1963. "Public Discussion," pp. 292-319, is a clear and helpful treatment of panels, symposiums, and forums.

Ehninger, Douglas, and Brockriede, Wayne, *Decision by Debate*. New York: Dodd, Mead, 1963. A good modern textbook on techniques of debating, and reflecting the contributions of Toulmin to argumentative theory.

Kennedy, Gerald, *While I'm On My Feet*. New York: Abingdon Press, 1963. A wise and witty commentary on many topics of interest by a Methodist Bishop, including reflections on preaching and lecturing.

Thomas, Norman, *Mr. Chairman, Ladies and Gentlemen . . . Reflections on Public Speaking*. New York: Hermitage House, 1955. One of America's most out-spoken and most frequently speaking public men deals delightfully with the art, drawing upon his own experiences.

*Vital Speeches of the Day*. Pelham, N.Y.: City News Publishing Co. Twice a month journal with complete texts of 8-10 speeches on current issues, by public officials, educators, and business and industrial leaders.

## EXERCISES

1. Plan a symposium for a community meeting in your home town. Include in your report a description of the situation or problem to be discussed, the over-all organization of the symposium, and the names and qualifications of the speakers you would invite.

2. Assume that you are responsible for planning a campus discussion on a current controversial issue of significance: (a) What subject would you select? (b) What kind of public discussion would you select—panel, symposium, debate, etc.? (c) Whom would you invite to take part? (d) What outline of topics would you follow?

3. Attend a public discussion meeting on the campus and pay special attention to the forum period: (a) How did the moderator get it started? (b) What kinds of questions were asked, and how many of each? (c) How did audience members participate other than by asking questions? (d) What special problems did the moderator encounter in handling questions and questioners?

4. Organize a panel discussion, following the sequence of steps described in this chapter. Assess your reactions afterward by commenting on questions such as these: (a) Did you feel that you participated as much as your preparation qualified you to do? (b) Did you find that any of your ideas were refined by exposing them to discussion by the whole group? (c) Did you find that the previously prepared outline hampered you? (d) Did you feel the same feeling of satisfaction after the panel that you usually do after a speech?

5. Attend a campus debate and evaluate its contributions to problem-solving. The evaluation might include a comment on the kind and quality of evidence presented, the relevance of the arguments to the analysis of the question made by each speaker, and the degree to which the debate really provided an intensive and comprehensive scrutiny of alternative courses of action.

6. Select three current problems of national significance, and choose one form of discussion to be used in a public meeting on each problem. In terms of the state of public thinking about each problem, persons available to participate, and so on, justify your choices.

# 11

# Speaking on Radio and Television

One of the illusions of the day seems to be that no one listens to broadcast talks in America, no matter what they may do on the BBC. But broadcasters are not known for sending signals out very long if no one listens. And it is a fact that approximately *twenty percent of network programming* today consists of speeches, interviews, panel discussions, and commentaries. In addition there are network and local newscasts; almost every radio station broadcasts one such five-minute talk to inform each hour. Finally, there are local station talks, appeals to give generously, attend faithfully, vote regularly, buy bonds, and donate blood. This means that many public officials and community leaders speak frequently on a nonprofessional basis, and that we also have a profession of radio and television talking. Some years ago Edward R. Murrow could report that "my father does not go so far as to say that there's something dishonest about a man making a living merely by talking. But he does think there's something doubtful about it." Times have changed.

Part of that change has been the penetration of the broadcast media into homes across the nation. They have, observed Lord Brain, re-created for modern democracies one of the great virtues of the Greek city-states: "all citizens can see and hear their leaders." And evangelist Billy Graham exults that "I can preach to more people in one night on TV than perhaps Paul did in his whole lifetime!"

For having this easy access to the ears and eyes of America, though, a price must be paid. *Radio and television talkers must give more strict attention to the basic principles of good communication than their platform counterparts.* In a political rally, a public lecture hall, or at a civic luncheon club, listeners are not likely to walk out, no matter how poor the speaker. But let a party orator spread his eagle on television and he will get tuned out, even by members of his own party. Let a distinguished scientist forget about the laws of audience attention in a radio talk and he's cut off with a flick of the wrist, no matter how much he may know about thermonuclear laws.

# ADAPTING SPEECHES TO RADIO

*Here is the rule:* the basic psychological principles applicable to public address do not change for radio and television speeches, they are just accentuated. *And here is how it works:* your problem is not how to hold an audience for five or ten or fifteen minutes in a radio talk, but how to hold it for *one minute at a time.* Especially in the opening minute you may be sized up in thousands of homes. If you can't command attention at once, and sustain interest, thousands of hands will reach out to switch stations. As someone put it, a radio speech is a race between arousing interest and being tuned out.

## Preparing the Speech

Radio speakers are not seen by their audiences, so they usually read from manuscripts rather than speak extemporaneously. They must make words and voice carry the whole burden that is shared by visual stimulation in public speaking. Thus they must not only master their subjects, but also master the uncommon art of committing good oral structure and style to paper. Good public speakers have an informal, conversational style. The best way to capture it on paper is to talk it out loud as you write. The best way to *lose* good platform style is to assume an unnatural and pretentious dignity, just because you are writing out your speech. If you are not stuffy or pompous in the open, don't get that way on the air! Here are some additional hints on how to do it, summarized from the counsel of experienced radio speakers.

1. *Command the listener's attention at once.* We say "command" because that's what you must do. There is no time to "ask" for attention, or "lead up" to it. The very first sentence must arrest the listener. One of the ways of supporting ideas should do it: facts, illustrations, specific instances, comparison and contrast, testimony, description, narration.

2. *Build the speech in a simple thought pattern.* You cannot watch your listeners and gauge their reactions. So you must take no chances: avoid complex thought structures right from the start. It may be useful to review the discussion of thought patterns in Chapter 6. It will also be useful to recheck what you've done to see that you have no more than two or three clearly related main ideas. Above all, recheck to see that your figures of speech, illustrations, specific instances, and anecdotes are cast into graphic language that will create mental images for your listeners.

3. *Use simple words and short sentences.* Allan Jackson, top CBS radio newscaster, offers advice to beginners about "hear" copy and "see" copy in *You Have to Write, Too!* "See" copy in the newspaper conveys its meaning to a reader but not to a listener. "The job of the writer of the broadcast copy is to write 'hear' copy, copy that is to be heard and heard only once. The listener will not have the opportunity of rehearing an ambiguous statement. . . ." To eliminate ambiguity eliminate complex and compound words, esoteric jargon, and literary locution.

Avoid long twisting sentences: make them short and straight—"subject, verb, object. Beginning, middle, finish. You won't stub your toe nearly so often," says Jackson, "and your listeners will be able to go along with you without performing mental gymnastics." Strip the elaborate phrases and dependent clauses from your talk, and remember that 20-25 words make a long sentence on the air.

Finally, remember that you are not writing *writing,* you are writing *talk.* You want listenable copy, not readable copy. So speak it to yourself as you write. That way you will get standard oral contractions into your script, such as "We don't" for "We do not," and "It's" for "It is. . . ."

4. *Put in pointers: transitions, summaries, and connectives.* Much of this advice sounds like that given earlier about public speaking before "live" audiences. It is so. But remember that your broadcast listeners are not seated row by row in a large audience; they are individuals, or perhaps two or three folks riding in a car, sitting in a living room, or even out on a beach. So talk to them as you would in the living room, even more than in public speaking hitching thoughts together with transitions and cumulating them with summaries. Use other pointers, too, like *but, also, hence, on the other hand,* and *therefore,* as connective phrases to show where we go next.

5. *Type your speech script in standard form.* Remember that you will have to *read* from your script, so be easy on yourself. Double or even triple space everything, use generous margins on all sides, and pica type if you have it. This will make the script as readable as possible. Use soft yellow typing paper or anything else that won't crackle into the microphone.

6. *Mark your script for clarity and emphasis.* Begin by recognizing that normal punctuation marks are designed for the silent reader, not the oral reader. Then devise your own system of markings that will help you *read aloud* with all the qualities of good talk. Some experienced radio speakers underscore words once for special emphasis in reading, twice for great emphasis; they use a slant mark for a short pause / and a double one for a longer pause //. For ease in pronunciation they type stressed syllables in CAPital letters. And to indicate "throwaway" or vocally unstressed words like *to, of, the,* and *a,* or whole subordinate phrases, they put parentheses around them (like this).

7. *Rehearse your talk—over and over.* Rehearse, just to read a script?

If you ask that question you don't know how badly most laymen read from the printed page. And you don't know that many real "pros" rehearse to the extent of tape-recording their speeches. Then they play them back and listen for any lack of clarity and variety, poor tone quality, inadequate emphasis, or faulty inflection. For novices this practice should be mandatory.

8. *Time your script.* Occasionally a two- or three-minute speech may be in a news "round-up," but more commonly a longer speech has its own time slot. Say you are scheduled from 7:00 to 7:15. Is this a fifteen-minute speech? Yes, but with allowances for a thirty-second station break, a thirty-second introduction by the announcer, and a thirty second closing announcement. If your "fifteen-minute talk" runs over thirteen and a half minutes, count on a dead microphone. What to do? Prepare by knowing your rate and adjusting your material. The average person speaks about 150 words a minute, plus or minus ten. This was Edward R. Murrow, at 145. Franklin D. Roosevelt was low at 117, and Walter Winchell is high at 215. You can practice reading your script until you get the rate that is right for you and for your material, then count words and mark times at the bottom of your pages, so that when you are on the air you will know where you should be at these intervals.

In their professionally definitive *Television and Radio,* Chester, Garrison, and Willis suggest another procedure.[1] They would have you type your script in lines of equal length, then determine your "lines per minute" rate by rehearsing a sample section of the script. Then they suggest marking the script in "minutes remaining" to the end of your time, and marking in the actual clock times for your broadcast assignment. Thus the end of your script for the 7:00-7:15 program would be marked "14." Working forward from the last line your next mark would show "13," or 1 minute to go. Earlier times marked might be "12," "11," "9," and "4," (or 2, 3, 5, and 9 minutes remaining). These writers also suggest that you put brackets around several two- or three-line cuts (about the middle of the speech, three-quarters through, and just before the closing paragraph) that you might make if, when you get to your check points, you find that you have slowed down your delivery and must make up time. Omitting a few lines, they argue, is better than ruining the ones you have by trying to speed them up.

## Making Friends with the Microphone

The subhead just above is the title of a useful booklet of suggestions for novice radio speakers compiled by the Columbia Broadcasting System. We borrow it here because it makes a good point: your aim is to make a friend—by informing, stimulating, or persuading—out of each listener, and

[1] (New York, 3rd ed., 1963), pp. 288-290.

you can reach your listeners only through the microphone. Here are four "friendly" tips.

1. *Sit down and speak up.* Usually the director will seat you at a table with the microphone suspended in front of you or on a table stand. You may think you would rather stand up, but don't say so. Experience shows that speakers are more likely to be conversational if they sit (and more oratorical if they stand) and the studio talk is *conversation.* The director will also give you technical advice about how to respond to his hand signals while you are on the air. One of these will tell you to back off from the microphone, another to get closer. According to the kind of microphone you use, and the degree of intimacy of tone he wants, the director will also tell you how far to stay away from the microphone. You do the talking, but let the expert tell you where.

2. *Remember the size of your audience.* We cannot overemphasize the two most significant differences between traditional public address and radio speaking. First, you talk to individual listeners rather than to large audiences. Second, your listener is in his living room, not a lecture hall. Thus your model is not William Jennings Bryan on the campaign circuit, but your best friend in front of his fireplace. It may help if you can imagine a friend or two sitting across the table from you in the studio, and talk as you would if they were there.

3. *Use your own voice.* Whose else? It isn't your *natural* voice if under the tension of speaking you tighten your throat muscles and thus heighten your pitch. It isn't your *best* voice if you talk in flat tones and unvaried rate. In no other form of oral communication does the voice have to carry such a heavy load in creating a favorable image of the speaker. If it is dull and lifeless . . .?

4. *Protect the microphone from distracting noises.* Thanks to you, a lot of extraneous noises can find their way into a soundproof studio. But if you really want to make friends with the microphone you'll try to hush these sounds. First of all, resist the temptation to pat, tap, or touch the microphone. It causes every sound that goes into it to be put out, with intense magnification. Table tapping has the same effect, but with greater reverberations.

Second, don't rustle the pages of your script. Crumpling paper in front of the microphone was once the way of making sounds like a forest fire crackle out of your speaker. Before you go on the air reduce the possibility of extraneous sound by removing paper clips from the script, checking to see that the pages are in the right order. On the air dispose of each sheet as you finish with it by sliding it quietly to one side.

Third, try not to clear your throat or cough into the microphone. Of course you have to do both sometimes. Just try to turn away from the microphone in time, but don't be thrown if one gets by you. Remember sitting with a friend before the fire, and say the same simple "sorry" you would to him in order to show that you know you inadvertently "coughed in his face." You will need to breathe when you are on the air, no doubt, but try not to do it right into the microphone. Better yet, never talk so fast that you get out of breath.

Finally, always assume that the microphone is open, unless the director or the announcer tells you it is dead. After concluding your speech on a great note of climax a breathless "How was I?" sounds a little strange to those listening.

## ADAPTING SPEECHES TO TELEVISION

In many respects planning and writing a television speech is similar to preparing a radio speech. Also in many respects television speaking is more similar to public speaking than is radio speaking. The reason for this seeming incongruity, of course, is that television restores sight to the listener. We know from repeated experiments that the visible code plus the audible code results in more effective communication than comes from either one separately. But what other effects are there from the addition of a picture to a voice? Consider these, and some of their implications.

1. *Each listener can see the television speaker with equal clarity.* The radio speaker cannot be seen at all. Like the public speaker, the television speaker can be seen, but every member of his audience sits in the same seat. When addressing a large crowd in an auditorium a public speaker tends to use expansive gestures that will be meaningful to those in the back rows, and they do not seem out of place to those who sit twenty feet away in the front row. But on the intimate television screen those gestures appear the same to every viewer, probably exaggerated and unnatural. After all, the television speaker's role is that of an an invited guest in the viewer's living room, and especially when he is only a foot tall such a guest would hardly shake a clenched fist under his host's nose. (As these remarks suggest, a normally animated public speaker faces a real dilemma when he has a large "live" audience and also a television audience.) Even facial expressions can be problems. Appropriate ones in a platform speech may appear as contortions when the camera moves in for a close-up. Finally, consider that while those alternating close-up and long shots may be dramatic, physical behavior that is appropriate for a speaker in a telescopic view may be inappropriate the next minute in a microscopic view.

What are the implications for the public speaker giving a television talk? *First,* he must be natural, but restrained in gestures and facial expressions, remembering that he is really talking intimately to little groups of two or three persons. As in radio speaking he may be seated behind a table or desk (but with no microphone in evidence; it will be out of sight on an overhead boom), or even in an easy chair. In any case his gestures will be inhibited by this setting as well as by the television medium. *Second,* the television speaker must become conscious of his little mannerisms of expression and action, usually unnoticed, but picked up and magnified by the camera. His best friend must tell him. *Third,* the television speaker, unlike the radio speaker, must be conscious of what he wears, and far more so than is the platform speaker. New studio lighting techniques have lessened this problem, but certain colors in suits, dresses, and shirts are still preferable, "noisy" patterns are discouraged, and so on. If you are going to make a television talk you can expect the program director to brief you on these matters.

2. *What to do about a script becomes a problem for the television speaker.* We have stressed the living room concept of broadcast communication. Nowhere does this cause more problems than with the radio speaker who is used to reading a script and then goes on television. In his own living room a man hardly expects a guest to converse with his eyes glued to a prepared text. His reaction is the same when he turns on the television and invites a speaker to visit with him. Nearly as bad as having the speaker look at his script *all* the time is having his head bob up and down all the time as he essays the impossible task of both reading a script and looking at his audience. (The worst feature is that usually it is on the final climax words of a sentence that the head bobs down so the speaker can see how the *next* sentence begins.) The public speaker may have the same problems, though they seem less obvious in a lecture hall than on a television screen. On the other hand, an experienced public speaker is likely to feel enough at home on a platform to talk without a complete manuscript, but anyone inexperienced in the television medium is likely to crave the security of a script.

How do television speakers handle this problem? *First,* we must note that many of them, including a surprising number of newscasters, continue to use a complete script. If they have time for sufficient rehearsal the more effective ones partially memorize the material, without making it *sound* memorized, and thus face the viewer directly a good part of the time. *Second,* some television speakers (and public officials who feel that they dare not speak without an exact text as a defense against later misquotation) use mechanical aids out of camera range. Once these were only cue cards, three by four feet, with the text printed large, and held alongside the camera so that they could be read while the speaker still faced his listeners. These cards are now often replaced by teleprompters, electrically operated devices mounted above or next to the camera, and unrolling a scroll about six lines at a time on which is reproduced a readable text. *Third,* the best television speakers cope with the script problem the same way the best public speakers do—by avoiding it. Instead of a script the speaker has an outline of his speech, perhaps supplemented by note cards with the full text of any long quotation he plans to use. The speaking outline, on the public platform or in the television studio, assures a set sequence of ideas, but makes for an extemporaneous style. The use of an outline is most advantageous in freeing the speaker—assuming that he has properly practiced his speech—to look most of the time straight at his audience. He thus approaches the directness of the platform speaker. If he is seated behind a desk, or standing behind a lectern, the outline may lie before him on standard typing paper. If he is seated in a chair, a set of note cards may be better, held in his hand or on his lap.

3. *The potential use of visual aids adds a new dimension to television speaking.* Public speakers seldom find charts, maps, and diagrams useful before very large audiences unless they can be put on slides and projected. Since the camera is always a kind of projector, the television speaker has an almost unlimited opportunity to use any visual aids that can help command attention, sustain interest, and depict or clarify his ideas. These aids may be charts, maps, diagrams, models, mock-ups, film clips, pictures, cartoons, and so on. Or he may make his own sketches on a blackboard or a drawing pad. Most commercial stations, and all educational stations and closed-circuit facilities, are likely to have specialists in preparing such aids.

The implications of these aids for the television speaker, as against his radio and platform counterparts, are very clear. *First,* he has at hand, and flexible enough to be adapted to almost any need, a variety of sensory stimuli, vocal, gestural, and pictorial. To twist the Chinese proverb, he has a picture *and* a thousand words. *Second,* aside from the cost of producing these visual aids, he must face the problem of using them expertly. To do so requires additional planning and rehearsing time. For a very complex set of aids the director and cameramen require detailed cue sheets, indicating his route as the speaker will move from desk to point to a map, then to the blackboard to make a sketch, across to a table to demonstrate a globe, and so on. And all the time he must remember the rules about not getting between his visual aids and his camera-audience. But, as in other ways, he can expect guidance from the program director when he has occasion to employ this special resource.

As astute observers have noted, in recent decades the status of politicians and their parties is increasingly being determined by how articulate they are in presenting their views to the public via radio and television. These mass media cannot yet substitute for platform speaking and whistle-stop campaigning, and probably never will, but they are powerful complements. Most of us are not likely to use radio and television as public officials, or even as candidates. But as community leaders, business and professional men and women, club officers, and campaigners for everything from the PTA to the Red Cross, we will more and more often be called upon to make radio and television talks. We will find that the basic principles of effective communication need only slight adaptation to apply to this kind of speechmaking.

## SUPPLEMENTARY READINGS

Chester, Giraud, Garrison, Garnet R., Willis, Edgar E., *Television and Radio*, 3rd ed. New York: Appleton-Century-Crofts, 1963. See "Talking on the Air," pp. 285-306, and "News Programs," pp. 393-412, in the most widely used textbook for courses in broadcasting.

Costello, Lawrence F., and Gordon, George N., *Teach with Television: A Guide to Instructional TV*. New York: Hastings House, 1961. A standard text for all aspects of educational television.

Eisenson, Jon, Auer, J. Jeffery, and Irwin, John V., *The Psychology of Communication*. New York: Appleton-Century-Crofts, 1963. For summaries of pertinent research studies see "Basic Psychological Factors in Group Communication," pp. 227-252, and "Psychology of Radio and Television," pp. 310-319.

Klapper, Joseph T., *The Effects of Mass Communication*. New York: The Free Press of Glencoe, 1960. An exploration and evaluation of studies on the effectiveness and limitations of mass media.

Kraus, Sidney, ed., *The Great Debates: Background-Perspective-Effects*. Bloomington: Indiana University Press, 1962. A comprehensive report and appraisal of the Kennedy-Nixon television debates of 1960, and the complete texts of the broadcasts.

## EXERCISES

1. Listen to a good radio speaker and report on what you think are the factors of his effectiveness. Include manner of speaking, articulation, speech content, manner of organization, and use of language.

2. Listen to a good television speaker. (a) Report on the things you *saw* that contributed to his effectiveness. (b) To focus on the technique of action, count how often the speaker changed his position or posture during a three-minute period. (c) Count the number of camera changes, of distance and angle, made during a three-minute period.

3. Recast one of your previous speeches in this course so it will be adapted for radio broadcast.

4. Recast one of your previous speeches in this course for telecasting. With marginal notes indicate what visual aids you would use. Also indicate special adaptations of posture and movement you would use.

5. Write out and record a one-minute newscast. Remember that the announcer's problem of reading aloud is like the actor's. He must *seem* natural, but cannot *be* natural. In everyday speech, sounds are often slurred and final phrases lost. If you talked in this "natural" way over the microphone, without the aid of gestures and sight, your voice simply would not make sense. An announcer, like an actor, must overdo to seem natural. The good announcer overdoes just enough to make it seem natural, whereas the "ham" overdoes in a way that seems overdone.

6. Write out and record a three-minute radio speech, either to inform or to persuade:

a. Type the manuscript, double spaced, and mark it for reading.

b. Time it carefully; and to make sure of not running over, cut it to 2 minutes 50 seconds. *Do not* write a 3½ minute speech then try to speed it up to 3 minutes, for the faster you read the less listeners comprehend. If you have a 3½ minute speech, read it in 3 minutes and the listener gets 1½ minutes worth. That is poor economy.

c. Above all, be earnest; talk directly to your unseen listeners.

# 12

# Evaluating Speechmaking

For the nearly 2500 years that we have had a theory of public address as a basis for effective speechmaking, we have also engaged in some form of speech criticism. "When the practiced and the spontaneous speaker gain their end," wrote Aristotle in his *Rhetoric*, "it is possible to investigate the cause of their success; and such an inquiry . . . performs the function of an art." It is an art of evaluating, not necessarily of doing, however, though the two are often confused. Doers traditionally taunt critics with "Can you do any better?" Indeed, the tradition is as old as Aristotle's rhetorical theories (c. 346 B.C.), for in his *Natural History* Pliny quotes Zeuxis, about 400 B.C., complaining that "criticism comes easier than craftsmanship."

No matter how uncomfortable performers of any kind may sometimes be made by their critics, the two will inevitably continue their coexistence. Especially do performers need thoughtful and analytical critiques that will help them better to meet accepted standards of excellence. It is given to few performers—public speakers, actors, or musicians—to be able to hear or see themselves truly, without distortion. Thus they must depend upon critics, formal or informal, for evaluations that can become guidelines for improvement. In one way or another the critic is a mirror in which the performer measures his image.

The critic provides *criticism*, a term that your dictionary probably defines something like *a reasoned opinion, expressed as an appreciation of art or technique, or as a judgment of truth or social value*. Some critics may express themselves in one or the other of these two ways, and some will use both. Let us look at each kind.

## WHO ARE THE CRITICS?

Critics of speechmaking seldom function singularly and we can best indicate their dual functions by hyphenated labels: scholar-critics, peer-critics, and citizen-critics.

## Scholar-Critics

Historians of public address tend to focus upon the speechmaking of significant individuals, among Americans such as Jonathan Edwards, Henry Clay, Jeremiah Sullivan Black, Samuel Gompers, and Franklin D. Roosevelt in the three-volume *History and Criticism of American Public Address*. Sometimes they concentrate instead upon a major public issue, or a significant political or social movement, as in *Antislavery and Disunion, 1858-1861: Studies in the Rhetoric of Compromise and Conflict*. Or upon speechmaking in a particular region, such as the South, or in a particular period, such as the Colonial. These studies are done by rhetorical scholars. Their purpose is, first of all, to re-create history, to tell us "what happened." In so doing they identify and judge speech communication as it relates to men and their times. Thus scholars ultimately serve a second purpose, the refinement of rhetorical theory. Using all of the tools of historical research and rhetorical criticism these scholars comb letters, diaries, newspapers, manuscripts, and public documents in order to discover and report facts and judgments in accurate, coherent, and critical narratives.

Out of the work of such a scholar-critic may come a revision of earlier judgments:

We may conclude, then, that history has sadly misjudged [Stephen A.] Douglas. The charges of inconsistency, insincerity, trickery, and carelessness have been made in the light of post-Civil War philosophy, after an examination of only a few of the printed speeches. Historians and critics have ignored the need to understand thoroughly the four elements [audience, occasion, speaker, and speech] that go into every speaking situation before judgment may be passed; they have failed to realize that it is dangerous to criticize isolated speeches that appear in print until the conditions under which the speeches were given have been reconstructed.

An examination of the individual audiences to whom Douglas spoke, the various influences that accounted for his beliefs, and the total number of campaign speeches now in existence shows conclusively that Douglas was not driven to the defensive by a superior opponent. It shows conclusively that his arguments were basically honest, sincere, and consistent. In fact, many of the things that have drawn the critics' disapproval prove to be masterly techniques of an unusually fine speaker, who was a past master at audience analysis and adaptation. Douglas should be remembered as one of the ablest speakers the United States has produced.[1]

Or the scholar-critic may provide a summary of the apparent reasons for an orator's effectiveness:

[1]Forest L. Whan, "Stephen A. Douglas," in William Norwood Brigance, ed., *A History and Criticism of American Public Address*, Vol. II (New York: McGraw-Hill, 1943), p. 824 (pp. 777-827).

Earlier in this study it was stated that [William Jennings] Bryan was lacking in the broad scope of argument, that he chose to speak from "heart to heart and not from mind to mind." Some have gone so far as to say that his speeches were utterly devoid of argument, that "you could drive a prairie schooner through any one of them." Generally, his speaking was highly emotionalized. That was his strength. A fair and objective conclusion is that he *could* argue when he felt arguments to be necessary, but he knew that an argument may often confirm others in their opinion rather than move them to change it. For this reason his appeals were to patriotism, justice, and reverence. Perhaps he carried the tendency too far, but his preference was from choice, not from necessity, and if one criticizes his choice, one must remember that in his choice lay his tremendous power as a speaker. . . .

Bryan's strength also lay in the simplicity of his style and the directness and precision of his diction. The cold print of Bryan's words, posterity's sole legacy, reveals, above all things, its imagery, its vividness, its simplicity.[2]

The student speaker may find guideline values in these judgments of the scholar-critics. From Forest L. Whan's study on Douglas he can learn the importance of audience analysis, and how to use it; he can find a moral in the account of how some critics jumped to conclusions before they reconstructed all of the available evidence, and he can gain an understanding of the role of debate in American politics. Myron G. Phillips on Bryan gives to the student speaker some understanding of the relationship between logical arguments and emotional appeals, and how both may be used with popular audiences; and he offers a "model" of effectiveness for the student whose own style may be pompous and dull, rather than simple and vivid.

The scholar-critic is writing history and passing rhetorical judgments. The judgments help to refine the theory of speech communication. They can also inspire the student speaker to want to do better and show him how some speakers did well. Read such studies when you can to sharpen your abilities to communicate and to extend your knowledge of history. Begin with the volumes of studies listed at the end of this chapter. For additional ones consult past and current issues of *Quarterly Journal of Speech* and *Speech Monographs*.

### Peer-Critics

As in the courtroom so in the public forum or the public speaking classroom, you are judged by a jury of your peers. Sometimes they may write out their evaluations, sometimes they may deliver them orally, and always they are making them silently and mentally. These evaluations begin with pre-speech expectations: you have an idea what you'll get from Vince Virtue or Archie Awful and you're open-minded about Nina New-

[2]Myron G. Phillips, "William Jennings Bryan," in Brigance, *Ibid.*, p. 917 (pp. 891-918).

comer. The final evaluation is expressed by voting, grading, ranking, applauding, and so on. But it is what comes between expectation and final judgment that is important for the student speaker and his peer-critics.

The peer-critic himself can always profit from hearing speeches. As we suggested in Chapter 1, we should constantly *listen to get meanings* and also *listen to evaluate speech communication techniques.* Observing and evaluating others is one of the basic ways of learning.

The student speaker profits most from his peer-critics. (When he sits in the audience with the class, incidentally, we consider the instructor to be a peer-critic, although an exceptional one in training, experience, and insight. If you think of him as a separate auditor, however, and quite different from your fellow student peer-critics, then you risk floundering between two audiences while you speak, adapting well to neither one.) Fellow students in a speech class may play several roles; for example, they may be learners about speech, and also learners about many other subjects as they listen to speeches. But here we are concerned with them only as peer-critics. Gradually throughout the school term these classmates increase their understanding of the communication process, the strategies open to a speaker in planning a speech, the techniques that make for greater effectiveness in speaking, and the components of ideas, organization, style, and delivery from which the end product must be fashioned. Thus they become increasingly sophisticated as evaluators, for the essence of criticism is understanding an ideal and being able to compare an actual performance with it. The more they understand about speech communication, and the more they have tried to perfect themselves as communicators, the more detailed, analytical, and reliable they can be in their judgments.

At a meeting of the Parent-Teachers Association, before a board of directors, or in a business conference, a speaker seldom receives an evaluation in terms of the standards and techniques of effective speaking. Such audiences are interested only in the *product,* not in the *process.* An audience of investors, listening to a stock market analyst, is concerned only with whether he urges them to buy or sell. Chances are, *these listeners do not even realize that by the strategies and techniques he employs, the speaker is influencing that buy-or-sell decision.* And least of all are they concerned with helping him to improve his speaking ability!

We would argue that in most respects the classroom speaking situation is as "realistic" as the board of directors meeting. You are as anxious as the market analyst to lead your hearers to respond in a particular way to what you have to say. *At the moment you are speaking* the challenge facing you in getting the attention and influencing the behavior of your listeners is as realistic in the speech classroom as anywhere else. The differences come when you stop speaking. Then your listeners become peer-critics whose evaluations can aid you in your development as an effective communicator.

Of course you will have to *want* these evaluations, and to *learn* from them. If you naturally avoid criticism, you will have to change your nature and seek it. If you tend to become defensive and concentrate upon rationalizing your failures rather than learning from them, you will have to develop a new attitude. If you become depressed when your performance is less than ideal, you must recognize that most of us can only *progress toward* perfection, and that we do that by practice, evaluation, improved practice, more evaluation, and then still better practice. And finally, if it consoles you, remember that today's peer-critic is tomorrow's speaker.

## Citizen-Critics

Malcolm Muggeridge, for over three decades a leader in British journalism, and a former editor of *Punch,* once observed that "the essence of a free and civilized society is that everything in it should be subject to criticism." We are all, he was saying, citizen-critics. We are skeptical, we take little for granted, and we want to be sure. On this side of the Atlantic Hubert Humphrey epitomized the same attitude when he reminded delegates to the National Student Association convention in August, 1965, that "the right to be heard does not include the right to be taken seriously."

As citizen-critics each one of us is a potential believer, member, buyer, or voter, listening to speeches for help in deciding what to believe, what to join, what to buy, or how to vote. Thus we evaluate preachers, teachers, advertisers, and campaigners of all sorts.

Unlike peer-critics, citizen-critics seldom focus sharply upon a speaker's techniques. Instead of asking "*how* did he do it?" they ask "is it *true?* is it *significant?* is it a *cause for my action?*" Citizen-critics do not listen in order to pick up ideas that would improve their own speaking, nor to advise speakers how to improve theirs. They are not concerned with an appreciation of art or technique, but with a judgment of truth and social value. In a reversal of the old axiom, the citizen-critic says "ask not how you played the game, but whether you won or lost!"

In a democratic society Everyman is a citizen-critic. And one of the goals of the speech course should be to help Everyman become an intelligent consumer as well as a producer in the communication process. Viscount Morley long ago set the standard for the consumer: "Any educated man or woman should know what is evidence, should know when a thing is proved and when it is not proved . . . should know how many interpretations the same rival propositions would fairly bear, and what weight is to be attached to rival authorities."

# HOW DO CRITICS WORK?

Our real purpose in this chapter is to suggest an approach to evaluating speechmaking. But first there are two necessary qualifications: 1. Because it is unlikely that in the immediate future you will be operating as a scholar-critic, we will confine ourselves from here on to your role as peer-critic and as citizen-critic. 2. Because it would be folly to suggest otherwise, we will deal with *an* approach to evaluation, not *the* approach. We believe in innovation and encourage the development of new approaches, new forms, and new terminologies. The ones we employ here just happen to have proven themselves to us.

### Criteria for the Peer-Critic

The peer-critic needs at least a few general virtues. Among them, we think, are these.

1. *His evaluations must be relevant.* They must be in terms of the kind of speaker John Doakes can aspire to become in the course of a semester, not the kind of speaker Adlai Stevenson was at his prime. This means the critic must be realistic as well as candid. It is no service to gloss over real deficiencies.

2. *His evaluations must be specific.* Their purpose is to help the speaker achieve a self-image. This he cannot do unless generalized evaluations are supported by specific examples. When "something's wrong," we cannot fix it. But when we cannot be heard in the back row, or our definition cannot be understood, we at least know where to begin.

3. *His evaluations must be constructive.* Some expert critics always try to balance their evaluations, finding something good to say about a speaker, even if it's no more than congratulations for showing up on the right day. To be truly constructive (helpful) evaluations must not only point out problems candidly and specifically, but also remedially. What can the speaker do to overcome or avoid his problems next time?

The peer-critic also needs the special virtue of staying within the limits of his own competencies. We naturally do not expect as sophisticated evaluations in the first weeks of the course as we do near the end: as his knowledge about the communication process increases, the peer-critic's range of topics for intelligent judgments is expanded.

Most speech textbooks and all instructors have some particular form of rating sheet or criticism blank to recommend. In order to keep our focus upon the *criteria* rather than upon the *format*, we leave to the reader and his instructor the development of a satisfactory instrument. What follows is our conception of the six possible main topics for evaluating speechmaking. We have even made them alliterative so they will be easier to remember: *subject, sources, substance, structure, style, symbols.* (Our own idea of a proper evaluation form is a blank sheet of paper, ruled off into six boxes with those one word labels, and a maximum amount of space in which to write specific and individualized comments.) We would not claim too much for these six main topics, but we have found that they lend themselves as well to evaluating informal discourse in conferences and committees as to more formal patterns of public discussion and public speaking.

Each peer-critic, guided by the circumstances of the specific speech situation, will have to work out a priority of values for the six topics. Seldom will each receive the same emphasis. In the early weeks of the course, for example, one instructor may feel that physical adjustment to the speaking situation is most important, and thus concentrate upon vocal and gestural *symbols.* If student speakers lamentably show a tendency for careless organization, then *structure* may seem the most significant criterion.

Moreover, each peer-critic, again adapting to the total speech situation, will want to work out his own series of questions to probe each of the topics. But the questions may well be different for each speaker, even when they are on the same speaking program. The complex of occasion, speaker, topic, and audience is in a constant state of flux in a speech class, and the same should be true of specific questions used for evaluation.

It may be useful to have a set of "stock" questions to open up each of the main topics. Our own suggestions for such questions appear in the list below. *But note:* not all of these questions will be suitable for any given speech situation, and you must select those that are most appropriate. *Also note:* not all questions are listed that could be asked; these are only starters, and as a peer-critic you must develop others that are adapted to the occasion, speaker, topic, and audience.

## TOPICS FOR USE IN PEER-CRITIC EVALUATIONS

SUBJECT
>    Is it significant? Does it really make any difference?
>    Is it narrowed to a specific purpose for this audience?
>    Is it relevant to the needs and interests of this audience?

SOURCES
>    Is his material adequate? Has he earned the right to speak?
>    Has he ignored significant sources of facts and opinions?
>    Does he reflect a real understanding of his material?

SUBSTANCE
>    Is it impressive? Does the speech really inform? Or persuade?
>    Are the main heads (or the major contentions) logical and coherent?
>    Is the supporting material relevant? Sufficient? Memorable?

STRUCTURE

> Is there a proper introduction? An adequate conclusion?
> Is the discussion clear? Easy to follow? Appropriate?
> Are there adequate transitions? Internal summaries?

STYLE

> Is the language concrete? Simple? Colorful? Appropriate?
> Are the sentences cast into true oral style?
> Are significant local usage patterns adhered to?

SYMBOLS

> Are vocal symbols distinct? Fluent? Flexible and varied?
> Are physical symbols (posture, gestures) meaningful? Reflect poise?
> Does the delivery support the substance of the speech?

## Criteria for the Citizen-Critic

"The function of all persuasive utterance is realized in some decision," wrote Aristotle, "for when we know a thing, we have reached a decision about it, there is no need of further argument." This decision-making is the function of the citizen-critic. He must make decisions about whom to elect, what church to join, which philanthropy to support, and what product to buy. But decisions do not spring, full-blown, from the minds of men. It is the function of rhetoric, of speech communication, to give form to economic, social, and political problems, and to establish alternatives. This is the way it is in a society that is governed through the ballot box. In clubs, schools, businesses, homes, and in our government, we believe in decision by discussion, majority rule in a climate of free speech. Thus the speech course contributes to society's welfare, not merely by making the student a more effective producer of speechmaking, but also by making him a more discerning consumer.

The citizen-critic also needs some general virtues, such as:

1. *He must be as objective as possible.* It has been said of Max Ascoli, editor and publisher of *The Reporter,* that "he will always be objective—and never impartial." That is, he looks for and weighs the relevant facts without prejudice, but with that done he is willing to take a stand on the issue.

2. *He must not make decisions prematurely.* No one should be pushed to make a judgment now, just because he will have to make one ultimately. Those who wish to spend all the time they can in examination of a problem, investigation of the facts, and reflection upon their bearing, should be encouraged.

3. *He must, when the time comes, be willing to decide.* The citizen-critic who serves on a jury must ultimately vote "Guilty" or "Not guilty." When election day comes the citizen-critic must finally choose among Tom, Dick, and Harry. Those who procrastinate indefinitely about mak-

ing up their minds, as George Bernard Shaw once said, die without wills.

How does the citizen-critic make the decisions that qualify him as a participating member of his society? We believe that these decisions depend upon the strength of propositions and upon their desirability. A *proposition's strength* is determined by the lines of argument that develop it and by the forms of support that sustain them. A *proposition's desirability* is determined by the motivational appeals that undergird it and by the speaker's credibility in presenting it. Put into a formula these relationships may be more apparent:

$$
\left.
\begin{array}{l}
\left.\begin{array}{l}\text{Lines of argument} \\ + \\ \text{Forms of support}\end{array}\right\} = \text{strength of a proposition} \\[2em]
\qquad\qquad + \\[1em]
\left.\begin{array}{l}\text{Motivational appeals} \\ + \\ \text{Speaker's credibility}\end{array}\right\} = \text{desirability of a proposition}
\end{array}
\right\} = \text{judgment}
$$

There is no magic in the formula, of course. To apply its four basic components properly, each must be amplified with a series of questions, as determined by the speech occasion, speaker, subject, and audience. Here are some sample queries, submitted with the clear notion that they must be revised or supplemented according to the needs of the specific speech circumstance.

## TOPICS FOR USE IN CITIZEN-CRITIC EVALUATIONS

LINES OF ARGUMENT
Have all significant issues been considered?
Are they adapted to listener attitudes?
Is there consistency in the whole presentation?
FORMS OF SUPPORT
Is the evidence relevant? Adequate? Convincing?
Is it consistent with what is already generally known?
Can it be checked by other observers?
MOTIVATIONAL APPEALS
Does the listener have specific needs, wants, and interests?
Will the proposition satisfy these needs?
Does it relate favorably to listener attitudes, beliefs, and desires?
SPEAKER'S CREDIBILITY
Is he of good general repute?
Has he special reason to know about this topic?
Does he seem sincere, poised, fair, and trustworthy?

# SPEECHES FOR EVALUATION

It is often alleged that speech texts inadequately represent speakers. Nathan Sargent, in 1853, for example, complained of Tom Corwin that "the *words* of his speech" were as unlike what came from his lips "as the remainder of a bottle of champagne after standing a week is unlike the sparkling beverage when first uncorked." For analyzing five of the six possible topics of the peer-critic, however, and most aspects of the four general topics of the citizen-critic, manuscripts or stenographic transcriptions of speeches are quite satisfactory. Looked at critically they may provide excellent learning devices for the student speaker. At this point in the chapter, therefore, we propose that you read the texts of four contemporary speeches, and that you evaluate each one, first *as a peer-critic,* then *as a citizen-critic,* and that you begin by using the topics we have just outlined for you.

## An Introduction to the Speeches

The four speeches reproduced below have been specially selected to provide you with an interesting yet convenient exercise in evaluation. *They are all, in the first place, about some aspect of higher education and by speakers who are concerned with its future.* If there is any topic upon which you may have some of the interest and understanding that comes from personal experience, it is higher education. Thus you will be a knowing critic without making a special study of a new subject area.

*In the second place, all of the speeches were given before similar audiences and within a brief time span.* The occasion, in each case, was the annual Chicago conference of the Association for Higher Education. Two of the speeches were delivered to the 1964 conference and two to the 1965 conference. The audiences were similar. In 1965, for example, the total attendance was 1800, including approximately 1450 faculty and administrators, 89 graduate students, and 37 trustees from 709 publicly and privately controlled colleges in 49 states, two territories, and seven foreign countries. In addition there were 418 delegates from 83 lay and professional organizations, such as government agencies, state education associations, communication media, and foundations. Though you are not a professor, a dean, or a trustee, you have spent some time associating with such persons thus far in your college career. You share certain basic points of view and common attitudes with them, and thus you will be able to project yourself easily into the original audience situation for these speeches.

*Thirdly, all of the speeches were deliberately designed to provoke discussion and evaluation.* The speaker, in each case, was an analyst for a group of 50 to 150 persons concerned with a specific problem in higher education. This means that he was the only member of the group with a prepared speech. His discourse was expected to provide the springboard for the group to plunge into informal discussion of the issues. Thus it can be said that these are everyday speeches, serving a very common function. For purposes of discrete classification two of them may be labelled to inform and two to persuade. Yet in each case the speaker has a basic point of view, whether explicitly or implicitly presented.

These speeches were first published in *Current Issues in Higher Education: Undergraduate Education,* The Proceedings of the Nineteenth Annual National Conference on Higher Education, April 19-22, 1964 (Miss Schleman, pp. 80-82; Mr. Coffin, pp. 86-90), and *Current Issues in Higher Education: Pressures and Priorities in Higher Education,* The Proceedings of the Twentieth Annual National Conference on Higher Education, March 7-10, 1965 (Mr. Conley, pp. 88-91; Mr. Butler, pp. 130-133). They are reprinted here by permission of the Association for Higher Education, a department of the National Education Association.

## HOW IS THE EDUCATION OF WOMEN
## DIFFERENT FROM THE EDUCATION OF MEN?

Helen B. Schleman[3]

Some significant differences in the education of women and that of men affect the long-range educational outcomes for women adversely. Girls and young women can, and do, earn high grades. Education fails, however, to achieve its fundamental goals and objectives for most women: in general, women do not develop their talents fully, achieve maximally satisfying lives, or aspire to contribute to the quality of human life as greatly as they could.

Slightly more than half as many girl as boy high school graduates go to college. The proportion of girls in higher education has increased only slightly in thirty years. Presently, a smaller percentage of advanced degrees is earned by women than in the 1930's.

Universities admitting only very top grade-earners as freshmen or to honors programs are embarrassed that more women than men meet their standards.

Lives of persons seeking psychiatric help are obviously less than satisfactory. More women than men seek psychiatric help.

Literature in the field offers a variety of explanations for these facts: insufficient finances, failure of counseling, early marriage, belief in the nonideological character of American women, sociologically normal waning of the feminist movement, the feminine mystique.

Realizing that motivation and expectation are (1) closely related and (2) different for women and for men, helps explain why women students generally fail to follow their excellent grades with excellent work performance.

Let's check personally the matter of motivation and expectation for girls. Is there any father here who, even though he knows his daughter to be academically brilliant, socially competent, and personally attractive, really expects her to become president of one of the large coeducational state universities or believes realistically that this is a possibility for any women within his lifetime? Or, indeed, if given a choice, is there anyone who would *not* prefer that his daughter become the happy wife of the

[3]Miss Schleman is Dean of Women, Purdue University. Her speech was made as the analyst of a 1964 conference discussion group concerned with the education of women as one facet of "The Future of Liberal Arts."

president and mother of his children, presiding with grace and charm over the social functions of the university, rather than the occupant of the often uncomfortable, but always prestigious, chair of the president? Has anyone's college-age daughter said that *she* wanted to be president of the University of California, or of General Motors, or governor of New York? What would you, or her mother, say if she did? If her aspirations are more modest than her abilities, what about your expectations for her? It should be emphasized that home and children constitute the big area of exception in this discussion. Aspirations of girls and families are almost universally high here—and generally without reference to academic ability.

In an infinite variety of subtle ways, you have communicated to your daughter what your hopes and dreams for her are. Your son has been aware of your aspirations for him, too. Intellectually, you have hoped for the rich fulfillment of the goals of education for each of them. Emotionally, your actual aspirations for them have probably been quite different. Intellectually, you know that gender is obsolete when applied to jobs. Emotionally, however, you probably have a feeling that certain activities are far more appropriate for one sex than for the other. Appropriate carries the feeling-tone of approval; inappropriate, of disapproval. One's true feelings seep through eventually, regardless of any effort made to conceal them.

Among student personnel workers it is axiomatic that the quality of student life reflects the honest expectations faculty and administrators hold for students. Philip E. Jacob in his study, *Changing Values in College*, confirmed our belief.

What about the subtle, unconscious communication of expectations— positive and negative—that are a built-in part of our mores, not to say specifically our educational system?

Whether the rat experiments relating to expectation have any relevance for humans we do not know, but they are startling enough to make us wonder. In the Rosenthal experiment, graduate students were given two evenly matched groups of rats with instructions to follow identical procedures in teaching them to run the maze. For purposes of experimentation, the students were told that the rats in one group were genius rats; in the other, stupid rats. Expectedly to the students, the "genius rats" learned faster than the "stupid rats." What is completely unclear, but devastatingly disturbing, is why the results corresponded to the expectations. Maybe it was sheer chance; on the other hand, maybe it wasn't. If it weren't chance, then indeed we should wonder about the possible relevance to human behavior.

Do we, as educators, say every day to girls on our campuses subtly, often unconsciously: "We don't really expect you to take the goals of education seriously. You won't make any significant contribution to the world outside of home and family anyway, so why exert to develop your intellectual capacities fully? You aren't going to use them." I am afraid we do.

We communicate to girls in many ways our lack of positive expectation for them. We do this unconsciously, not deliberately, but we do it. The long-range achievement of most girls, by comparison to that of their brothers, takes on the same color as the achievement of the "stupid rats" who knew only relatively negative expectations from their teachers. Maybe, too, this is sheer chance, but maybe it isn't.

How does educational practice tell girls, unconsciously, about our lack of expectation for them? One of the most obvious ways is that we don't show them many models of women who are loved, honored, respected, and rewarded for their intellectual achievements in educational matters. There are a few women models visible, of course, but nothing like the abundance of men models that boys see everywhere.

Let's be specific about what we mean by models. Fifteen or sixteen hundred representatives of higher education are in Chicago for the 19th National Conference on Higher Education to discuss undergraduate education, the most important of enterprises. It involves hundreds of thousands of professional workers serving millions of young people, approximately a third of whom are young women. But few women are registered for this Conference. Likewise, women in leadership or policy-making positions on campuses are scarce. Women representing coeducational institutions at gatherings of this sort are few and far between. Note the women that are in the Conference program. Of forty-two discussion group and information sessions, five have women analysts. Of 223 analysts, panelists, chairmen, recorders, and resource personnel, nineteen are women. The Planning Committee of nine included one woman. Whatever the reasons for so few women participating, the fact says clearly to thousands of women students back home that women are not expected to participate significantly in higher education.

Administrators complain that they can't find competent, experienced women for top jobs. If true, it's understandable. What visible evidence does a girl have that it is reasonable for her to aspire to a vice presidency, academic deanship, department chairmanship, or full professorship—let alone a presidency? If we accept the psychologists' assertions that models are important in educational motivation, then we need some, at least, on campus for women students. President Lyndon B. Johnson's example of deliberately—and not especially quietly—appointing women to high government posts could well be followed by other administrators in other fields. Eventually, it will have to be if we as a nation are to compete in the world arena on comparable terms.

## THE UNIVERSITY AND THE SOCIAL ORDER:
## A PROBLEM OF INEFFECTIVENESS

William Sloane Coffin, Jr.[4]

Here is a text from the late Whitney Griswold: "Every basic institution bears a direct responsibility for society's moral health. The university bears a large and exceptionally important part of this responsibility."

What can we say of our moral health? Not long ago a foreign observer remarked, "You Americans are so obsessed with the luxuries of life that you are forgetting the necessities." What he had in mind might have been what *Newsweek* recently termed the "good nonlife" in America, the way our culture makes the middle class safe, polite, obedient, and sterile.

A couple of centuries ago most college graduates went into the service of the church or state. Since then the range of vocational choices has widened, and properly so. Still, is it not disturbing to recall that, at the founding of our nation when we had a total population less than Los Angeles County today, we turned out a generation of statesmen named Washington, Hamilton, Franklin, Jefferson, Adams—and you could name a list as long as your arm? Yet today, with population sixty times as great and with statesmanship needed as never before, how many people can you name of the caliber of our first generation of statesmen?

And why are there not more? Because, as Plato said, "What is honored in the country will be cultivated there."

"Cease to do evil, learn to do good. Seek justice, correct oppression." So said the Prophet Isaiah. But how many of our graduates are actively seeking justice, actively correcting oppression? Our society is organized with a view first and foremost to business—profits first, people afterward. You have heard the Civil Rights debate: what is more real, real people or real estate?

There is an increasing number of people for whom the affluent society is neither a reality nor even a hope: most Negroes, and millions of whites. And now they are finding their strength and finding the structures of society strangely vulnerable. So, if things do not change radically, soon, Samsonlike, they are going to strive to bring the structures of society crashing down in a cloud of dust. And woe to the privileged who judge

[4]Mr. Coffin is Chaplain, Yale University. His speech was made as the analyst of a 1964 conference disscussion group asking "To what extent should the undergraduate college accept responsibility for the development of democratic values by students and faculty through active involvement in public affairs?"

them, for surely it is the role of society's leaders that they should bring forth the captives out of bondage.

Traditionally, two institutions—the church and the state—have transcended society. But I suggest that the problem of both is ineffectiveness. In the churches with breath-taking regularity Sunday after Sunday the wine is turned into water.

And the university seems equally ineffective. Never before have we had a level of attendance so high, never a level of performance so high, and yet never before have we had a level of influence so low. Our problem is not that we are incompetent, only that we are somehow insignificant; not that what we say is not impressive intellectually, only somehow unimportant historically.

Why does our teaching lack consequence? I suggest we look in four areas of university life. The first is ourselves. We teachers are not a committed lot and are in danger of becoming even less so as our intellectual competence increases. Our fear of being naïve prohibits the possibility of being moved, so that increasingly we end up going through the motions but not the emotions.

If you want to assess the degree of timidity of an academic community, assess the degree of risk in what follows whenever a professor says, "Now I am really going to stick my neck out."

The poet Heine wrote in a letter: "When I lately stood with a friend before the Cathedral Amiens, he asked me why we can no longer build such piles. I replied, 'Dear Alphonse, men in those days had convictions. We moderns have opinions, and it requires something more than an opinion to build a Gothic cathedral.' "

For instance, in November 1954, when public hearings were held in Virginia as to whether the public schools should remain open and public, 143 people testified. When Jeffersonian principles were at stake, how many professors from Mr. Jefferson's own university raised their voices? Not one. How many raised their voices during the McCarthy era? And how many college presidents have spoken out in support of the Civil Rights Bill, or in opposition to the mindless militancy of the Right?

"The teacher as pedagogue has an obligation to stand up and be counted, if only for the sake of stimulating thought and debate. But as preceptor, he also has the duty to set an example of moral and intellectual courage." So said Kingman Brewster recently.

Too often safety is treasured above truth, and our students know it. And they know you can't talk about love of truth if you fear to take a stand, for love and fear cannot be mated.

Of course there are prudential considerations that are real, particularly for college presidents. But let them find others to say for them what they cannot say themselves. And let them back up these individuals with the simple statement that the university guarantees members of the faculty no less freedom than that guaranteed them by the nation. If they don't do at least this much, then let them make no judgments on the cynicism of their students regarding the power of money, for the students know they are bought.

A second area where I think our teaching lacks consequence concerns the curriculum. Albert Camus, in his play, *Caligula,* has Cherea say: "To lose one's life is a little thing, and I will have the courage when necessary. But to see the sense of this life dissipated, to see our reason for existence disappear, that is intolerable. A man cannot live without meaning." It was Socrates who said, "To philosophize is to learn how to die." He knew where to look for meaning. But how many philosophers consider death the burning business of philosophy? How many educators are concerned with the great implacables of life? Is it not melancholy fact that most are paid to avoid these issues as we educate, not to make a life but to make a living; and that even those not paid to avoid them still manage to sidestep them with an agility that is positively breathtaking? Small wonder, then, that our students find so little of higher education meaningful; we are not dealing with areas where meaning is to be found.

A third area concerns vocational decision. Not long ago a great trial lawyer addressed a class at Harvard Law School and asked, "How many are going to become criminal lawyers?" One hand in front, and one in the back of the room. Then he asked, "How many are going to become corporation lawyers?" A forest of hands. "So," said he, "you all want to enter the guiltless society."

There is a distinction between an attractive job and an important one, and it runs through all our professions today. If a man is going to become a teacher, where is he going to teach? In Chicago, New York City, in the slums—or in some nice preparatory school? And if he is going to be a minister, is he going to be the pastor of a well-to-do suburban church, or a slum priest?

A man can join something a little more controversial than the Heart Fund. Among all the people for whom I have voted as a school or college trustee, never have I found one who has listed the Urban League, or the NAACP, or the Human Relations Council, or any of the Civil Rights groups as an extracurricular vocation—and in a day when this is the number one problem of the nation.

While universities and churches are concerned with how people spend their money, they aren't concerned with how they make it in the first place. Universities know that the acquisition of knowledge is second to its use, yet still allow public relations aspects to dictate which moral concerns they will make their own; so in every college I know sexual morality is considered far more important than vocational morality.

The last area is the extracurricular. I recently went to lunch with a law student who had just decided to join the Civil Rights section of the

Justice Department. He pointed out a teacher at a neighboring table. "On account of that man I am going into the Justice Department." My heart leaped with joy: a teacher with influence! He explained, "He was my twelfth grade teacher, and on the first day of class said, 'Fellows, there are things in this world on which you cannot turn your backs, and this year is going to be devoted to finding out what they are.' What happened in class was nothing. But he dragged us into town, into the slums. He dragged us through the court so we could see the whores, and drunks, and all the other lost people in this society who get judged at 9 A.M. in what constitutes an exercise in futility. It was at that time I pledged myself to do something for the poor."

In other words, are values taught or caught? Are they learned abstractly in the classroom, or are they experienced concretely outside?

From all sides we are urged not to self-sacrifice, but to self-preservation. Don't give, take. Don't climb out on a limb, cling close to the trunk. Look out for every bit of self-advantage you possibly can. We absorb these values on the deep emotional level, and it is naïve of the academic community to think that in the classroom, on a purely intellectual level, these values can be confronted and overcome.

Take, for instance, the issue of Civil Rights. Everybody says all men are created equal, but who feels the monstrosity of inequality? Usually only those who become concretely involved in the Civil Rights struggle. Let's open the gates and let more experience in, open the gates and encourage our students to go out. We cannot allow ourselves to be caught in the contradiction of having an extracurricular life on a residential campus enhance values which are opposed to the very values we are trying to stimulate in the classroom. Yet this happens all the time. Fraternities, for instance, are monuments to irrelevance in 1964; and yet how many colleges have done much about them? Rushing could be put off till the sophomore year. Better yet, the junior year. By that time many have seen the light. Or one can take the bottom quarter of all fraternities and put them automatically on social probation.

And what of the summer vacations? College students shouldn't be lifeguards to get sun tans—that's greasy kid stuff! To stimulate them to do something else, colleges ought to have one full-time man, a live wire to play a brokerage role in collecting all the interesting kinds of experiences students could have at home and abroad, during and after college that would enhance the values the college is trying to stand for. For values, once again, are caught as well as taught and therefore must be deeply experienced so they become part of the whole person.

The relationship I would like to see between university and society is that of a lovers' quarrel, with the accent equally on lover and quarrel. For there are two things neither society nor the university can risk: alienation or identification. The mood for this quarrel is wonderfully reflected in the opening words of Alan Paton's *Too Late the Phalarope*:

Perhaps I could have saved him with only a word, two words out of my mouth. Perhaps I could have saved them all, but I never spoke because he spoke hard and bitter words to me, and shut the door of his soul to me and I withdrew. I should have hammered on it. I should have broken it down with my naked hands. I should have cried out, not ceasing. For behind there was a man in danger, the bravest and gentlest of them all.

## PRESSURES FROM STUDENTS FOR EMANCIPATION FROM INSTITUTIONAL CONTROLS—AND VICE VERSA

William H. Conley[5]

The topic for consideration is so charged with emotion that few have the temerity to make a definitive statement about it. During this entire year the headlines of the national press have alerted readers to an unrest on many campuses which has expressed itself sometimes in a manner which is, to say the least, dramatic. From civil disobedience and a strike conducted by an aggressive minority which caused a great university to grind to a momentary halt, to the usual routine complaints of editorials in college newspapers, one may observe that students are exerting pressures on various institutional controls. Freedom from restraint has, of course, always been a goal of the later adolescent. Over the years the collegian who fancied himself a budding genius not infrequently adopted some of the exaggerated individualism of the true genius without having his substance.

Although the so-called rebellion of college students is not peculiar to this generation, some of the forces underlying it are sufficiently different to warrant consideration if we are to understand and cope with current pressures. There are several causes we should keep before us.

First, we are living in a period of exponential and pervasive change which creates an instability in the minds of all thinking persons. The college student with his keen awareness of developments yet his lack of maturity is probably more affected than anyone else. Never has the rate and magnitude of change been equalled. In the fields of science and technology change is so rapid it can be indicated only by the power of a number. The expansion of knowledge in all fields is so revolutionary that it shakes even some advanced scholars. And students realize that before they complete their academic courses in some subjects the matter will be out of date.

Second, and closely related, is a lack of clear understanding of goals. Many courses of action—moral, academic, social, and political—are available to today's student. Without commitment to immediate goals, and without firm ultimate goals he is influenced by various extrinsic pressures. The time preference of youth is for the present. What appears desirable

[5]Mr. Conley is President, Sacred Heart University. His speech was made as the analyst of a 1965 conference discussion group focusing on student pressures, one of a series of twenty-six groups studying pressures of various kinds on higher education.

today is likely to be chosen and acted upon. Such decisions are regarded as irrational by the more mature. Until students can set goals for themselves or be assisted in formulating a set of objectives to guide their actions there will be many who will rebel against the very institutional controls which exist for the purpose of assisting them.

Third, the depersonalization of education in our large institutions must be regarded as a major and underlying cause of unrest and pressure. The individual becomes lost in the crowd. He has no identity in the mass. He is not looked upon as a whole person who is a member of an intellectual community seeking rounded development in a critical period in his life, but as a "number" enrolled in several courses which when added together result in the awarding of an academic degree. Mechanized and depersonalized guidance services have, to be sure, been made available on some of the big campuses but at best they can only care for the serious cases of maladjustment and deal vaguely with groups of ordinary students. In such a situation there can be no community of learners and learned, and the student can feel little organic unity in a learning society.

Fourth, the quality of the process of educating is frequently frustrating. There continues to be poor teaching in the lower division years on too many campuses. Many of the persons who are directing the learning activities of freshmen and sophomores are primarily interested in the completion of their own graduate work. They have little concern with the motivation of the undergraduate and are willing to devote only a minimum amount of time to teaching. Moreover, while resenting the menial tasks—teaching and paper grading—which they are required to perform in exchange for graduate training and for meager living, they recall the frustrations of their own undergraduate years and, perhaps unconsciously yet vociferously, become an efficient cause of student unrest. In some cases they have actually advocated rebellion.

The graduate assistant is not solely responsible for all the poor teaching on the campus. Not a few of our famous professors find little time for undergraduates. While on the campus they may be engrossed in organizing a research program for which a new government or foundation grant may be solicited. The "scholar in action" in the classroom, the ideal of the thirties, is likely to be the "scholar in absentia" in the sixties. It is little wonder that the students who looked forward to the stimulation of great teachers, to the experience of working with great minds, are disappointed to find that their learning experiences are directed by other students only slightly more mature.

Students and faculty cannot be charged with the total blame for campus unrest. The administrative officers of colleges and boards of control have been in many cases unwilling to adapt to changed conditions. Some of their regulations, necessary in bygone days, continue on the books and are occasionally enforced. During such a period of enforcement student resentment may erupt. Some regulations are irrational because they are unrealistic. They stand as a challenge to students much as a 25 mile per hour speed limit does on a superhighway.

These special causes for unrest are behind the pressures for emancipation from institutional controls. It should be clearly understood that the pressure is not and cannot be for total freedom. Institutional controls are necessary. They must exist and be enforced if the college or university is to achieve its objectives. Institutional controls must be ordinances of reason, promulgated by the authorities, for the common good. The ordinances are essential in the academic realm, in the area of personal and social behavior, and in the political and economic life of the campus. They must be regarded as essential guidelines to assist students in educational and maturing processes.

The primary objective of a college is the intellectual development of students through knowledge in an environment which contributes to their continuing total development. The civilized intellect should be a major outcome. It is one which knows things as they are, has been introduced to the total reality, can judge and reason. It can analyze and synthesize, discriminate and discern. It has a developed intellectual taste and can appreciate. It can extrapolate and perhaps create. The civilizing of the intellect requires breadth and depth of knowledge presented in organized learning situations with opportunity for reflection. The university adds to the objective of the college development in greater depth and creativity through apprenticeship in research. It also provides preparation for the learned professions.

An essential condition for the attainment of these objectives is a climate of tranquility. This does not mean complacency nor intellectual contentment. There must be freedom from emotional disturbance and from strife so that reflection is possible and encouraged. When colleges stand in the marketplace in the midst of change, when students are frustrated and aimless, institutional controls are more necessary than ever to protect students from internal and external pressures which interfere with their education. No student is an island. His personal and social behavior affect the learning society of which he is a part. A desire to be free from the restraints of the family must not lead to a license to conduct himself without regard to the influences on the group of peers. Institutional controls are required to protect every student from actions of individuals which interfere with the rights of all to an education in an environment conducive to learning.

Institutional controls have also come into existence for other reasons which depend upon the philosophy of the individual institutions. Some colleges accept a responsibility of standing *in loco parentis* and enforce regulations which they consider to be those which intelligent parents expect. They hold that the college should be a transition between home-family controls and the personal freedom of mature adult living. Institutional controls are looked upon as essential to the formation of adults. This may be distasteful to students, but it must be understood that students in such schools are there because of their own choice or parent's choice. Student pressure to change the schools should be directed at parents rather than the schools. Again, institutions with religious orientation have controls for moral and spiritual formation. These may be displeasing to some students, but it is not the role of students to change the stated objectives of a privately supported college which they are free to attend or not attend.

On the other hand debatable controls exist in many institutions. Administrations are so conscious of the public image of a school that arbitrary regulations may be enacted. The fear that student expression may alienate prospective donors or legislators who vote on budgets may result in controls which actually impede education and interfere with the attainment of objectives of school and student. The concern that the press may associate student incidents with the quality of the school leads to what might be called infantile requirements.

We should keep before us the understanding that the adolescent and immature adult usually presses for freedom from restraint; that at this period in history there are special causes of student unrest on college and university campuses, i.e., the exponential and pervasive change going on about us, lack of clear understanding of goals by collegians, depersonalization of education due to bigness, the inferior quality of college teaching, and the failure of colleges to adapt to changed conditions. We must also recall that institutional controls which are reasonable and for the common good are essential for the attainment of the objectives of the college and of the students, that some controls exist because of the unique philosophies of institutions. But there are other controls which are debatable. This last group may evoke student pressure for modification. Student pressure should utilize recognized channels for change, should aim at objectivity, and should be within the rights and duties of citizens.

## PRESSURES ON HIGHER EDUCATION
## FOR THE EDUCATION OF DISADVANTAGED GROUPS

Broadus N. Butler[6]

When we view the matter of pressures and priorities from the perspective of the education of disadvantaged groups, the first priority is that education in the interest of national survival, rather than education for the promotion of the general welfare in the old sense, is the real and ultimate immediate imperative. Of first importance is the fact that our national human dream and our domestic economy must be sustained. Education of the disadvantaged is as indispensable to the future of our domestic economy and of our intranational strength as technological advancement is to the future of our international relations and our military strength. No nation is or ever has been invulnerable to the paralysis and decline which can result from inability to solve basic domestic human problems in times which combine record prosperity, rapid technological change, domestic restlessness, and international tension.

Here in 1964-65, our nation has taken full cognizance of the weight of poverty and disadvantage upon both the domestic and international prospects for our nation's future. We have finally realized that we are just not permitted to believe ourselves invincible, even though prosperous, in this Nuclear Age.

So serious is the problem of poverty in world perspective that there are only two countries in the whole world whose average per capita income is more than $2,000 according to a recently published UNESCO world map of economic status. These are the United States and tiny Kuwait. By contrast, half of Latin America, almost all of Africa, most of the Middle East, Far East, and Southeast Asia subsist on less than $200 per year per capita. The rest of the world, including the whole of Europe, falls somewhere in between and preponderantly in the lower than $1,300 per capita category. Moreover, when we view the distribution of wealth within the wealthy countries as well as the poor countries, we see how inadequate even the words "average" or "per capita" are to describe the problem of world poverty.

[6]Mr. Butler is Assistant to the Commissioner, United States Office of Education (though his speech was made in his private capacity and with no official support or indorsement). His 1965 speech was made as the analyst of one of twenty-six discussion groups considering various pressures on higher education.

The dimensions of American domestic problems are inseparable from the complexities of world problems. The interrelationships are such that even though it would have been inconceivable to the average American just a few years ago that Cuba would be the main threat to the security of the entire Monroe Doctrine region today, she is. It would have been equally unbelievable that all of our military skill and statesmanship would be unable to resolve the problems in Vietnam and in many other small pockets of tension in the world where Communist manipulation of racialism and of the contrast between American affluence and their poverty militate against the United States and against the possibility of progress toward effective world peace. Unless America does in fact resolve her twin domestic problem of race and poverty, the antipathy of the world itself may undo us.

The underprivileged have never been and are not now exclusively Negro; nor, indeed, have the privileged ever been exclusive of Negroes. So the problem has not ever been one exclusively of race, although it has been exceedingly involved in the projection of the matter in that way.

Let us look at some simple figures which will themselves tell a nonracial story, but a story of a national problem which cannot be solved until we completely redefine the present way that racial symbolism functions in our educational system and generally in our nation.

Half of all Americans represent a figure that is five times larger than the entire Negro population of the country, yet half of all American families earn less than $5,600 per year. Twenty-two percent of adult Americans earn less than $4,000 per year, and this percentage translated into numbers is more than twice as many people as there are adult Negroes altogether in the country. Five percent of Americans earn less than $1,000. This picture is even more serious when we take into account the difference in quality between urban poverty and rural poverty.

The Secretary of Labor recently estimated that 30 million Americans in nine million families are in the category of chronic poor. Of these 30 million, he said, three million are non-white, which means that 27 million are white. Indices vary; but, by most of the current scales, from 40 to 50 million Americans may be listed in the poverty group. These numbers are themselves twice to two-and-one-half times the total Negro population of the nation. Yet in proportionate or percentage figures, and here is where the impact of inequality and race have taken their toll, almost 50 percent of American Negroes live in poverty. Seventy-five percent of Negro families in the U. S. have incomes less than that $5,981 median income for white families. Sixty percent of Negro families in our country have incomes less than $4,000 annually as compared to 28 percent of white families. One reason for this is the median income of white high school graduates ($5,969) is higher than the median income of Negro college graduates ($5,571). Several cities and states have recently reported that the average income of the white high school dropout is higher than the average income of Negro high school graduates.

But when we look at the lowest scale of literacy, the figures reverse. Of 11 million total illiterates in the nation, some three-fourths of them, or nearly eight million are white. Fifty-five million Americans have less than secondary education. Of these, 22 million adult Americans lack eight years of schooling and 8.3 million have less than five years of schooling and are considered functional illiterates. Of the 8.3 million, only two million are Negro. Functional illiteracy is highest in the South, but the problem is national. The *Denver Post* reported last May that the industrialized states of New York, California, Pennsylvania, Illinois, Ohio, New Jersey, and Michigan account for 35 percent of Americans with less than five years of schooling.

These figures are too massive to be viewed racially. Nevertheless, we cannot approach them without the recognition that even though the Negro population in them is small in proportion to the total, it is not small in proportion to the Negro population of the nation; and it is not insignificant in relationship to the historical function of Negro symbolism in any matter relating to our national destiny. Even in the critical matter of the rapid urbanization of the nation, we are finding the urban Negro public school populations exceeding white populations in our nation's capital and in an increasing number of our largest cities. This phenomenon has created adverse reactions by whites in both their attitudes toward public education and their local support of public schools in our major cities. This is both unfair and unfortunate. But we are rapidly coming to a recognition that while the facts as absolute facts are certainly not racial, the willingness to approach a resolution of the problem which these facts present to the nation is so inextricably bound to historical racial attitudes and symbolism (and to our habit of racially interpreting all human facts in our national life) that we cannot solve the one without the other. Even the absence of an appropriate inclusion of Negro, Mexican, Oriental, and American Indian imagery in American history in proper perspective has made it necessary for these students to constantly battle against their own sense of alienation. Particularly has the Negro student had to fight against the ascribed self-image of nothingness and nobodyness. This alienation and this nothingness our nation has determined in dollar costs to be a luxury which we can no longer afford, especially since everyone will have to pay the price. When the list of the poorest states was computed, the first nine of the list, not unexpectedly, were those Southern states which are most associated in the minds of the nation as traditional regions of weak education and strong racial segregation. It is noteworthy, though, that the major economic enterprises of these same states are either Northern owned or Northern controlled.

President Johnson has indicated that if we can raise the level of per capita income of just one million of the poor in these and other states by $1,000 per year, the gross national product stands to increase by 14 billion dollars. Public assistance costs also stand to be significantly reduced. One economist, Professor Vivian Henderson, places the annual dollar cost of segregation to Southern states alone at more than three billion dollars. A recent national figure placed the cost of racial discrimination to the nation at 20 billion dollars annually. This is why so much priority is given to the elimination of this alienation and this nothingness among our people; not only because both are exceedingly costly, but because the reversal of the trend can produce inestimable positive gains. Even the per capita cost to the taxpayer of detaining juvenile delinquents provides a dramatic illustration of the difference that can be made. Juvenile detention costs almost four times as much public dollars as the public dollar cost of higher edution for the same youths of the same talent where investment in this talent directs them into, rather than away from, socially constructive channels. Compare an annual per capita public state college cost of $1,000–$1,200 in public dollars in one state to an annual reform school per capita cost of $3,800–$4,200 per year in the same state, and you will see the difference.

What has all of this to do with higher education? First and foremost, it is to our college doors that will come the masses of students whom we have already prevented from dropping out of school and to whom we are promising fulfillment of their renewed hopes that education will lead to a better life.

Even more important, it is in institutions of higher education that attitude formation of the most respected and authoritative order for good or bad reaches the highest degree of sophistication. It is here that teachers are trained and their attitudes toward what is respectable to know, to do, and to communicate—as well as what to teach—are crystallized. It is here that they prepare to impart these attitudes along with their subject matter lessons to the nation's children and youth.

It was from students in our colleges and universities that the nation received one of the major impulses toward the present direction, and it is from them and their institutions that the nation will now expect responsibility and guidance on the critical points of difference between the wise and unwise courses through the present social change. For these reasons, the priorities as well as the pressures are upon institutions of higher education to steer themselves, the nation's teachers, students, schools, school systems—and ultimately the nation's communities—from attitudes of segregation, divisiveness, and monolithic interpretation of American culture to attitudes of integration, inclusiveness, and a recognition of the positive values inherent in the very heterogeneity of our American peoples and our diverse national cultural heritage. The privilege as well as the responsibility is upon higher education also to realize the positive value of this heterogeneity to the self-esteem and dignity of the kaleidoscopic array of American peoples. For even with her 30 million chronic poor, and for all her other faults, America is still the most productive and democratic so ciety that the world has ever seen. This is education's mantle and charge to protect and to enlarge.

In all this, the question of importance is not the fine detail of the accuracy of the figures. The question is not even whether we can solve the problem in 1965; the question is, however, whether or not we have time to wait beyond 1965 to get started.

## SUPPLEMENTARY READINGS

Auer, J. Jeffery, ed., *Antislavery and Disunion, 1858-1861: Studies in the Rhetoric of Compromise and Conflict*. New York: Harper & Row, 1963. An integration of rhetorical criticism and historical analysis in studies of twenty-six speaking situations relating to the central theme.

Bosmajian, Haig A., ed., *Readings in Speech*. New York: Harper & Row, 1965; paperbound. Especially relevant to evaluating speechmaking are William Norwood Brigance, "What Is a Successful Speech?" pp. 14-19; Daniel Katz, "Psychological Barriers to Communication," pp. 20-34; Richard Murphy, "The Speech as Literary Genre," pp. 99-115; Lester Thonssen and A. Craig Baird, "The Character of the Speaker," pp. 119-129.

Brigance, William Norwood, ed., *A History and Criticism of American Public Address*, 2 Vols. New York: McGraw-Hill, 1943; Vol. 3, ed. by Marie K. Hochmuth. New York: Longmans, Green, 1955. The most extensive available collection of critical and biographical studies of major orators, written by leading scholar-critics in the speech profession.

Cathcart, Robert, *Post-Communication: Critical Analysis and Evaluation*. Indianapolis: Bobbs-Merrill, 1966; paperbound, 125 pp. Especially helpful for peer-critics, with detailed and carefully exemplified procedures for analyzing, interpreting, and evaluating the speech.

Hillbruner, Anthony, *Critical Dimensions: The Art of Public Address Criticism*. New York: Random House, 1966; paperbound, 180 pp. A detailed analysis of the function of the scholar-critic as he deals with individual speechmakers; many examples of method, drawn largely from Brigance and Hochmuth, above.

## EXERCISES

1. Assume the role of the *peer-critic*, read one of the "speeches for evaluation," and write an analysis of 150-300 words on each of the criteria suggested on

pp. 207-208. Your instructor may assign one of these speeches to you, and he may also wish you to present your analysis as an oral report. (He may also wish to assign each criterion to one student, and have them present their analyses as short speeches in a symposium. Or the students may take part in a panel discussion on each of the speeches.)

2. Assume the role of the *citizen-critic*, read one of the "speeches for evaluation," and write an analysis of 200-400 words on each of the criteria suggested on p. 209. Your instructor may assign one of these speeches to you, and he may also wish to hear your analysis as an oral report. (He may also wish to assign each criterion to one student, and have them present their analyses as short speeches in a symposium. Or the students may take part in a panel discussion on each of the speeches.)

3. Apply the criteria for the *peer-critic* to classroom speakers, and the criteria for the *citizen-critic* to public speakers on your campus outside of the classroom.

# Index